CRISIS IN URBAN GOVERNMENT
A STUDY DECISION-MAKING

By the same author:

Functioning of Village Panchayats
Educational Administration in Zilla Parishads in Maharashtra
Political Thought and Leadership of Lokmanya Tilak (edited)
District Planning in India (co-authored)
Profiles of Indian Government and Politics (edited)

CRISIS IN URBAN GOVERNMENT
A STUDY OF DECISION-MAKING

N.R. INAMDAR

CONCEPT PUBLISHING COMPANY, NEW DELHI 110059

ISBN 81-7022-330-X

First Published 1991

Published and Printed by
Ashok Kumar Mittal
Concept Publishing Company
A/15-16, Commercial Block, Mohan Garden
New Delhi 110059 (India)

Lasertypeset by
Microtech Advance Printing Systems (Pvt.) Ltd.
H-13, Bali Nagar
NEW DELHI 110015

DEDICATED
to the Memory of
PROFESSOR D.R. GADGIL (1901-1971)
Eminent social scientist and a
pioneer of empirical social science
research in India

CONTENTS

LIST OF TABLES

PREFACE

THE RESEARCH work *Crisis in Urban Government: A Study of Decision-Making* was done during late sixties and early seventies. The drafting of the chapters could however not be completed until recently due to urgent research preoccupations. The lapse of time, I am sure, would not affect the validity of the conclusions of the work even as of today.

The author is thankful to the Indian Institute of Public Administration, Pune Branch, for the financial assistance towards the project, and to Shri S.M Golwalkar (now Senior Lecturer in Fergusson College, Pune), for assistance in the investigation in the project. Without the cooperation of the office-bearers, corporators and officials of the Poona Municipal Corporation, the work would not have been possible; thanks are due to them. The author also expresses his thanks to Professor V.K. Kshire of Poona University for reading the manuscript. The author wishes to thank Shri Naurang Rai of the Concept Publishing Company, New Delhi for the ready publication of the book.

N.R. INAMDAR

1

INTRODUCTION

DECISION-MAKING AND POLICY ISSUES

THE DICTIONARY meaning of 'Decision' is "resolution" as applied to the legislative sphere. This meaning would be applicable to a municipal government, in the present study, the Poona Municipal Corporation. The other two meanings of the term, namely "final judgement" or "settlement" and "verdict of a judge", would not apply here.

The 'decisions' in the Poona Municipal Corporation, the theme of our study, therefore, were the "resolutions" adopted by the Committees of the Corporation in the first instance and those adopted by the Corporation, that is, the General Body, later. It is not necessary at this place to indicate the legal inter-relationship between the resolutions of the Committees and the General Body. That would be done in the chapters on these segments of the main theme.

In the organisational vocabulary 'decision-making' has been considered an integral part of the process of managing organisations.[1] We, in this study, propose to analyse both the decision-making mechanism and the decision-making process as well as the interaction between the mechanism and the process, which three constitute the substance of the process of managing or, to use a batter term in our context, governing the organisation of the Municipal Corporation under study.

This study of the decision-making in the Poona Municipal Corporation deals with the alternatives conceived during the process of decision-making on various functional subjects and individual items and choice from these. The study has left out of its purview the implementation or execution of the decisions, which, being a vast theme, would require an independent study.

'Policy', as distinguished from 'Decision', is "plan of action" or "statement of aims and ideals of a government or a political party", in our study, of the Poona Municipal Corporation, which is an urban local government. Various policies of a sizable urban government, like, Poona, concern roads, water supply, lighting of public roads and places, public health and medical care, execution of town-planning schemes and preparation of a development plan for the city, slum improvement, housing for the flood affected and slum-dwelling families, creation of recreational facilities and other related matters. Because of several factors, an urban government, even a big-sized, like, Poona, is not in a position to formulate long-term policies for, say, five or ten years, relating to the functions mentioned above. The first reason is that, barring purely municipal functions, like, the construction and repair of roads, city lighting, water supply (but not dam construction for water storage), public health and medical care (latter again to a limited extent) and the like, other functions are in the domain of main functions of the State Government whose creature urban local government is. In the second place, the financial resources of an urban local government are limited, the sources of local taxation being few, most important of these being property tax and octroi. With more efficient mobilisation of the tax resources, the financial condition of an urban government would improve to a certain extent, but not so much that it could execute all the expected functions effectively. In the third place, an urban local government does not possess the necessary expertise in all these functions, e.g., town-planning, urban development planning, etc.

Neither the political parties or groups in the city nor the Poona Municipal Corporation as a public body has followed the practice of pronouncing any policies for a term of the elected body. This has deterred us from including a study of the policy aspect *per se* in this project.

DECISION MECHANISM AND DECISION PROCESS

The decision mechanism in the Poona Municipal Corporation is mostly patterned on the structural scheme of the Bombay Municipal Corporation established in the 1980s of the last century. It was supposed to be a product of the ingenuity of Sir Pherozeshah Mehta, the moving spirit behind the then Bombay Provincial and Bombay Municipal politics. Except the Committee pattern, the other structural features of the Poona Municipal Corporation (created in 1949) are modelled on those of the Bombay Municipal Corporation. While the borough and the district Municipalities set up under the Bombay Provincial Acts during the '20s exercised freedom to appoint their own Chief (Executive) Officers, the Bombay and Poona Municipal Corporations (and later species) had as their Commissioners civil servants deputed for a term by the Provincial (now State) Governments.[2]

Both these categories of municipal legislation governing the Municipal Corporations and the borough/district Municipalities are marked by a division of authority in decision-making between the Committees and the Corporation (the General Body), on the one hand, and the primary consultative role for the Committees, on the other. The bifurcation of deliberative and executive functions, the former wielded by the elected members through the Committees and the Corporation and the latter exercised by the appointed officials, is still another feature of the structural schemes embodied in these two types of municipal legislation. All these three features have been taken from the respective patterns of contemporary municipal government in England. The spirit of voluntary civic service inspired the (Municipal) Councillors in England. The delegation of an amplitude of functions (including policing) of the Central Government to the local governments vested considerable authority and responsibility in the local bodies and indirectly among the Councillors. In India, also, eminent personalities, like, Pherozeshah Mehta, Tilak, Patel, Jawaharlal Nehru, made the debut of their political career in municipal government. However, after Independence, the spirit of selfless civic service has been giving way to the motivation of personal power-mongering and/or financial gain, exceptions excluded.

The English local government has also had the benefit of officials with a fair degree of knowledge, experience and efficiency, and a well-knit party system. The Municipal officials are all appointees of the Municipal bodies themselves, but even then they have, by and large, accounted themselves creditably in their performance. Organised national political parties participate in the local government affairs in which they project their national policies as applied and applicable to the local circumstances.

Recently, the English local governments have also experienced the strains of the motivation of self-interest among the elected members as well as the officials. The lack of co-ordination and coherence among the different Committees and the Councils/Corporations, on the one hand, and between the elected bodies and the administration, on the other, has originated new Committees, such as the Executive Committee, Planning Committee, Central Committee, Policy and Resources Committee.[3]

In India, political parties have contested the elections to the Municipal Corporations like Bombay and Poona, but neither have they been able to project coherent policies in the Municipal administrations nor to infuse discipline in their own or the Municipal proceedings.

The Municipal bureaucracy in India suffers from defects of absence of adequate expertise, appointments on the basis of favouritism and general lethargy and apathy in day-to-day working. The bureaucracy in the Municipal Corporations has shown somewhat better performance than the one in the smaller Municipalities.[4]

Innovations in the pattern of Committees have been of late tried in India, as, for example, the Co-ordination Committee comprising the leaders of the political parties and groups in the Poona Municipal Corporation.[5] But such new mechanisms are not durable nor are they armed with statutory powers. By and large, it could be observed that the two patterns of Municipal government for the large cities and towns, respectively, conceived and devised during the past decades of the 19th and the early ones of 20th centuries have been retained without major reforms after Independence. Direct elections for the Municipal Presidents have been tried in Madhya Pradesh and recently in Maharashtra (in latter were discontinued after a five-year experience). In West Bengal, in the Calcutta Municipal Corporations, the Mayor-Council system has been introduced recently.[6]

The set of checks and balances devised in the urban local bodies of both the varieties has made for slow, uneventful working of the whole decision-making mechanism and process and their parts and stages. This slow and cautious process of decision-making and implementation might have been suited to the colonial times when safeguarding the interests of the colonial masters was the uppermost objective pervading the governments at various levels including the one at the local, notwithstanding the professed "self-governing" nature of the Municipal government.

VARIOUS MODELS

The consensual model of local self-government operating in ancient and, to an extent, in medieval India could not be applied to the local bodies constituted under the British rule. It did not suit the ideal of electoral democracy inducted in the country from England. It also did not subserve the colonial interests of the alien rulers of keeping alive and fomenting the conflicting communal and caste divisions embedded in the Indian society. The English-educated upper and middle class elites also aspired to collect whatever experience they could have in these newly created species of "self-government".

The French model of prefectural government also enthused a few public personalities and civil servants by the close of the last century. In Bombay city one section of political elite was keen to institute the prefectural system in the city Municipal administration. But the colonial government must not have relished delegation of more functions and authority to the city government (the police had already been withdrawn). So the idea was short-lived and stillborn. The district administration headed by the Collector and Magistrate was a sort of prefectural government in the rural areas without even a semblance of democratic appearance. Since then, before Independence, in the urban government no new idea was conceived and tried for experimentation. Weak functional and financial base and bureaucratic stranglehold were the twin maladies from which the urban governments suffered before Independence.

The American models were much farther both before and after Independence. Before Independence, USA's assertion of national identity, within the country, composed as the nation was of diverse ethnic constituents and, outside in the comity of nations, inspired the national leaders and the nationalist movement in their strivings towards the nation-making. Individual liberties and federalism in the American Constitution also provided ideals worthy of emulation in free India. Although local democratic experiments were admired by Tocqueville and Bryce in their widely read classics on American democracy, the various urban government models set up in the USA did not stir active thinking before and also after Independence. It is only recently after visits to the local governments in the USA by political dignitaries, officials and scholars that interest has been evinced in experimenting with some of the features of the American urban governments such as the Mayor-Council plan and the City Manager pattern.

The structural model adopted in the colonial times is just not attuned to tackle the problems and issues that are facing the urban government after Independence.[7] The 'pull' and 'push' factors both have placed thousands of incoming people within the boundaries of the cities. Most of these people find themselves houseless; they have created new slums or are sheltered in the existing ones. The roads, lanes, highways, prepared for a lakh of the city population, are bursting at seams with tens of lakhs of people. Hawkers, pedlars and mini-shopkeepers situated in smallest possible cubicles encroach the roads and the pavements. Vacant reserved plots and spaces are occupied by trespassers. Lands essential for gardens, sports grounds, schools and such other essential facilities are de-reserved and diverted with impunity. Hospitals and clinics needed by the poor families cannot be set up for want of resources. Thanks to three dams nearby, Poona city is well placed in respect of water supply, but most of the towns and cities are half-thirsty due to an acute shortage of water supply. The children of the poor are in need of school facilities which the urban governments cannot provide in sufficient quantity and with modicum of quality. Underground drainage and sewage works happen to be a luxury in the case of most of the towns. Newly amalgamated suburbs or outlying villages have to suffer the burden of increased local taxation without the compensating civic facilities of water supply and drainage, etc. Most, important, a citizenry conscious of its civic obligations (obviously proud of its privileges) is conspicuous by absence. Public health and sanitary regulations are regularly observed in breach; traffic regulations and rules are violated without compunction. Cities and towns are supposed to have urban development plans; by the time they are prepared and commissioned into action they have become outdated.

RESEARCHABILITY OF THE THEME "DECISION-MAKING"

The research into the decision-making mechanism and decision-making process in the Poona Municipal Corporation would bring out the pace of their movement and the quality of the decisions arrived at in terms of the target issues.

Not much research has been conducted in the decision-making mechanism and process in Indian urban government. The decision-making mechanism and process in the *Panchayati raj* institutions which are comparatively recent political and governmental institutions have been researched to an extent.[8] Only few articles have been published in journals[9] on decision-making in Indian urban government.

In the Indian urban governments, studies of their constitutional and legal positions *vis-a-vis* the Provincial Governments was a set theme for research before and after Independence. It is only recently that winds of change are blowing. Political leadership of the urban local bodies has of late attracted the attention of the scholars.[10]

The pursuit of the theme of decision-making in the present study is, therefore, timely; it would fill a salient gap in the urban government studies in the country.

SCOPE OF THE STUDY

The decision-making mechanism and process in Poona Municipal Corporation was studied for the period 1961-1967. Two general elections to the Corporation were held during 1962 and 1966-67. So we could not only study the reflections of the Municipal affairs – the successes, failures and problems faced by the Corporation – in the election process, but also witness the changes in the configurations of the political parties and groups and Independents and their alliances. We could also investigate into the impact of the politics, including electoral politics of 1961, on the Municipal decisions. We could not do this in respect of the Municipal elections of 1966 as we had closed the period of our study at 1967.

As mentioned earlier, the decision-making mechanism and process in the Poona Municipal Corporation was gleaned from the decisions of the Committees and the Corporation. As would be observed later, except the Standing Committee and the Transport Committee, the decisions (resolutions) of the other Committees are referred to the Corporation for final decision. The resolutions adopted by the Corporation *suo motu* are necessarily referred to the respective Committees for consultation. Sometimes there are references back to the Committees for a fresh look or amendments in specific respects.

METHODOLOGY

The records of the proceedings of the meetings of the Corporation and its Committees were the primary source of our research materials. The annual reports, accounts, budgets and other statistical materials of the Corporation were also helpful to us in drawing on supplementary information. The Municipal handbooks prepared every year by the Municipal Secretary's office giving information regarding the number of meetings of the Corporation and the Committees, the attendance at these of the Corporators and other matters also came handy to us. The office notes drafted by the Municipal officials furnished us with hitherto unknown facts. The Municipal Act, Rules and Byelaws were also examined minutely.

Interviews and discussions with the officials, including the Municipal Commissioner, the Deputy and Assistant Commissioners, Municipal Secretary and heads of various departments, gave us rare insights into the decision-making process, not available through the above records. Interviews and discussions were also held with the Corporators and elected office-bearers of the Committees and the Corporation, so also the leaders of the political parties and groups and knowledgeable Independent Corporators.

Further, we observed the meetings of the Corporation and Committees for a period of one to two year(s). This enabled us to be acquainted with the behavioural aspect of the elected elements among themselves and in relation to the officials. Some decisions – these expectedly were few – were influenced by this relationship between the elected elements and the particular officials. It was not possible for us to follow up the decisions of the Committees observed by us during 1966-67 through the decisions in the Corporation as our investigation closed in 1967. We compensated this deficiency by studying the decisions of the Corporation including references back to and from the Committees during the period 1962-67, selectively. However, we perused the proceedings of all the meetings of the Corporation and the *Ad hoc* Committees during 1962-67, and of the sub-committees during 1962-65. The constraints of time, financial availability and access to records were the limitations of the study.

Newspapers which covered the proceedings of the Municipal meetings as well as the Municipal happenings were also perused by us so as to fill in the gaps in our information.

CHAPTERISATION

The structure of the Poona Municipal Corporation and its Committees and their relationship with the administrative officials is delineated in the Chapter 2. Chapter 3 analyses the elections and the composition of the Corporation and its Committees. The decisions of the Coordination and *Ad hoc* Committees are discussed in the next two chapters, i.e. Chapter 4 and 5. The decisions of the statutory committees are analysed in detail in Chapter 6, while those in the Corporation are discussed in Chapter 7. Both these chapters are longish, they are, in fact, the crux of the theme. The concluding chapter, i.e. chapter 8 brings to the finale the treatment of the theme of the study by enlightening its various aspects and dimensions.

NOTES

1. B.L. Maheshwari, (1980). *Decision Styles and Organisational Effectiveness*, Vikas, New Delhi, p.2.
2. N.R. Inamdar, (1972), "Maharashtra", in A. Avasthi (ed.), *Municipal Administration in India*, Lakshminarain Agarwal, Agra.
3. Martin Cross and David Mallen (1978). *Political Realities, Local Government and Politics*, Longman, London.
4. *Rural-Urban Relationship Committee Report*, Vol. I, (1963), Government of India.
5. See Chapter, 4.
6. Abhijit Dutta (ed.), (1985). *Municipal Executives in India*, IIPA, New Delhi.
7. See J.F. Bulsara's book on Urbanisation (Popular, Bombay); also B.V. Pandit, (1969). *Urbanisation and Municipal Administration in Jalgaon District*, unpublished Ph.D. Thesis, University of Poona.
8. For example, N.R. Inamdar, (1970), *Functioning of Village Panchayats*, Popular Prakashan, Bombay; N.R. Inamdar and V.K. Kshire, (1985), *District Planning in Ibid*, Oxford & IBH, New Delhi and Iqbal Narain, *et al.* (1976), *Education and Panchayati Raj in Rajasthan*, Impex, Jaipur.
9. For example, M. Bhattacharya, (1973). "Municipal Decision-Making", *Nagarlok*, Vol. 4, Oct-Dec.
10. For example, S.L. Kaushik, (1986). *Leadership in Urban Government in India*, Kitab Mahal, Allahabad.

2

THE STRUCTURE

INTRODUCTION

THE BOMBAY Provincial Municipal Corporations Act, 1949, provided for the constitution of the Standing Committee and Transport Committee, the Special Committees, the *ad hoc* Committees and the sub-committees of the Standing and the Transport Committees. The setting up of the specific Special Committees in each corporation city was left by the Act to the individual Corporations to suit their respective needs. The Co-ordination Committee existing in the Poona Municipal Corporation since 1963 is a non-statutory informal body specially devised by the Corporation to meet its growing work-load and urgent problems and policy matters.

Position of Committees

The Committees in the Poona Municipal Corporation occupy an important position in the structure of the Corporation. They participate in the deliberative function of the Corporation. Two of the Committees, the Standing and the Transport, also share the decision-making authority of the Corporation in some respects. None of the Committees are vested with *executive powers* regarding the core of the administrative functions. But the Standing Committee exercises direct control over the Municipal Secretary and the Municipal Chief Auditor and their establishments, kept out of the purview of the jurisdiction of the Municipal Commissioner. Similarly, the Transport Committee is the controlling and overseeing authority in respect of the Transport Manager and his operational and ministerial establishments.

Committees – Standing, Transport, Special and Ad Hoc

Among the Committees, the Standing and the Transport Committees stand above the Special Committees (four Subject Committees, namely, the Public Works Committee, the Medical Relief and Public

Health Committee, the Law, Revenue and General Purposes Committee, and the City Improvement Committee) in wielding real authority. The Special Committees, laid down by the rules under the Bombay Provincial Municipal Corporations Act, 1949, and not by the Act itself, play an advisory or recommendatory rather than a prescriptive role even in regard to the deliberation of the policies and administrative matters of the Corporation. The *ad hoc* Committees that can be appointed by the Corporation from time to time are a category by themselves. Their proposals and recommendations possess even less assertive force than those of the Special Committees, their constitution itself being dependent on the *ad hoc* needs of the Corporation.

Co-ordination Committee

A class by itself, the Co-ordination Committee, recently functioning in the Corporation, is a purely informal device to settle some of the urgent or irritating issues faced by the Corporation. It lacks the statutory authority of either the Standing or Transport Committee or of the Special Committees. Its real influence derives from its informal character and is very much due to the cordial relations between the Administration headed by the Municipal Commissioner and the elected element in the Corporation.

Sub-Committees

The Sub-Committees of the Standing and the Transport Committees, though provided in the Act, do not enjoy any independent powers. They are set up voluntarily by the Standing or the Transport Committee. They are, at the best, a mechanism to facilitate the deliberation and decision-making by the Standing or Transport Committee. At the worst, they create time-consuming bottlenecks in timely decision-making by the parent Committees.

FUNCTIONS* AND POWERS

(A) Standing Committee

The Standing Committee is the most powerful of the Committees in the

* The duties (obligatory and discretionary) and taxation powers of the Poona Municipal Corporation as mentioned in the Municipal Corporations Act are cited in Appendix I.

Poona Municipal Corporation. It wields authority overall the subjects of municipal administration except the Transport Undertaking operated by the Corporation. Over the City Motor Bus Transport Undertaking (entitled 'Poona Municipal Transport') the Transport Committee exercises authority comparable to that exercised by the Standing Committee in all other subjects.

Powers

The Standing Committee exercises four types of power:

(a) Powers which are unique, not shared even by (the General Body of) the Corporation: Exercised over the Municipal Secretary and the Municipal Chief Auditor;
(b) Final Decision-making Powers over different subjects (excluding Transport) within certain limits, especially in financial and personnel matters;
(c) Consultative powers over a variety of subjects, including financial and personnel matters; and
(d) Powers regarding the Budgets of the Transport and other departments framed by the Transport Manager and the Municipal Commissioner, respectively, before passing them on to the Corporation for adoption.

It could be seen that all these powers exercised by the Standing Committee are material, hence its dominant position among the Committees of the Corporation. The Transport Committee is equally decisive, but in regard to the operations of the Transport Undertaking only. The operations of the Transport Undertaking also are subject to the review of the Standing Committee is regard to its budget and loans.

We shall first deal with the decision-making powers referred to in (b) above.

Powers regarding Municipal Personnel

A significant decision-making power relates to the Municipal personnel. For the sake of convenience of analysis the relevant authority of the Standing Committee in regard to the staff of the Municipal Secretary and the Municipal Chief Auditor is dealt with last while analysing the statutory provisions mentioned in (a) above.

It is obligatory on the Municipal Commissioner to place, from time to time, before the Standing Committee for sanction a statement setting forth the number, designations and grades of the officers and servants to be maintained by the Corporation and the amount and nature of the salaries, fees and allowances to be paid to each [B.P.M.C. Act, Section 51(2)(3)]. It may be noted that it is incumbent on the Corporation to appoint the City Engineer, the Medical Officer of Health, the Municipal Chief Auditor, the Municipal Secretary and the Deputy/Assistant Municipal Commissioner. The above provision regarding approval by the Standing Committee of the statement of personnel obviously refers to the officers and servants other than these heads of departments as well as the Transport Manager and his establishment and the staff of the Municipal Secretary and the Municipal Chief Auditor. However, the ultimate power of sanctioning the creation of permanent offices with a minimum monthly salary (exclusive of allowances) of Rs. 100 or more is vested in the Corporation, and of those with the said salary of Rs. 800 or more is vested in the State Government [B.P.M.C. Act, Section 51(4)]. But the sanction of the Standing Committee is essential for the renewal of temporary appointments carrying a monthly salary of more than Rs. 100 (exclusive of allowances) up to six months (each time) after the first tenure of six months. This, together with the budget-making power, gives to the Standing Committee a decisive lever over the Municipal personnel (excepting those in the Transport Undertaking who are regulated by the Transport Committee).

The approval of the Standing Committee is also necessary for the temporary appointments for loan works carrying a monthly salary of Rs. 400 or more (exclusive of allowances) for the first six months. The sanction of the Corporation for the renewal of such appointments is, however, called for, since the power of appointing Municipal officers, whether temporary or permanent, whose minimum salary is or exceeds Rs. 400 is vested in the Corporation.

The Standing Committee is the appellate authority in regard to the punishment of reduction, removal or dismissal – ordered by the Municipal Commissioner in respect of personnel appointed by him. Moreover, the cases of dismissal of Municipal officers or servants drawing monthly salary of above Rs. 200 have to be approved by the Standing Committee. Cases of suspension of the officers appointed by the Corporation (namely, those drawing monthly salary above Rs. 400 as well as the statutory officers) are provisionally decided by the

Standing Committee subject to the final decision by the Corporation. The exercise of appellate authority in regard to severe punishment, like reduction, removal or dismissal gives the Standing Committee a high status in the image of the Municipal employees.

The Standing Committee grants leave for more than one month to the officers appointed by the Corporation, the remaining cases being within the purview of the Municipal Commissioner/Transport Manager. The Standing Committee here acts on behalf of the Corporation because the matter is lower in order of importance.

Financial Powers

The Standing Committee wields considerable financial powers, besides the budget-making power. These concern contract acquisition and disposal of property, accumulation of and withdrawal from Municipal and special funds, accounts and audit, and taxation. The consideration of some of these matters does not brook delay and involves various complications which can be thoroughly discussed only in a compact body, like the Standing Committee. Some decisions involving larger amounts or of momentous significance, however, require to be sanctioned by the Corporation.

Every contract bearing expenditure above Rs. 5,000 is to be approved by the Standing Committee. The Commissioner is obliged to report to the Committee the contracts of expenditure in the limit of Rs. 1,001 to Rs. 5,000. The Commissioner has to invite tenders for works or supply of materials or goods worth more than Rs. 3,000, but the Standing Committee can authorise the Commissioner, for reasons to be recorded in proceedings, to enter into a contract without inviting tenders or without accepting any tender received by him. This grants the Commissioner the much-needed manoeuvrability regarding choice of contractors within the confines of the contract-sanctioning authority of the Standing Committee.

The Standing Committee determines the maxima of rates of prices for acquisition of immovable property by the Commissioner either for particular cases or classes of cases. The approval of the Committee is also essential for the application of the Commissioner to the State Government for proceedings to be taken within the meaning of the Land Acquisition Act, 1894, for acquiring immovable property or easement that could not be acquired by agreement. The sanction of the Standing Committee is also stipulated in certain cases of disposal of property, both movable and immovable. The jurisdiction of the Committee in case of movable property is over the value of Rs. 501 and Rs. 5,000 and in case of immovable property it is for a period of more than one year, and over value of Rs. 50,000 in respect of sale or lease in perpetuity or of Rs. 3,000 in respect of annual rental. The transactions above these limits are within the purview of the Corporation. Thus, the Standing Committee has vital *locus standi* in all cases of acquisition of property and over certain ranges in cases of disposal of property.

The Standing Committee is in a position to issue directions to the Commissioner regarding retention of cash balances, because the Commissioner is expected to credit all moneys received in the Municipal Fund as deposits in banks as well as to make all payments in excess of Rs. 100 in cheques. The Standing Committee is authorised to approve the deposit of any portion of the Municipal Fund with a bank or other agency at any place beyond the Poona city. For the investment of surplus funds in banks or public securities also, the sanction of the Standing Committee is required. These provisions are devised to act as a check on the irregular handling of cash funds.

The Act prescribes the purposes for which the Municipal Fund is to be applied as also the restrictions on the expenditure from it. Whenever any expenditure is incurred by the Commissioner on objects exempted from the list of prohibited items [Section 86(2)], such as compensation, special sanitary measures, information is to be furnished to the Standing Committee which would take necessary action or recommend the Corporation to take it for covering the additional expenditure. The relevant authority of the Standing Committee is to recommend to the Corporation to increase any amount of budget grant or make an additional budget grant to meet any special or unforeseen requirement subject to the stipulation of keeping balance of Rs. 1,00,000 intact in the Municipal Fund. The Standing Committee is authorised to sanction expenditure of unexpended portions of budget grants during the next two following years on the original objects of the grants even if the amounts of the grants have not been taken into account in the opening balance of the Municipal Fund entered in the budget estimates of any of the two following years. This indicates that except in regard to increase in budget grants or insertion of additional grants the Standing Committee wields wide powers over utilisation of budget.

The Standing Committee may reduce the amount of a budget grant at any time during an official year. If such reduction exceeds Rs. 500, the Corporation may pass an order on it which is binding on the Committee and the Commissioner. This provision seems to have taken into account difficulties of Municipal departments in the wake of such reductions in budget grants. It has no doubt struck at the roots of the authority of the Standing Committee, but it has asserted the overriding authority of the Corporation in the matter.

In regard to the transfer of budget amounts, the Commissioner, the Standing Committee and the Corporation exercise powers in an ascending order of importance. The Commissioner is in a position to make the transfer of any amount not exceeding Rs. 5,000 within a minor head from one subordinate head to another or from one primary unit to another if such transfer does not involve a recurring liability. Every such transfer exceeding Rs. 5,000, however, requires to be reported forthwith to the Standing Committee. Secondly, the Standing Committee may sanction the transfer of any amount within a budget grant from one minor head to another or from a subordinate head under one minor head to a subordinate head under another minor head or of any amount above Rs. 5,000 within a minor head from one subordinate head to another or from one primary unit to another. Finally, it is within the authority of the Corporation to sanction the transfer of any amount from one budget grant to another on the recommendation of the Standing Committee. The Standing Committee obviously shares the authority over transfer of budget grants with the Commissioner and the Corporation, but the Corporation acts only on the recommendation of the Standing Committee. The Commissioner needed to be given that much discretion (up to Rs. 5,000) in regard to the transfer of budget grants within minor heads.

The Standing Committee can bring to the notice of the Corporation prospective contingency of shortfall of income to meet the expenditure and then the Corporation is bound to order any measure to proportion the year's income to the expenditure by way of economy of expenditure or supplementary taxation. Such contingencies are these days ever likely to arise in view of mounting responsibilities and growing expenditure of the Corporation.

It is the authority of the Corporation to constitute from time-to-time special funds from the corpus of the Municipal Fund to earmark expenditure for special purposes. The Standing Committee is, however, granted authority, according to the rules under the Act, to give directions regarding the disbursement of compassionate allowances from the Fines Fund as well as the provision of benefits and amenities from the Welfare Fund to the families of Municipal employees or employees themselves.

The Standing Committee determines the manner and forms of maintaining the accounts of the receipts and expenditure of the Corporation. The Committee also determines the form of, and the nature of information to be contained in, the annual administration report of the Corporation. The Committee is entitled not only to receive but also to review the annual administration report and statement of accounts prepared by the Commissioner. Over the audit of accounts also the Standing Committee possesses vital powers, but to that we shall come later while dealing with the Committee's relationship with the Municipal Chief Auditor.

Taxation Powers

Apart from the general authority over taxation in the budget, in regard to the assessment of specific taxes in particular cases the Standing Committee exercises significant powers. Instead of the prescribed water tax on particular premises, the Standing Committee may approve charge for the water supplied by measurement at specified rate or by the size of the water connection with the Municipal main. In lieu of such charge by measurement of size of water connection also, the Standing Committee may choose to compound with any person for a renewable term of up to five years on payment of a fixed periodical sum. The Standing Committee may lay down specific conditions in these particular cases of charge by measurement or size of water connection or of a fixed periodical sum. The Standing Committee also fixes the rate by measurement for water supplied to premises used solely for public purposes by Government. In regard to the assessment of the conservancy tax also the Standing Committee has similar powers. The special rate at which the conservancy tax is to be paid in respect of a hotel, club, stable or other large premises, generally, is approved by the Standing Committee.

For the tax on vehicles and animals, the Standing Committee may like to compound with any livery-stable keeper or other person keeping vehicles or horses or bullocks for hire, or with any dealer having stables of horses kept for sale, for the payment of a lump sum for any period up to one year at a time.

The Standing Committee is also authorised, instead of requiring payment of octroi due from a person, mercantile firm or public body to be made at the time of entry of the goods into the city direct, to order keeping of an account-(current) of the octroi due from the party concerned.

When the several holdings comprised in any building or land assessed to general property tax are treated as one property for such assessment, the Standing Committee may lay down general conditions for sanction of a drawback of one-fifth part of the general tax by the Commissioner.

The Standing Committee's approval is also necessary to write off from time-to-time a sum due on account of any tax or of the costs of recovering any irrecoverable tax amount.

Besides these important powers with regard to the assessment or collection of specific taxes, the Standing Committee is vested with powers over minor financial matters. A few of these are: The determination of fee for acceptance of the notice to be given to the Commissioner for transfers of title of persons liable to payment of property tax; giving directions to the Commissioner regarding classes of plants and machinery contained in any building or land for fixation of rateable value of the building or land; approval to the fixation of fee to be paid by a non-owner or non-occupier of property to inspect and take extracts from the assessment book; approval to the offer of a nominal bid by the Commissioner in the case of an immovable property of an assessee of a Municipal tax put up for sale for non-payment of such tax.

Loans

The Standing Committee is vested with a few powers in regard to the borrowing of loans by the Corporation. All coupons attached to debentures issued by the Corporation have to be signed by the Chairman of the Standing Committee and the Commissioner. The Standing Committee also fixes the share of the cost on account of the salaries and allowances of Municipal employees engaged in part on the preparation of plans and estimates or the construction or supervision or on the maintenance of the accounts of the works financed from the loans raised by the Corporation. This enabling provision is stipulated because normally no portion of a loan for works is to be utilised for 'administrative' expenses.

An invaluable authority of the Standing Committee is in regard to framing of regulations concerning conditions of service of Municipal employees, scope of work of the Municipal Chief Auditor and miscellaneous matters, like, determination of the standards of fitness of buildings for human habitation or regulation of future construction of certain classes of buildings in particular streets or localities.

Policy-making

The Standing Committee also participates in policy-making in regard to the administration of matters, like, improvement schemes, building regulations, etc.

Consultative Powers

The Standing Committee not only exercises decision-making authority in important matters affecting financial, personnel, municipal property, city improvement and other aspects of municipal administration, but is also consulted by the other bodies in the Corporation on issues within its purview. If an issue which involves framing of a new policy or departure from an existing policy comes up before the Corporation it is referred to the Standing Committee for working out its financial or personnel implications. The Corporation may give due consideration to the opinion of the Standing Committee on such issue. The Special Committees may also be required to refer any of the matters before them to the Standing Committee for its opinion. If the matter is within the sphere of competence of the Standing Committee it is settled in it, but if it is within the jurisdiction of the General Body of the Corporation (as, for example, in the case of increase in a budget grant or an additional budget grant), the Corporation decides it finally. The Special Committees are definitely put in a dock before the Standing Committee on questions within the orbit of authority of the Standing Committee. The Standing Committee can also initiate matters that go to the Corporation for final decision.

Budget-making

The budget-making power of the Standing Committee is a species of the financial power vested in the Committee. It gives the Committee an opportunity to review and plan the administrative operations of the Corporation in a broad perspective. It also lends the Standing Committee an upper hand over the Special Committees insofar as their administrative plans during the ensuing year are subjected to the approval of the Standing Committee. This enables the Standing Committee to act as an effective bridge between the Corporation and the Administration. It does this by setting before the Corporation a conspectus of the Municipal administrative activities during the prospective year.

Though the Corporation possesses the authority of final sanction of the budget it is the Standing Committee which frames it on the basis of the proposals prepared by the Commissioner. Thus, the initiative for reflecting the financial needs of the Administration in the budget proposals rests with the Commissioner but the Standing Committee is in a position to exercise its judgement and discretion in framing the budget taking cue from the Commissioner's proposals. The Standing Committee also decides the form of the budget to be followed by the Commissioner while presenting it to the Corporation. For example, the budget expenditure is to be classified into major, minor and subordinate heads as well as primary units. The Corporation can remit the budget to the Standing Committee for suitable modifications, but is free to adopt it making whatever changes it likes. This pinpoints the screening and scrutinising role of the Standing Committee in relation to the budget, confirming at the same time the budget-sanctioning authority of the Corporation.

The budget has to provide for, besides the estimated income and expenditure, balances and expenditure on account of the Special Funds, the minimum revenue balance of Rs. 1,00,000, the payment of loans, the estimated tax income and the stipulated annual contribution from the Municipal Transport in lieu of the Corporation's investments in the Transport Fund.

The Standing Committee is also expected to act as a watchdog over the investments of the Corporation in the Municipal Transport through its power of screening the budget of the Municipal Transport (distinguished as Budget 'B' from Budget 'A' of the Corporation *per se*). The Standing Committee can intimate the Corporation the results of its screening of the Transport budget through a report accompanying the said budget.

The Standing Committee secures about one-and-half month for the scrutiny of both the budgets, of the Corporation and the Municipal Transport. The Corporation also gets ample time of two months for the discussion of the two budgets. But it has to adopt the taxation measures by 20th February and the whole budgets by the end of March. In case budget estimates are not finally adopted by the Corporation by the end of March, the estimates as recommended by the Standing or the Transport Committee, as the case may be, are deemed to be budget estimates finally adopted by the Corporation until the estimates are so adopted.

Municipal Secretary and Chief Auditor

The Municipal Secretary and the Municipal Chief Auditor, the two of the main props of the Municipal administration in Poona, work under the direct control of the Standing Committee. Out of the two, the Municipal Chief Auditor is more independent of this control by the Standing Committee. In the exercise of functions, the Chief Auditor does not depend upon the Standing Committee, the authority for his functions being vested in him by the Act and the Rules under the Act. But, just as the Auditor-General of the Government of India is responsible under the Constitution to the Parliament through its Public Accounts Committee, the Municipal Chief Auditor is statutorily responsible to the Standing Committee and through it to the Corporation in the discharge of his audit function. He is required to place the audit reports before the Standing Committee for necessary action. But he can make the Standing Committee forward his audit reports on irregularities in accounts as well as his views on the manner of the exercise of audit to the Corporation for final action. Thus, the Chief Auditor has access to the Corporation, though an indirect one, through the supervising Standing Committee.

The Municipal Secretary, on the other hand, is under the direct oversight of the Standing Committee, as he is in charge of the Secretariat for the legislative business of the Corporation. It is a sound principle of governmental organisation that the arrangements for the exercise of the legislative function are looked after and controlled by the legislature itself. It is, therefore, in keeping with this principle that the Municipal Secretary and his office should be under the direct authority of the Corporation. The Corporation being a large body, the control over the Municipal Secretary and the Secretariat is wielded by its Standing Committee. This facilitates not only the administration of the Secretariat but also the exercise of control over it.

The appointments of the Municipal Secretary and the Municipal Chief Auditor are made by the Corporation on the advice of the Standing Committee. They have to fulfil the conditions regarding qualifications and experience laid down by the Corporation and approved by the State Government. Similarly, they draw salaries prescribed by the Corporation and approved by the State Government. While the appointment of the Municipal Chief Auditor is subject to the confirmation by the State Government that of the Municipal Secretary is not subject to this condition. While these officers can be suspended by the Standing Committee, subject to final action in this regard by the Corporation, punishment of any kind can be ordered only by the Corporation. All this implies that while for all practical purposes these two officers work under the Standing Committee their appointment and conditions of tenure are handled by the Corporation.

The Municipal Secretary as well as the Municipal Chief Auditor are governed by the general direction of the Standing Committee in the appointments and the conduct of work in their offices, supervision over it as well as disciplinary action over the employees there. This means that the Municipal Secretary and the Municipal Chief Auditor do not possess much control over their own offices which would have an adverse effect on the quality as well as output of their work. The Municipal Secretary is to be incharge of the management of the proceedings of the Corporation, the Standing Committee, the Special Committees and the Sub-Committees. He also holds the custody of papers, documents and records of these elected bodies. All these functions are onerous and arduous and as such require certain amount of freedom of operation in their discharge. Likewise, the Municipal Chief Auditor performs very vital functions that are invaluable for the efficient working of the democratic administration of the Municipal Corporation. He prepares weekly, *ad hoc* and annual audit reports on the accounts of income and expenditure of the Corporation. Besides the absence of freedom over subordinate personnel, there are two other obstacles in the effectiveness of Chief Auditor. The exact scope and extent of audit of accounts relating to different items of income and expenditure, particularly the former, is determined by the Standing Committee and the Corporation. So the audit may not cover all the accounts of the Corporation if the Standing Committee and the Corporation choose to leave out certain items of receipts from the purview of audit. Second, it is up to the Standing Committee and the Corporation to take necessary remedial or preventive action on the audit reports. This absence of compulsiveness, about the scope of audit and the follow-up action on audit, reduces the value of audit in the administration of the Corporation.

The area of operation of the Municipal Secretary and the Municipal

Chief Auditor extends also to the proceedings of Transport Committee and the audit of the Transport Fund, respectively. But in the exercise of their functions *vis-a-vis* the Municipal Transport they are responsible to the Transport Committee, and not to the Standing Committee.

(B) Transport Committee

The Transport Committee holds very nearly the same position *vis-a-vis* the Municipal Transport Undertaking (P.M.T.) and the Transport Manager, as the Standing Committee *vis-a-vis* the other subjects of Municipal administration and the Municipal Commissioner. The Transport Committee has been assigned an independent position on par with the Standing Committee because it was thought that a business undertaking, like the Passenger Motor Transport, should operate with utmost autonomy to attain maximum efficiency. The Transport Manager is also granted a statutory status equal to that of the Municipal Commissioner on the same account. In some respects, for example, power of creating temporary posts in the Transport Undertaking, the Transport Committee enjoys higher powers than the Standing Committee (to create posts up to monthly salary of Rs. 200 as compared to those up to monthly salary of Rs. 100). In one important respect only, namely the budget, the Transport Committee is subordinate to the Standing Committee. The budget framed by the Transport Committee is scrutinised by the Standing Committee and then placed before the Corporation with a statement of its own views on it. The authority of the Transport Manager to operate the Transport Undertaking is affected only during his absence or on his failure to exercise it when the Commissioner takes it over.

There would be no two opinions on the propriety of granting to the Transport Committee and the Transport Manager a nearly autonomous sphere for the operation of the Municipal Bus Transport Undertaking. But the calibre expected of the Transport Manager as indicated in the rules is too low for the efficient operation of the Bus Transport Undertaking of the size existing in the city of Poona. Or else he should have been placed under the Commissioner, as far as personnel hierarchy was concerned, without affecting his semi-autonomous powers in regard to the operation of the Transport Undertaking.

(C) Special Committees

Distinct from the Standing and the Transport Committees, but certainly lower in status, are the Special Committees provided for in the Act. The Special Committees are expected to play an essentially advisory role in regard to the subjects of Municipal administration in their respective jurisdictions, decisions concerning which are taken by the Commissioner, the Standing Committee or the Corporation. The Act lays down the nature of the role and functions of the Special Committees bearing their number, broad subjects and respective jurisdictions for the Corporation to decide. The Corporation, accordingly, has framed rules prescribing the number and respective jurisdictions of the Special Committees.

The Special Committees constituted so far by the Corporation are four:

(a) The Public Works Committee;
(b) The Medical Relief and Public Health Committee;
(c) The Law, Revenue and General Purposes Committee; and
(d) The City Improvement Committee.

It is obvious that there is no finality about this number of Special Committees which the Corporation is free to increase according to the needs of the situation in future.

A Special Committee's advice assumes obligatory force only when the Corporation delegates a matter to it for final decision and the final decision is adopted by the Committee by at least half the total number of members of the Committee. Such matters have been only five in number, two of which are within the jurisdiction of the Medical Relief and Public Health Committee, two within that of the Law, Revenue and General Purposes Committee, and one within jurisdiction of all the Special Committees. The two matters within the competence of the Medical Relief and Public Health Committee are to make payments for the maintenance and treatment of persons undergoing anti-rabies treatment as indigent persons *and* to paupers, lunatics and lepers. The Law, Revenue and General Purposes Committee, in its own right, can take a decision in regard to instituting suits in respect of decision of claims to property *and* expressing concurrence with the nomination by Government for evaluating Government properties. All the Special Committees can call for any extract from proceedings of or any return, statement, account or report connected with any Committee or Sub-Committee formed under the Act. The secondary importance of a handful of matters which the Special Committees can decide confirms the essentially advisory role of the Special Committees. In all other matters the proceedings of the Special Committees are subject to confirmation by the Corporation. Even otherwise, the advice of a Special Committee obviously is not binding on the Commissioner, the Standing Committee or the Corporation, within whose charge final decision in all other matters rests.

Overlapping Jurisdictions

In spite of the clarifications by the Corporation regarding the respective jurisdictions of the four Special Committees through its resolutions (dated 24th January, 1952 and 19th February, 1952), there are bound to be some matters with overlapping jurisdictions of more than one Special Committee. The Public Works Committee has been allotted business pertaining the City Engineer's Department and questions concerning it: roads, buildings, water supply and water works, parks and gardens, fire-bridge, workshop, mechanical branch and other works of the Engineering Department; public safety and convenience; Lands and Estates Department and questions concerning it; inspection of works and calling for reports from the Municipal Commissioner. The Medical Relief and Public Health Committee has been assigned all questions relating to Municipal outdoor dispensaries, hospitals, maternity homes, medical and nursing assistance and medical institutions to which monetary assistance is given by the Corporation's Health Department (including street cleansing, conservancy, etc.) and all other questions concerning it. The Law, Revenue and General Purposes Committee looks after the questions relating to the interpretation and amendment of the Municipal Act and other Acts, Bye-laws, Regulations, Rules relating to all matters of Municipal administration; Assessment and Collection Department; Election matters; Octroi, Accounts and Licence Departments and all miscellaneous questions not falling within the purview of any Special Committee. The City Improvement Committee has been put in charge of questions relating to the general improvement of the city, master plan, town planning schemes, industrial estates, housing schemes, etc.

It is clear from this list that on a number of matters more than one Special Committee can claim exclusive advisory status. Matters pertaining to city improvement vitally affect the Public Works Committee, so it might join issues with the City Improvement Committee that has been entrusted with improvement matters.

Similarly, the engineering implications of health works, especially relating to conservancy and drainage, would engage the attention of the Public Works Committee and as such may have its own point of view to offer to supplement the one offered by the legally authorised Medical Relief and Public Health Committee. In regard to use of roads, the Standing Committee might claim hearing with the Public Works Committee. In regard to the regulations and taxation matters the Standing Committee might be in a position to assert its standpoint over the view of the Law, Revenue and General Purposes Committee. All this implies these conflicting claims regarding jurisdiction have got to be adjusted through conventions regarding discussion of different policy and administrative matters.

In regard to certain aspects, reference to certain Committees is made compulsory under the rules. But this does not resolve the issue as to which Committee's view is to prevail. All proposals affecting finances have got to be routed by a Special Committee through the Standing Committee. Plans and estimates of new works are to be directed by the Special Committee to the Corporation through the Public Works Committee. And proposals involving amendment of the Municipal Act, Rules, Regulations, etc., have to be submitted by the Special Committees through the Law, Revenue and General Purposes Committee. These obligatory references were, of course, implicit in the detailed item-wise analysis of the assignments of the Committees made in this chapter so far.

The Standing Committee can authorise by the vote of at least two-thirds of its members present at the meeting a Special Committee to take decision on a matter on its behalf, but the resolution has to be reported to the Corporation which might cancel it any time. But, taking into account the jealous vigilance of the Committees to guard their own territories, it is doubtful whether at all this provision would be acted upon. To ward off delay, a Special Committee can, by a resolution supported by at least half the total number of members, direct the action on its decision without waiting for confirmation of its proceedings by the Corporation, but the Corporation might not subsequently confirm the proceedings of the Committee in which case the action of the Committee's resolution is to be cancelled. This again reinforces the intrinsically advisory role of the Special Committees.

(D) Ad-hoc and Sub-Committees

The Ad-hoc Committees of the Corporation and the Sub-Committees of the Corporation and the Sub-Committees of the Standing and the Transport Committees are also purely advisory. Their sphere of review and proposals are confined to the terms of reference laid down by the Corporation's parent Committees.

COMPOSITION

Consideration Regarding Size

Two considerations seem to be underlying the size of membership of the Committees – Standing, Transport and Special. The first is the facility of discussion. If the size of membership a Committee ever reaches about ten it would affect the informality and directness of discussions in it. The second is that, as far as possible, all the members of the Corporation should continuously secure an opportunity to participate in the deliberative business of these Committees. The issue of the size of membership of the Committees is also linked with the term of membership. If the size of the Committees is large, the term could be made longer because it is then assured that members secure adequate experience in particular Committees to which they are assigned. In fact, these are the two alternatives for choice: larger size and longer term *or* smaller size and shorter term. Both these alternatives enable each of the councillors to receive experience of different Committees during his four-year term of councillorship. But a shorter term ensures the participation of each of the councillors in the deliberations of the Committees. Another factor weighing in favour of a shorter term is that it prevents growth of vested interests in particular Committees by members. But it obstructs members acquiring insights into the functions and working of particular Committees of their charge, unless they opt for continued membership of the same Committees to which they were assigned during the preceding term. Deep experience in selected Committees *or* diverse experience in different Committees is a difficult choice for a majority of councillors.

The size of the Standing Committee is 12 members and its term is two years. To enable a larger number of members to garner experience of the important work of the Standing Committee, half the number of membership, i.e. six, is renewed every year. Woeful is the *lot* of the members who have to retire just one year after the constitution of the Standing Committee on the general elections of the Corporation. In keeping the term of the Standing Committee at two years, a comparatively (as compared to the one-year term of the Special

Committees) longer experience of the decision-making authority of the Standing Committee is assured for their members. The term of the members of the Transport Committee is four years, the tenure of the Transport Committee remains continuous. The underlying reason seems to be the same, namely, to enable the Committee's members to have a longer spell of decision-making experience in the Transport Committee. The overlapping membership due to the retirement of only one-half of the membership every year and every two years makes for continuity of experience throughout the tenure of both the Standing and the Transport Committees, respectively, during the four-year term of the Corporation. But, unlike the Standing Committee, the size of the Transport Committee is smaller, namely nine, including eight elected members and one *ex-officio*, the Chairman of the Standing Committee, being on par with the size of the Special Committees. The term of the Special Committee is, however, shorter, namely, one year, to facilitate the sharing of experience of their advisory work by as many councillors as possible. Another provision contributing to the same result is that a councillor is prohibited to hold membership of more than two Special Committees.

Unlike the Standing and the Special Committees, the membership of eight seats in the Transport Committee is thrown wide open to "persons who, in the opinion of the Corporation, have had experience of, and shown capacity in, administration or transport or in engineering, industrial, commercial, financial or labour matters", irrespective of whether they are corporators or not. The object behind this stipulation seems to be laudable, to make available to the Transport Committee persons whose experience in related fields would be a valuable asset in the decision-making process of the Committee. But, since no strict definition of "experience" or "capacity" is laid down, the provision makes possible the continuation of the members of the Committee who cease to be corporators after fresh general election to the Corporation. This not only would slacken the Corporation's control over the second of its two powerful Committees charged with the policy-making in regard to its vital Transport Undertaking, but also would introduce an undesirable practice of associating with the Committee's work those remotely qualified for it.

Cumulative Voting

The method of voting for election of members of the Committees is cumulative. This enables even minority groups in the Corporation to secure representation in the Committees. Consequently the Committees have in them representatives of diverse groups in the Corporation, some in majority and others in small minorities. This places majority group in a risky position in the Committees, because sometimes it may not obtain a clear majority in the Committees. But this promotes the Committee's deliberative work on account of the reflection in them of different shades of opinion represented in the Corporation. Different Committees may, however, have varying quanta of representatives belonging to varied groups in the Corporation.

Election of Chairman

The Chairmen of the Committees are elected every year by relative majority among the two highest scoring candidates at re-votings on the elimination of the lowest scoring candidates, one at each time. This is a very simple method of voting to operate and also a clear index of the majority opinion in the Committees as far as preference for the Chairmanship is concerned. A Councillor is barred to hold simultaneously chairmanship of more than one Special Committee. But the bar does not extend to holding at one and the same time the Chairmanship of the Standing Committee and a Special Committee. Whether this loophole occurs by oversight or because of genuine intention is a matter of conjecture.

Casual Vacancies

The tenure of the casual vacancies of membership or chairmanship of the Committees is the unexpired part of the regular term. This is quite in keeping with the general plan of periodic elections to the Committees. The Committees' membership is vacated in case of absence for more than two months on medical grounds or sanction by the concerned Committee and for more than four months on any ground whatsoever.

Ad-hoc and Sub-Committees

The composition of the Ad-hoc Committees or Sub-Committees is not regulated by any conditions except an obvious one that their members belong to the parent bodies and that in the case of each sub-Committee the number of members should at least be three.

MEETINGS

The meetings of the Standing and the Transport Committees have to be held more frequently than those of the Special Committees since the business before them is more urgent and decisive than that before the Special Committees. The meetings of the Standing Committee are held at least once in a week and of the Transport Committee at least once in a fortnight. No such definite frequency is prescribed in case of the meetings of the Special Committees. Special meetings of all these Committees can be convened to transact urgent or pending business at the instance of the administration or the Mayor/Chairman/members. The timings of the Committees' meetings have to be adjusted to the meetings of the Corporation and the convenience of the members as well. Further, the attendance at the meetings of the Committees is not compensated by the payment of an allowance unlike the attendance at the meetings of the Corporation and of a conveyance allowance in case of attendance at the meetings of the Transport Committee.

Quorum

The quorum at the meetings of the Standing Committee is five and at those of the Transport and Special Committees four. The difference in the quorum in the case of the Standing and the other Committees is due to their differing strength, namely 12 and nine. But its proportion to their total membership is uniform, namely just one (or one-half) less than the exact half. It is arguable that the quorum for the meetings of the powerful Standing and Transport Committees should have been higher than one-half of the total membership, but then perhaps adjourned meetings would have been more frequent and this would have come in the way of timely decision-making.

Chairman

The Chairman is authorised to regulate the discussions in the Committees. He also enjoys the privilege of casting a second or decisive vote in case of a tie in voting on resolutions or motions that have to be carried by majority of members present and voting. The voting is by show of hands and not ballot. This makes for speedier dispatch of business before the Committees, but on delicate matters, like appointment of or disciplinary action on personnel or acquisition of property or road-widening, this might inhibit free expression of views by members. A motion regarding adjournment of meeting or postponement of the consideration of a question is granted precedence over other business. This procedure might be called for on certain occasions, but a fear is expressed that it might be a frequent phenomenon. Motions to cancel or alter adopted resclutions are not to be entertained (within three months of such adoption in the case of the Special Committees) unless supported by at least half of the total membership of the Committee. Members lose membership if they participate in the proceedings on matters with which they or their partner are connected. Joint meetings of the Special Committees may be held to discuss matters of common interest or concern. No provision exists for joint meetings of the Standing Committee and the Transport Committee as also of the Standing/Transport Committee and the Special Committees. Officials concerned with the matters to be discussed in the meetings have a right to attend and participate in the proceedings of the meetings but are not allowed to vote. This is a healthy and indispensable provision in view of vesting the executive authority of the Municipal Corporation in the Commissioner in the case of all Municipal subjects except the Transport Undertaking and the Transport Manager in the case of the Transport Undertaking.

Sub-Committees

In the case of the meetings of the Sub-Committees of the Standing and Transport Committees only two stipulations need to be noted. Normally Sub-Committees meet and adjourn as they think proper, but the Chairman of the Standing Committee/Transport Committee may, and has to, upon the written request of not less than two members of a sub-committee, call a special meeting of the Sub-Committees. This is to obviate the dysfunctioning of the Sub-Committees. Secondly, no business is to be transacted at a meeting of a Sub-Committee at which decisions are taken (and they are taken by majority) unless at least two-thirds of the members are present from the beginning to the end of the meeting. The Sub-Committees are small bodies, hence their decisions have to be carried by a clear majority of their total membership.

The minutes of the proceedings as well as names of the persons present at the meetings of the Committees (including the Ad-hoc Committees and Sub-Committees) are to be maintained by the Municipal Secretary. Attending to the meetings of the Committees as also of the Corporation is the core of the functions of the Municipal Secretary. Receiving material for these meetings and disposal of decisions at these are other related functions. Looking after the establishment of the Secretariat is his fourth function.

CONCLUSION

The foregoing analysis might create an impression that the Committees, especially the Standing and the Transport, dominate the Municipal scene in Poona. There are two other statutory organs which occupy the municipal scene along with the Committees. These are the Corporation and the Municipal Commissioner.

The Corporation shares with Standing and the Transport Committees the policy-making authority. The Special Committees as well as the Ad-hoc Committees render advice to the Corporation and the Standing and the Transport Committees (to the Transport Committee to a very little extent). Any new policy or a departure from any existing policy can be proposed and adopted only by the Corporation. The Corporation also controls the purse, for it sanctions the budgets of the Transport Undertaking and the Municipal Corporation. It also decides significant financial proposals, like acquisition and disposal of property (above certain limits). It regulates the appointment, tenure and conditions of service of the higher personnel of the Municipal Corporation. It is the sub-legislative authority for the city in the sense that it adopts the rules and bye-laws, but the minor sub-legislation in the form of the regulations and the standing orders is framed by the Standing Committee and the Commissioner respectively. The city development plans and schemes are undertaken by the Corporation. The Corporation, however, exercises its authority in all these respects after the deliberative screening by the Committees.

The Commissioner wields the executive authority of the Corporation. And as such the initiative for most of the administrative issues that come for decision to the Committees and the Corporation rests in the hands of the administration headed by the Commissioner, (the Transport Manager in the case of the Transport Undertaking). Even in working out the implications of new policies or departures from existing policies the Corporation and the Committees are helped by the Administration by providing necessary information and guidelines. In other discussions also the Administration furnishes data to the elected organs and helps keep these on the track.

The Committees, the Corporation and the Administration are regulated in their working by the legal framework. But the legal framework does not exhaust the mainsprings of the actions of these bodies, especially the Committees and the Corporation. Politics in the broad as well as narrow senses influences the functioning of these organs. Political parties participate in the Municipal and the Committees' elections and as such have their impact on the functioning of these elective bodies. Citizens approach the Corporators with their grievances and demands which the Corporators, in their own way and style, seek to fulfil. This affects the functioning of the elected bodies as well as the administration.

The functions of the Poona Municipal Corporation are obligatory and discretionary as defined under Sections 63, 64, 65 and 66 in Chapter VI of the Bombay Provincial Municipal Corporations Act, 1949 (Bombay Act No. LIX of 1949). The provisions of control over the Municipal Corporation by the State Government are detailed in Sections 448-452 of the Act in Chapter XXVIII. The relevant statutory provisions relating to both these aspects of functions and State Government control are cited in an Appendix to the book.

3

ELECTIONS AND COMPOSITION

ELECTIONS TO the different permanent Committees are held for varying terms. Elections to the Standing Committee are held every year but only one-half of the total number of 12 members in the Standing Committee are elected every year. Similarly the elections to the Transport Committee are staggered; every second year one-half of the total number of eight members are elected. The difference between the system of elections to the Standing Committee and to the Transport Committee consists in the continuous life of the Transport Committee irrespective of the holding of the general elections to the Corporation periodically, and unlike the Transport Committee, the overhauling of the Standing Committee is after every general election to the Corporation. On the other hand, the total membership of the Special Committees is completely renewed every year. The total strength of each of the four Special Committees, namely the Public Works Committee, the Medical Relief and Public Health Committee, the Law, Revenue and General Purposes Committee and the City Improvement Committee, is nine seats. Thus, the Standing Committee is the largest of the three types of Committees in the Poona Municipal Corporation. Next come the Special Committees and last stands the Transport Committee. The elections to the various Committees are held after the elections of the Mayor and the Deputy Mayor who are elected every year.

The elections are held by secret ballot and the Mayor is in-charge of the elections to the Committees. The method of election to the Committees is cumulative voting. This method facilitates the election to the Committees of representatives of minor parties or groups. It is a salubrious provision in the sense that representatives of all the important parties or groups are in a position to participate in the working of the Committees of the Corporation. As we have seen in the previous chapter the Committees are not only policy-making organs of the Corporation but also centres of decision-making on important matters. This highlights the significance of the participation of all the important parties or groups in the functioning of the Committees of the Corporation.

ELECTIONS

(A) The Standing Committee

The elections to the Standing Committee are contested with vigour and enthusiasm. This is natural because the Standing Committee is the most important Committee in the Corporation. The respective strength of the different parties or groups in the Corporation is broadly reflected in the results of the elections to the Standing Committee. The defections and vague affiliations of some of the Corporators, however, affect the certainty of the extent of representation of the different parties and groups in the Standing Committee.

General Election, 1962 – As a result of the general elections of the Corporation in 1962 no political party or group commanded an absolute majority in the Corporation. The Congress had secured 23 seats, the Nagari Sanghatana, a coalition of diverse political parties and groups, such as the P.S.P., S.S.P., P.W.P., the Hindu Mahasabha and Independents, had obtained 28 seats, while the Janasangh had won five seats and the Independents as many as nine seats.

Elections during 1962-68 – In the elections to the Standing Committee during six years, 1962-68, the strength of the Congress party varied between four and five seats, the strength of the Nagari Sanghatana marked variation between five and six, while the Janasangh secured between zero and two seats, and the Independents obtained between zero and three seats. These variations in the seats won by the different parties and groups in the Standing Committee are due to, first, the wavering of the affiliations of the Independents as well as of a few of the Nagari Sanghatana Corporators; secondly, the shifting alliances among the different parties and groups and also among individual Corporators; and, thirdly, the odd strength of the different parties and groups as compared to the number of seats in the Committee as well as the number of absentee Corporators belonging to different parties and groups at the elections.

The results during all the six years of the Standing Committee indicated that the Congress or the Nagari Sanghatana could command an absolute majority in the Standing Committee only in alliance with the Janasangh and the Independent members. This factor as well as the non-political nature of the matters coming for decision before the Standing Committee were responsible for the functioning of the Committee on non-political lines on most of the matters before it.

Election in 1962-63 – In the election of the Standing Committee in 1962-63, 14 candidates had filed their nominations but later on one of them withdrew his nomination with the result that the contest was held among 13 candidates of which the Congress fielded four, Nagari Sanghatana six, Janasangh one and Independent two. In the result of the contest one of the two Independents was defeated. The Congress secured four seats, the Nagari Sanghatana six, the Janasangh one and the Independent one. It may be noted that this was the first election to the Standing Committee after 1962 elections to the Corporation and so 12 seats had to be filled during this year.

1963-1964 – During 1963-64, eleven candidates had filed their nominations for six seats, out of whom four Corporators withdrew their nominations. So the contestants were: Congress three, Nagari Sanghatana three and Janasangh one. The outcome of the contest was that the Congress secured two seats, the Nagari Sanghatana three and the Janasangh one.

1964-65 – During 1964-65, twelve Corporators had registered their nominations but three of them withdrew their nominations. Out of nine contestants (Congress three, Nagari Sanghatana three and Independents three), six were elected as follows: Congress three and Nagari Sanghatana three.

1965-66 – In 1965-66, twelve Corporators had filed their nominations, out of whom three took back their applications. Among the contestants, three were Congressmen, two were Nagari Sanghatana, one was Janasangh and three were Independents. Those elected were Congress two, Nagari Sanghatana two, Janasangh one and Independent one. This year, in the beginning three candidates were elected on the strength of their higher number of votes, while the remaining three vacancies had to be declared filled by choosing lots from four candidates who had secured an equal number of votes.

1966-67 – In the elections, 12 candidates had registered their nominations, out of whom three withdrew. Among the nine contestants were: Congress three, Nagari Sanghatana three and Independent three. The results showed that the Congress secured two seats, the Nagari Sanghatana two and Independents two.

1967-68 – In the elections during 1967-68, the last year of our study, nine candidates had filed their nominations, out of whom two withdrew their applications. The contestants were: Congress two, Nagari Sanghatana two, Janasangh two and Independent one. The results showed that the Congress secured two seats, Nagari Sanghatana two and Independent two.

Wavering in Voting

The elections in the Standing Committee for six years revealed that the different parties and groups did not poll votes strictly according to their potential strengths. In 1962-63, only the Janasangh polled the exact number of votes they commanded, while the Independents polled 15 votes less than their potential strength. The Congress also polled 18 votes less which might have been cast for the Nagari Sanghatana candidates. In 1963-64, the Congress secured a surplus of 18 votes over their actual strength; the Nagari Sanghatana secured only two surplus votes; the Janasangh was the largest beneficiary gaining 22 surplus votes over its actual strength; the independents' votes were cast for the Janasangh and/or Congress candidates. Similarly, in 1964-65, the Congress secured 24 surplus votes, the Nagari Sanghatana three less and the Independents eight surplus. It is likely that the Janasangh votes were cast for Independents because it had not filed any candidate. It is also likely that some of the Independents might have cast their votes for some of the Congress candidates. In 1965-66 again, the Congress got 24 surplus votes which might have been obtained from Independents, the Nagari Sanghatana secured 16 less votes which might have been cast for the Janasangh candidate who secured 25 surplus votes. The Independents got 20 less votes which might have been cast for the Congress candidate as noted above. In 1966-67, the Congress obtained 13 surplus votes, the Nagari Sanghatana a deficit of 42 votes and the Independents secured 37 surplus votes. It is likely that the Janasangh, not having fielded any candidate, might have cast its votes for an Independent candidate. Some Independents' votes might have been cast for the Congress while some Nagari Sanghatana votes for an Independent candidate. During 1967-68, the Congress obtained 26 less votes, the Nagari Sanghatana also a deficit of 32 votes, while the Janasangh obtained a surplus of 18 and the Independents a surplus of 32 votes. This indicates that there might have been a shift from the Congress and the Nagari Sanghatana to the Janasangh and the Independents. This amply corroborates our hypothesis noted above that there were changes in the voting patterns of different parties and groups on account of the shifting loyalties of the Independents and some of the Nagari Sanghatana and the Congress Corporators. There was, however, a hard core of majority of the Congress and Nagari Sanghatana Corporators, who stood firm in the loyalty to their own parties. Another factor responsible for the changing pattern of voting was the number of absentee Corporators. During 1962-63, 65 Corporators were present, out of whom 64 voted. During 1963-64, 64 members were present but 63 actually voted. During 1964-65, all the 65 Corporators were present and voted. In 1965-66 also, all the 65 Corporators were present and voted. In 1966-67, 63 Corporators were present and actually voted, while during 1967-68, 62 Corporators were present and voted.

In the elections to the Standing Committee, within the Nagari Sanghatana different political parties secured representation in varying strengths during the six years. It seems that there was an overall understanding among the different groups within the Nagari Sanghatana regarding representation in different Committees, including the Standing Committee.

(B) Transport Committee

Elections in 1963, 1965 and 1967

In two elections to the Transport Committee held in 1965 and 1967 no party/group commanded an absolute majority. In 1963 elections, however, the Congress enjoyed an absolute majority in the overall strength of the Transport Committee. In 1963, five candidates had finally filed nominations, out of whom Congress were two, Nagari Sanghatana two and independent one. The results indicated that the Congress and the Nagari Sanghatana secured two seats each. In 1965, six candidates contested elections. These six were: Congress one, Nagari Sanghatana three and Independents two. In the result, the Congress won a seat, the Nagari Sanghatana two seats while an Independent one seat. In 1967 elections, six candidates had filed nominations, out of whom one was Congress, two Nagari Sanghatana, one Janasangh and two Independents. The results show that one seat each was secured by the Congress, the Janasangh, the Nagari Sanghatana and the Independent.

Vacillating Voting Pattern

The elections to the Transport Committee revealed a much more vacillating pattern than the elections to the Standing Committee. There were not only shifting alliances among parties but the candidature of individual Corporators also influenced the voting by Corporators belonging to different parties or groups.

The Chairman of the Standing Committee was an *ex-officio* member of the Transport Committee. His party affiliation also affected the political balance in the Transport Committee. Actually, the alliances in the working of the Transport Committee during these six years were marked not on the basis of the political divisions, but of attitude towards the management of the Transport Undertaking by the Manager. The potential power wielded by the members of the Transport Committee was much wider than exercised by even the members of the Standing Committee. The reasons were: First, the Transport Undertaking was the closed concern in the sense that much control was not exercised over day-to-day management by the Corporation or the Municipal Commissioner and, secondly, the Transport Committee was a smaller body and its term was longer, namely four years, as against two years of the Standing Committee. The elections to the Transport Committee during six years also revealed that though non-Corporator experts could be elected to the Committee according to the provisions of the Act, no such expert was ever elected during this tenure of the Corporation.

At the elections to the Transport Committee also, as at the elections to the Standing Committee, it was found that there were shifts of the votes belonging to different parties or groups during the 1963 elections. The Congress secured eight surplus votes while the Nagari Sanghatana only one surplus and the Independents obtained seven less votes than their potential strength. Similarly, at the 1965 elections, about 44 votes from the Congress party might have been cast for the Nagari Sanghatana and the 20 votes, commanded by the Janasangh, for the Independents. During the 1967 elections also, 48 votes belonging to the Nagari Sanghatana might have gone in favour of the Janasangh candidate.

It is also notable that there is difference between the number of votes polled at the elections to the Standing Committee and the votes polled at the elections to the Transport Committee. This might have been, firstly because of the smaller number of seats open for contest and consequently because of less opportunity for smaller groups to contest these seats, and, secondly, because of more individualised working of the Transport Committee.

Strength of Political Parties and Independents

The overall strength of the different parties in the Transport Committee showed marked changes during the six-year tenure of the Corporation. During the year 1962-63 there was one Nagari Sanghatana member and one Janasangh member as compared to the remaining members of the Congress. During 1963-65, the Congress had five members as against Nagari Sanghatana's three. The Standing Committee Chairmen, who were *ex-officio* member of the Transport Committee, belonged to the Janasangh and the Independents up to September 6, 1962, and during 1962-63, respectively. During 1963-64, the Standing Committee Chairman belonged to the Janasangh, while during 1964-65 and 1965-66 he belonged to the Nagari Sanghatana. During 1965-66, as a result of the fresh elections of four members, the composition of the Transport Committee during these years was Congress three, Nagari Sanghatana four and Independent one. During 1966-67, the Standing Committee Chairman was an Independent. As result of the 1967 elections, the Transport Committee for the next two years comprised Congress two, Nagari Sanghatana three, Janasangh one and Independents two. During 1967-68, the Standing Committee Chairman was an Independent having a leaning towards the Congress party. Thus, the gains of different parties or groups in the elections to the Transport Committee during 1963-65 and 1967 were very much different from the gains of the different parties in the elections to the Standing Committee during the six-year tenure of Corporation, except that in 1967 there was a sudden slump in the strength of Nagari Sanghatana due to the defection of a group of five members from the Sanghatana to independent position. But this defector group leaned on the Congress quite often. It is also to be noted that the number of members present at the elections to the Standing Committee was different from the numbers present at the elections to the Standing Committee during different years.

It is thus clear that during the years 1965-68 no party or group commanded an absolute majority in the Transport Committee; however, during 1962-65 the Congress enjoyed an absolute majority in the Committee.

(C) Special Committees

Uncontested Elections more than Contested Ones

In marked contrast with the elections to the Standing Committee and the Transport Committee, the elections to the Special Committees, namely the Public Works Committee, the Medical Relief and Public Health Committee, the Law, Revenue and General Purposes Committee and the City Improvement Committee, were a smooth and unruffled affair. Contests were held to the Special Committees only thrice during the whole tenure of all the four Special Committees for the six-years of our study: for the City Improvement Committee in 1963-64, for the Public Works Committee in 1964-65 and for the Law, Revenue and General Purposes Committee in 1964-65. The remaining 21 elections to the Special Committees were uncontested. It is worthwhile to delve into the reasons for this phenomenon. First, the Standing Committee and the Transport Committee were the prize Committees for the Corporators. The membership of the School Board also was sought by the Corporators much more avidly than the membership of the Special Committees. The Special Committees had a mere advisory role in the Corporation. They did not possess any power of final decision-making either in regard to personnel matters or financial/functional matters. Secondly, the respective strengths of different parties and groups would be already decided in the elections to the Standing Committee and the Transport Committee, so the different parties and groups were aware by the time of the elections to the Special Committees of their real strength in the Corporation. That is why these parties and groups preferred to allocate the seats on the Special Committees among themselves by mutual agreement.

Elections in 1962-63: During 1962-63, the elections to all the four Special Committees were uncontested. In the Public Works Committee the Congress secured three, Nagari Sanghatana four, Janasangh one and Independent one. In the Medical Relief and Public Health Committee, as well as the Law, Revenue and General Purposes Committee and the City Improvement Committee, the same composition was reflected.

1963-64 Elections: During 1963-64, there was contest in election to the City Improvement Committee among 11 candidates (Congress four, Nagari Sanghatana four, Janasangh one and Independents two). Those elected were Congress four, Nagari Sanghatana four and

Janasangh one. In the Public Works Committee the Congress secured four, Nagari Sanghatana four and Janasangh one. In the Medical Relief and Public Health Committee, Congress got three, Nagari Sanghatana four and Independents two; and in the Law, Revenue and General Purposes Committee Congress obtained three, Nagari Sanghatana four, Janasangh one and Independent one.

1964-65 Elections: During 1964-65, elections to the Public Works Committee and the Law, Revenue and General Purposes Committee were contested by 10 candidates (Congress four, Nagari Sanghatana four, Janasangh one and Independent one). Those elected were Congress three, Nagari Sanghatana four, Janasangh one and Independent one. In the elections to the Law, Revenue and General Purposes Committee the contestants were 10: Congress three, Nagari Sanghatana four, Janasangh one and Independents two. Results showed that Congress secured three, Nagari Sanghatana three, Janasangh one and Independents two. The composition of the Medical Relief and Public Health Committee during this year was Congress four, Nagari Sanghatana four and Independent one; and that of the City Improvement Committee was: Congress three, Nagari Sanghatana four, Janasangh one and Independent one.

Election in 1965-66: During 1965-66, the strength of different parties and groups was as follows: Public Works Committee: Congress three, Nagari Sanghatana three, Janasangh one and Independents two: Medical Relief and Public Health Committee: Congress four, Nagari Sanghatana two and Independents three; Law, Revenue and General Purposes Committee: Congress three, Nagari Sanghatana four and Independents two; City Improvement Committee: Congress four, Nagari Sanghatana two, Janasangh one and Independents two.

Election in 1966-67: During 1966-67, the composition was as follows: Public Works Committee: Congress four, Nagari Sanghatana three, Janasangh one and Independent one; Medical Relief and Public Health Committee: Congress four, Nagari Sanghatana two, Janasangh one and Independents two; Law, Revenue and General Purpose Committee: Congress three, Nagari Sanghatana three, Janasangh one and Independents two; and City Improvement Committee: Congress four, Nagari Sanghatana three and Independents two.

1967-68 Elections: During 1967-68, the composition was as follows: Public Works Committee Congress three, Nagari Sanghatana three, Janasangh one and Independents two; Medical Relief and Public Health Committee: Congress two, Nagari Sanghatana four, Janasangh one and Independent two; Law and General Purposes Committee: Congress four, Nagari Sanghatana two, Janasangh one and Independents two; and City Improvement Committee: Congress six, Nagari Sanghatana two and Independent one.

During the six years 1962-68, the strength of the Congress in the Special Committees generally varied between two and four seats (only once in Improvement Committee, in 1967-68, the Congress got six seats), the strength of the Nagari Sanghatana indicated the same range of seats, the Janasangh secured between zero, and one seat and the Independents between zero and three (only once in Medical Relief and Public Health Relief Committee, in 1965-66, they secured three seats).

Gains of Smaller Parties

The respective strengths of the Congress and the Nagari Sanghatana in the Special Committees were not equal to those in the Standing Committee. The main reason was that these two major parties negotiated with other groups, namely the Janasangh and the Independents, regarding allocations of seats in the Special Committees. Another reason was the smaller size of the Special Committees, as a result of which the larger parties, namely the Congress and the Nagari Sanghatana, secured less number of seats than their actual voting strengths. Obviously, the smaller groups, namely the Janasangh and the Independents, gained in majority of elections to the Special Committees a higher percentage of seats than in the Standing Committee.

PARTICIPATION OF THE CORPORATORS IN THE COMMITTEES' MEMBERSHIP

It is worthwhile to study the extent of participation by the Corporators in the membership of the different Committees. Of course, this would not reveal the actual participation of the Corporators in the proceedings and the discussions in the Committees. But one indicator of the extent of opportunity available to the Corporators for participation in the working of the Committees is their membership of these Committees.

Vast Majority Participated in Membership

There were two Corporators who did not participate in any of the

Committees of the Corporation. One of them was a woman member who participated fully in the working of the School Board, the other was a lawyer Corporator, who also got an opportunity to participate in the proceedings of the Corporation in a more honoured manner, viz. by occupying Deputy Mayorship of the Corporation twice during the six-year tenure. Five Corporators enjoyed only one Committee membership term each. These included two all-India leaders of the all-India parties, who naturally had very little time for Committee work, a Corporator who expired during the second year of the Corporation's tenure, a Congress Corporator who was Chairman of the School Board and also occupied Mayorship once and a Congress Corporator whose sole Committee term was rather surprising. Four Corporators had a lease of two Committee membership terms each. Two of these occupied membership of the Standing Committee and the Transport Committee, respectively. There were not less than 10 Corporators who secured three Committees membership terms each. Of these, three Corporators only did not hold membership of the Standing or the Transport Committee. There were as many as 10 Corporators who got the opportunity of serving four Committees membership terms and only one of them did not hold membership of the Standing or the Transport Committee. Fourteen other Corporators received the honour of engaging themselves in five Committees membership terms each. Only three of them did not hold membership of the Standing or the Transport Committee. There were as many as 13 Corporators who held six Committees membership terms each. Only six of them did not occupy membership of the Standing or the Transport Committee. Two Corporators enjoyed more than six Committees membership terms each. Both of them belonged to the Congress and one of them was also a member of the Standing and the Transport Committees during his tenure of Committee membership. This breakdown clearly indicates that, except half a dozen Corporators, the vast majority had an ample opportunity to participate in Committee membership.

Year-wise Participation

Let us now examine the inclusion of the Corporators in the Committees during each year of the six-year tenure of the Corporation. During 1963-64, seven Corporators were members of the two Committees and one Corporator enjoyed membership of three Committees. During the earlier year, i.e. 1962-63, no Corporator occupied membership of more than one Committee each. During 1964-65, four Corporators were members of the two Committees each, the rest being members of only one Committee each. During the next two years, i.e. 1965-66 and 1966-67, as many as eight Corporators enjoyed membership of two Committees each. During 1967-68, 12 Corporators had a spell of membership of two Committees each while another Corporator occupied membership of three Committees. This means that, on the one hand, about one-fifth of the Corporators secured an opportunity to work in two Committees and, on the other, on the lowest side, about one-sixteenth got this opportunity.

Preference for the Same Committee

The preference of the Corporators for the same Committee's membership for more than one term is also worth studying as it would reveal the interest of the Corporators in particular Committees. There were as many as five Corporators who occupied membership of the Standing Committee for more than one term. Out of these, four enjoyed two terms each and one – the leader of the Congress party – represented his party in the Standing Committee for all the six years of the tenure of the Corporation. It should be noted that the term of the Standing Committee is for two years unlike the term of the Special Committees which is for one year. The membership of the Standing Committee was a matter of privilege and as such all these five Corporators could be considered as important Corporators.

No Corporator, however, enjoyed membership of the Transport Committee for more than one term. This is obvious because the term of the Transport Committee is four years and so there was a keen competition among the Corporators for the membership of the Transport Committee. Furthermore, even if the membership of the Transport Committee overlasted the term of the Corporation and members ceased to be Corporators, they continued to enjoy the membership of the Transport Committee.

Sixteen Corporators, the highest number among all the Committees, secured membership of the Public Works Committee for more than one term. Out of these, two Corporators held membership for more than two terms each. The membership of the Medical Relief and Public Health Committee for more than one term was held by 13 Corporators, out of whom three occupied it for more than two terms. Slightly less number of Corporators, viz. 12, occupied membership of the Law, Revenue and General Purposes Committee for more than a single term and four of these engaged themselves in the Committee for more than two terms. Thirteen Corporators obtained an opportunity of serving the City Improvement Committee more than once and three of these were members of this Committee for more than two terms.

It is also interesting to observe that 14 Corporators held membership of more than one same Committee for more than one term. Only one of them occupied membership of same three Committees for more than one term.

There were four Corporators who enjoyed the membership of the Standing Committee as well as the Transport Committee during the six years tenure of the Corporation. Two of these were the Congressmen both of them being very senior Corporators, and two Nagari Sanghatana Corporators. It can be assumed that these four Corporators were of significance in their own parties. Five other Corporators were members of either the Standing or the Transport Committee as well as the School Board. Four of these belonged to Nagari Sanghatana and one was an Independent.

Membership of Two or More Committees in the Same Year and of Same Committee for more than one term

It is still more interesting to note that 24 Corporators, i.e. two-fifths of the total membership of the Corporation, held membership of the same Committee for more than one term and also membership of two or more Committees during the same year. These 24 Corporators were more privileged than the Corporators mentioned in earlier paragraphs because they had an opportunity to serve not only the same Committee over more than one year but also of serving more than one Committee during one year.

Continuous Spell Over Six Years

How far did Corporators enjoy a continuous spell of Committee membership during the six years tenure of the Corporation? Thirteen Corporators enjoyed a continuous spell of Committee membership for all the six years, 26 had a break in Committee membership for one year and 12 Corporators' continuity was broken for two years continuously or intermittently. There were 14 Corporators, whose Committee membership was broken for more than two years. It is worth noting that in some cases these disruptions in Committee membership were due to the concerned Corporators occupying honourable positions, like Mayorship or Deputy Mayorship or membership of the School Board. Some remaining Corporators, however, might have preferred to wait o. take respite for a year or two.

High Honours and Committee Membership

Did the conferring of high honours, like Mayoralty or Deputy Mayoralty, bar the Corporators from holding Committee membership? It does not seem so, except in the case of an Independent Corporator who was Deputy Mayor twice and was not elected member of any Committee even once. Two Mayor Corporators held Committee membership for only one term, but one of them was an all-India leader of an all-India party and the other held membership of the School Board and even its membership for a few years. The other eight Corporators, who either became Mayor or Deputy Mayor, held Committee membership for three to six terms.

Specialisation

How many of the Committee members were specialised in the functions of the respective committees? There were six medical practitioners in the Corporation; out of these, five Corporators held membership of the Medical Relief & P.H. Committee for one to three terms. One Corporator served the Medical Relief & P.H. Committee thrice, another for two terms and the remaining three for one term each. Another Corporator was a proprietor of a drug shop. He was also an M.Sc. He held membership of the Medical Relief & P.H. Committee thrice consecutively. For four years, the Medical Relief & P.H. Committee included Corporators belonging to the relevant profession. For two years, there was not a single Corporator belonging to this profession in this Committee. During 1962-63 and 1964-65 there were three medical practitioners and one druggist post-graduate degree-holder in this Committee. During 1963-64 there was one medical practitioner and one M.Sc. druggist Corporator in the Committee and during 1966-67 only one medical practitioner was included in the Committee. The other Committee which had a sprinkling of concerned specialists was the Law, Revenue and General

Purposes Committee. Seven Corporators were lawyers. Out of these seven Corporators, however, only four were included in the Law, Revenue and General Purposes Committee. One of these held membership of the Committee thrice and the remaining three twice each. The three remaining lawyer-Corporators were not at all included in the Law, Revenue and General Purposes Committee. During 1962-63 and 1967-68 two and three Corporators each in this Committee were lawyers and during the remaining four years one Corporator each in this Committee was a lawyer. There was not a single engineer-Corporator nor an administrator-Corporator in the Corporation during the six years 1962-68. From this, it may be inferred that only two, the Medical Relief & P.H. and the Law, Revenue and General Purposes Committees, were partially composed of the concerned specialists. The other two Special Committees did not have even a sprinkling of the concerned specialists. In the Standing and the Transport Committees, however, Corporators having experience of the work as Corporator were included.

Parties' Leaders as Members

In the Standing Committee, throughout all the six years, the leader of the Congress party in the Corporation was included. This was rather remarkable as compared to the position of the leaders of the other parties or groups. The leaders of the Janasangh group was included in the Standing Committee during the two years 1962-63 and 1963-64. In the Transport Committee, important Corporators of different parties or groups were included but these were not the leaders of the respective parties or groups.

ELECTIONS OF CHAIRMEN OF COMMITTEES

Term

The Chairmen of the different Committees in the Corporation are elected every year. The term of the members of the Standing Committee is two years but of Chairmen it is one year. Similarly, the Chairman of the Transport Committee is for every year, even though the term of the members of the Committee is four years. The Chairmen of the four Special Committees are obviously elected every year since the whole of the membership of the four Special Committees is renewed every year.

Vice-Chairman

The Standing Committee and the Transport Committee have only Chairman, but the four Special Committees have also Vice-Chairman. This difference between the Standing and the Transport Committees, on the one hand, and the Special Committees, on the other, is rather inexplicable. Why Special Committees have the office of the Vice-Chairman is not understandable. If at all Vice-Chairman was necessary, he should have been provided for in case of the Standing Committee and the Transport Committee as well, because the business of these two Committees is heavy, urgent and moreover decisive.

Unanimous and Contested Elections

Compared to the elections of the Chairmen of the Special Committees, the elections of the Chairmen of the Standing and the Transport Committees are keenly contested. During the period of our study, for one-half of the number of occasions of elections to the Standing and the Transport Committees contests took place, while for the remaining occasions unanimous elections were held. It has been noted above that elections of the members of the Special Committees are also held unanimously in general. The reasons which account for the unanimous elections of the members of the Special Committees are also applicable to the generally unanimous elections of the Chairmen of the Special Committees. The spirit of accommodation and give and take is evident in the elections of these Chairmen and generally the minority groups are given weightage in the elections of these Chairmen. Only twice, the elections of the Chairmen of the Special Committees were contested: once in 1962-63 in case of City Improvement Committee and for the second time in 1963-64 for the Medical Relief & P.H. Committee. All others elections of the Chairmen of the Special Committees were unanimous.

Standing Committee Chairmanship

During 1962-63, the election of the Chairman of the Standing Committee was very keenly contested. The strength of the Nagari Sanghatana and all other combined groups, including the Congress, the

Janasangh and the Independents, was equal, but a prominent member belonging to the Nagari Sanghatana came late on the election scene when election had already taken place. Some knowledgeable persons suggested that there was a secret understanding between this member of the Nagari Sanghatana and the Independent member who was elected Chairman of the Standing Committee. The single Janasangh member supported the Independent backed by the Congress. So during 1962-63 an Independent member was elected Chairman of the Standing Committee. During the next year 1963-64, however, a Janasangh member was elected Chairman unanimously. This time, the Janasangh commanded two votes in the Standing Committee and the Nagari Sanghatana mustered six votes while the Congress had four votes. Besides, the Nagari Sanghatana and the Janasangh had struck a deal distributing the Mayoralty to the Nagari Sanghatana and the Standing Committee Chairmanship to the Janasangh. At the election for the next year 1964-65, the strength of the Janasangh was reduced to one and this Janasangh member also defected from the parent party because his candidature for the Deputy Mayorship was not supported by his party. Consequently, the defector-member from the Janasangh backed the Nagari Sanghatana candidate. Thus, the candidate of the Nagari Sanghatana mustered seven votes as against the Congress nominee's five, and was declared elected. In the succeeding year 1965-66 also, the Nagari Sanghatana commanded majority support, so the Congress nominee withdrew from the contest as a result of which the Nagari Sanghatana nominee was elected unanimously. During 1966-67, the contest was held between two Independent members, one of whom had during the previous year defected from the Nagari Sanghatana and joined an alliance with the Congress under the leadership of another defector Nagari Sanghatana Corporator. The two Independent contestants secured an equal number of votes (6 : 6), but the temporary Chairman of the meeting, the previous Chairman of the Committee, gave his casting vote to one of the contestants, who was declared elected. During our study (1967-68), however, the election was unanimous. On this occasion, a defector Corporator from the Nagari Sanghatana, who was in alliance with the Congress as an Independent referred to above was elected unanimously because he was backed by a majority of members. It is to be noted that the temporary Chairmanship of the election meeting was also contested very keenly because in case of equal voting the temporary Chairman had the right to cast his second vote. The results of the elections of the

Chairman of the Standing Committee revealed that the Independents were elected Chairman thrice, the Janasangh once and the Nagari Sanghatana twice, the Congress not securing Chairmanship even once, but among the three Independents one was supported by the Congress and the remaining two by the Nagari Sanghatana. On account of the inability of the Congress and the Nagari Sanghatana to muster an absolute majority in the Standing Committee, the minority groups of Independents and the Janasangh secured the Chairmanship for the number of occasions disproportionate to their respective strengths in the Committee.

Transport Committee Chairmanship

At the elections of the Chairman of the Transport Committee, contests were held thrice and unanimous elections took place thrice. Unlike in the case of the Standing Committee, in the case of the elections of the Chairman of the Transport Committee, the Congress was successful in obtaining as many as four terms of Chairmanship, the Nagari Sanghatana secured Chairmanship once and the independents also once. This was because during the first three years, viz. 1962-1965, the Congress was in majority in the Transport Committee and again during the last year 1967-68 it commanded majority. The Nagari Sanghatana could never muster majority on its own in the Transport Committee. During 1962-63, in the Transport Committee, the Congress had six members, the Nagari Sanghatana one and the Janasangh one; besides, the Standing Committee Chairman, who was an *ex-officio* member of the Transport Committee, was an Independent supported by the Congress. Hence, the Congress nominee was elected unanimously because there was an overwhelming majority in his favour. During the next year 1963-64 also, the Congress had five members as against Nagari Sanghatana's three and the Janasangh's one, that of the Standing Committee Chairman. The Congress nominee was elected by five votes against four secured by the Nagari Sanghatana nominee. During the succeeding year 1964-65 also, another Congress nominee was elected by five votes against four secured by the same Nagari Sanghatana nominee as during the last year. During the next year 1965-66, however, the Congress lost this majority in the Transport Committee, having been reduced to three votes as against Nagari Sanghatana's four and the Standing Committee Chairman also being the Nagari Sanghatana nominee. So, an Independent member was elected chairman unanimously. During the next year 1966-67, the election was most keenly contested. This time, the Nagari Sanghatana and the Congress commanded an equal number of votes, viz. three, the fourth Nagari Sanghatana member having defected from the parent group. At the first meeting of the Transport Committee held on 14 December, 1966, the Nagari Sanghatana nominee and the Congress nominee, who was the defector from the Nagari Sanghatana, got an equal number of votes., viz. four. The Chairman of the meeting, who was the previous Chairman of the Committee, declined to give the casting vote. At the next meeting of the Transport Committee held on 17 December, 1966, the Nagari Sanghatana nominee was elected by five votes against three secured by the Congress nominee. The change in the alignment at the second meeting was caused by the defection of the third Congress member in favour of the Nagari Sanghatana nominee. This defector from the Congress belonging to a sub-caste among the scheduled castes did not see eye-to-eye with the Congress nominee belonging to another sub-caste of the scheduled castes who was himself a defector from the Nagari Sanghatana. During the last year of our study, viz. 1967-68, however, the election of the Chairman of the Transport Committee was unanimous because the Congress had by then an absolute majority in the Transport Committee. This analysis of the elections of the Chairman of the Transport Committee disclosed that there were shifting alliances not only of minority groups with major groups but there were also changing alliances of individual members of the Transport Committee.

Chairmen of Different Committees

Out of the 36 Chairmen elected during the six years tenure of the Corporation, Congress secured 10, Nagari Sanghatana also 10, the Janasangh four and Independents 12. The Congress obtained a lion's share in the Chairmanship of the Transport Committee (four), the Medical Relief and Public Health Committee (three) and the City Improvement Committee (three). Except in the City Improvement Committee, the Nagari Sanghatana secured Chairmanship in all the Committees, but were over-shadowed by the Independents in the Standing Committee and the Law, Revenue and the General Purposes Committee. The Janasangh was represented in three Committees, the Standing, the Law and General Purposes and the Improvement. The Independents obtained Chairmanship of all Committees; they secured as many as three Chairmanships each in the Standing and the Law and General Purposes Committees and four in the Public Works Committee. Thus, it would be clear that the Janasangh and the Independents secured chairmanships more than what the proportion of their strengths called for due to the spirit of accommodation evinced by the major groups.

Vice-Chairmanship

The Vice-Chairmanships of the four Special Committees (total 24) for six years (1962-1968) were distributed as follows: Congress 10, Nagari Sanghatana five, Janasangh seven and Independents two.

It is also notable that during one and the same year, the Chairmen and the Vice-Chairmen of the Committees belonged to different parties or groups. Similarly, in very few cases, the same person was elected as Chairman or Vice-Chairman of a Committee for consecutive years.

Year-wise Elections of Chairmanships and Vice-Chairmanships

Let us examine the distribution of Chairmanships and Vice-Chairmanships for each year. During the first three years, the Congress secured one Chairmanship each; during the last three years it obtained two, three and three chairmanships, respectively. This implies that the Congress gained strength especially during the last two years. The Nagari Sanghatana was at the peak of its power in 1964-65 when it secured as many as four Chairmanships; during the earlier two years, it got one and two chairmanships respectively and during the last three years one, one and zero Chairmanships, respectively. So it seems that during 1967-68, Nagari Sanghatana reached the lowest ebb of its strength. The Janasangh obtained one, two and one chairmanships during 1962-63, 1963-64 and 1967-68, respectively, but scored nil during the middle three years, viz., 1964-67. The Independents obtained as many as three Chairmanships during the three years (1962, 1965 and 1966) and one Chairmanship each during 1963-64 and two during the last year. This indicates the pivotal position occupied by the Independents including different minority groups in the Corporation.

Let us review the distribution of the Vice-Chairmanships of the Committees. During 1964 the Congress bagged the highest number of Vice-Chairmanships, viz. three, in 1963 and 1965 two each, and in 1962, 1966 and 1967 one each. The Nagari Sanghatana tallied nil

Vice-Chairmanship during 1963 and 1964; in 1962 it got two such honours; and in 1965, 1966 and 1967 one each. The Janasangh secured one each in five years; in 1963 however, it obtained two Vice-Chairmanships. The Independents secured one Vice-Chairmanship in 1966 and 1967 each. It is seen that almost all the political parties in the Corporation were represented in the distribution of Vice-Chairmanships of the Committees, which was more or less an outcome of accommodation among the different parties and groups and also among many different individuals.

It is rather depressing to find that only two Chairmen and only one Vice-Chairman were professional experts in the fields of respective Committees. An Independent lawyer-Corporator was Chairman of the Law, Revenue and General Purposes Committee in 1962-63 and a Janasangh lawyer-leader was Chairman of the City Improvement Committee in 1967-68. The lone expert Vice-Chairman was a Nagari Sanghatana Medico-Corporator who occupied the post in the Medical Relief & P.H. Committee in 1962-63. Among the Chairmen of the Standing Committee also only one could be spotted out as being an experienced person; he was a Janasangh leader elected as Chairman of the Standing Committee in 1963-64: this leader had been a Corporator for seven years in Poona. It could, of course, be pointed out that in the Transport Committee a few members were experienced Corporators, but they were by no means experienced in the field with which the Transport Committee was concerned.

PROFILES OF THE COMMITTEES' MEMBERS

The biographical data* of the members of the Committees would not only throw light on the personal characteristics of the members but also give clues for the proper understanding of the working and the decision-making processes of the Committees. It is true that all the features of the biographical data of the members would not influence the decision-making processes in the Committees, but on occasions and in particular cases some of the biographical data of the members would

* The party-wise breakdown of the Corporators in this section is different from that in the earlier sections, because the analysis in this section is based on the bio-data collected in 1968 while the account in the earlier sections gives the actual or inferential positions of the members from time to time. The official publications, such as the annual reports of the Municipal Corporation, have not mentioned the Corporators' party-affiliations.

be pertinent. The caste position of the Committee members in a majority of the decisions of the Committees is not relevant, but in the cases of a few decisions, as, for example, regarding appointments, promotions and disciplinary matters, award of contracts, acceptance of tenders for works, the caste position of the Committee membership would provide instructive guidelines. The age of the Committee members is not very much relevant in understanding the decisions of then Committees. The professional education of the members would enable them to follow the intricacies of the different matters coming before the Committees for discussion and decision. The training as a lawyer or as a medical practitioner or as an engineer would stand in good stead of the members to understand the complex issues before the Committees. So also the education in humanities or in sciences would equip the members adequately for following the different issues before the Committees. It has been, however, a matter of experience that some of the members who were not fortunate to have higher education knew the ins and outs of the matters before the Committees on account of their long experience as Corporators or Municipal Councillors. Lack or paucity of education is not necessarily a handicap in this context, provided the members concerned are willing to put in hard work in studying the law and the cases. Similarly, the experience of social or political work widens the horizons of the Committee members. Political work might prove as an obstacle in dealing with non-political civic issues before the Committees, but a proper perspective would soften the political preferences or biases of the concerned members. But, again, experience of social or political work is not a desideratum for efficient work as a Committee member. On account of the comprehensive functions of the Municipal Corporation, political parties have infiltrated into the Corporation as well as into the Committees, but in the day-to-day working of the Corporation as well as the Committees the party affiliations have got to be set aside if the work in the Committees and the Corporation is to be given due justice. Sometimes party discipline helps in decision-making but it may also be a handicap in dealing with non-political civic issues. It is very difficult to judge in abstract the worthwhileness of party discipline in the process of the working of the Municipal Corporation or its Committees. It is only in the context of specific issues and cases that judgement could be expressed on the desirability of party considerations or party discipline. The constituency from which a Corporator is elected is bound to colour his outlook regarding different issues before the Committees and the Corporation, like slum clearance, additional water supply, drainage lines, road widening, housing and so on, but the welding together of the Corporators in the framework of party discipline would provide a coherent frame of reference for judging the various issues confronting the Committees and the Corporation.

For the sake of analysis in this section, 64 Corporators were taken into account. The total membership of the Corporation during the tenure of study was 65. One Corporator expired in the early years of the tenure, so he was excluded from the total tally.

Age

The middle age groups between 35 and 50 predominated among the Committee members. Their number was 33. The number of members between the ages 40 and 60 was 36. Younger members were few: up-to the age of 35 they were six and up-to the age of 40 they were 19. The older members above 60 were nine and above 50 were 25. The detailed breakdown of membership among different age-groups was as follows:

Below 30	:	Nil
31 to 35	:	6
36 to 40	:	13
41 to 50	:	20
51 to 60	:	16
Above 60	:	9

The Nagari Sanghatana Corporators were comparatively younger than the Congress Corporators. The Nagari Sanghatana Corporators below 40 were 12 and the Congress Corporators below the same age limit were five. The Janasangh Corporators were older than either the Nagari Sanghatana or the Congress Corporators. It was found that the Janasangh Corporators above 50 were four out of the total number of six while the Nagari Sanghatana Corporators above 50 were eight out of 27 and the Congress Corporators 11 out of 23. The middle-aged (i.e., between 41 and 60) Committee members were: Congress 16 and Nagari Sanghatana 12. The Nagari Sanghatana and the Congress Corporators above 60 were two and five respectively, and the Independent Corporators were in the age-group of 36 to 60.

It was found that the Committee members in advance age-groups had longer experience as Corporator or legislator. Among the Corporators above 60 were seven with previous experience as Corporator and one Corporator with experience as member of the Legislative Council. Nearly 75 per cent of the Committee members above 60 had this kind of experience. Among the Corporators in the age-group of 50 to 60 about 50 per cent were experienced as Corporatiors or legislators. There were four legislator-Corporators in this age-group, one being member of the Legislative Council, one of Legislative Assembly and two Members of Parliament. Among the Corporators belonging to the age-group of 40 to 50, about 35 per cent (i.e., Corporators six and M.L.A. one) had this experience. Further, among the Corporators belonging to the age-groups of 35 to 40 and 30 to 35, about 30 per cent had this experience.

Education

The Committee members who had not completed even the course in primary education were 15. Out of these, two were practically with no education. Those who had completed their primary education were three. The members who could not complete the secondary education were 13 while those who completed it were nine. The members who could not complete higher education were five, but those who completed it were eight. These eight included four medical degree-holders or diploma-holders (two M.B.B.S., one Ayurveda Visharad and one L.M.P.), three B.A. and one Sanskrit degree-holder. It was satisfying to find that the additional degree/diploma-holders were 11, five with L.L.B. (one of these with M.A. also), three with B.T. (one of these with M.A. also), two with additional medical degree/diploma and one M.Sc.

It would be interesting to examine the correlation between education and caste or community. Among those with incomplete primary education course were five scheduled caste/tribe, one backward class, one Muslim, six Marathas and castes of similar status and one non-Brahmin but with status lower than that of Maratha. Those who could complete primary education were three – all Marathas. Among the members who could not complete secondary education were one Brahmin, 10 Marathas and castes of similar status, one scheduled caste and one backward class. The members who could complete secondary education were four Brahmins, one Marwari trader, four Marathas and castes of similar status. Five Marathas and castes of similar status had their higher education incomplete. Among those who had completed higher education were four Brahmins, three Marathas and castes of similar status and one Christian. Those with additional degree or diploma were eight Brahmins, three Marathas and castes of similar status.

It was found that the members who were involved in political work were distributed over all the different educational groups. Similarly, members who had previous experience as Corporator were also diffused over different educational groups. The members with legislative experience were also distributed over different educational groups: one literate, two with secondary education incomplete, one with higher education incomplete and three additional degree/diploma-holders.

Could any definite correlation be seen between education and constituency? Constituencies, like Sadashiv Peth and Shaniwar Peth, returned educated Corporators, while constituencies like Mangalwar Peth and Yerawda were represented by Corporators with not much of higher education. But other constituencies elected Corporators with higher as well as lower education.

It is also interesting to find out the extent of coincidence of higher education and higher caste or community or longer experience as Corporator or legislator. Among additional degree or diploma-holders, five were Brahmins and three non-Brahmins. Among the first degree-holders, three were Brahmins and three non-Brahmins. Similarly, the coincidence of low education and low caste or community or higher experience as Corporator or legislator could be found among two Marathas and one scheduled caste member. It should, however, be noted that low education did not necessarily go together with lack of social or political work experience.

Among the Congressmen, those with incomplete primary education and incomplete secondary education together were in a large majority. Among the Nagari Sanghatana members, however, additional degree-holders were the most important group consisting of nine; the next important group was with incomplete secondary education (six), and further next with incomplete higher education (four). Among the Janasangh members those with completed secondary education and first degree-holders were in equal strength of three. Among the Independents those with completed secondary education were the most important group, viz. three. Others were dispersed over other educational categories. If we cast a glance at the educational group-wise distribution, we would note the following details: The Congress members were the predominant group in those with incomplete primary education (12 out of 15) as well as in the group of completed primary education. In the group of members with incomplete secondary education, Congress and Nagari Sanghatana mustered equal strength of six, while Independents were represented by one member. In the group of those who had completed secondary education, Janasangh and Independents had three members each while the Congress had two and Nagari Sanghatana one. Among those who had incomplete higher education, Nagari Sanghatana dominated with four as against one member of the Congress. Among the first degree-holders were Nagari Sanghatana and Janasangh with three each and Congress one less than the others. Among the additional degree-holders, the Nagari Sanghatana members were in an overwhelming majority with nine against one each of the Congress and the Independents.

Among the degree and the additional degree holders, the white-collared professionals were in majority; while among other groups, merchants/traders, agriculturists, etc. were represented in large numbers. Among merchants/traders there were a few members with higher education and also with an additional degree. The social workers and the agriculturists (excepting one) did not possess higher education, while four political workers were highly educated.

Caste/Community

The Marathas were the largest caste or community among the Committee members with the strength of 23. The Brahmins were the next numerous group with 17 members. The non-Brahmin non-Maratha Hindu with status similar to that of Marathas were six and those with status lower than Marathas were nine. The scheduled caste members were five. The trading community was represented by two members. There was a lone Muslim and also a single Christian member.

The Census data from 1951 onwards do not mention the caste-wise break-up of the City's population, hence it is not possible to compare the caste composition of the members with the caste distribution of the City's population. It can only be stated that the members belonging to minority castes like the Brahmin or the trading community could be elected only from the wards which included substantial number of electorate of the respective castes. The multi-member constituencies facilitated the election of such minority group members.

Let us examine the representation of the different professions in the castes or communities. Among the 17 Brahmin members, lawyers were four, secondary teachers three, medicos three, merchants three, property-holders one and political workers three. Among the 23 Maratha members, merchants or traders were 17 (including two pensioner/teachers), agriculturists four, medico one and property-holder one. The six non-Brahmin non-Marathas with status similar to that of Marathas were distributed as follows: merchants three, agriculturist one and medicos two. The distribution of castes lower than Marathas was: merchants or traders four, agriculturist one, property-holder one, factory worker one and political or social workers two. The two trading community members were one housewife and one contractor. All the five scheduled caste members were social workers. The lone Muslim member owned a small shop and the lone Indian Christian member was a journalist.

The Committee members who were not involved in active political work were to be found among the trading community, scheduled castes and the Indian Christians. Except Muslim and Christian, among members of other castes or communities experience of the Corporation or legislative work was represented. Among the Brahmins there were eight such experienced members while among the Marathas there were 13. Only among the scheduled castes there was only one such experienced member and in the other three remaining castes there were six experienced members.

The Brahmin population was concentrated in a few constituencies like Sadashiv Peth, Shaniwar Peth, Shivajinagar, Narayan Peth, Budhwar Peth, etc. Brahmin Corporators could be elected only through these constituencies, similarly about the trading and scheduled caste communities. The Maratha and allied castes members could, however, be elected from amongst almost all constituencies because their population was dispersed in large numbers over almost all constituencies.

Among Brahmins, all the party groups were represented with seven members belonging to Nagari Sanghatana, five Janasangh, three Congress and two Independents. Among the Marathas there were no Janasangh Corporators. The Congress was predominant with 14 Maratha members, Nagari Sanghatana with eight and Independent with one. Among the castes lower than Marathas all groups were represented; the Congress with three and Nagari Sanghatana with four members had nearly equal representation in these castes. Among the scheduled castes, the Congress had a lead with three members and Nagari Sanghatana and Independents had one each, the Janasangh not being represented in these castes at all. Among the Muslims, the Congress alone was represented with the lowest number belonging to it. Among the Indian Christians, however, Nagari Sanghatana alone counted claiming the single member belonging to the community. Among the trading community, Congress and Independents had one member each.

In the Congress party, Marathas were in large majority with 14 members, the Brahmins, castes lower than Marathas and scheduled castes were with three members each, and other groups, except Christians, with one member each. In Nagari Sanghatana, Marathas had eight members, Brahmins seven, other non-Brahmins five, castes lower than Marathas four and scheduled castes and Christians one each. In Janasangh, there were five Brahmins and one belonging to a caste lower than Maratha. Among the Independents, Muslims, Christians, non-Brahmins and non-Marathas were not represented.

Profession

Among the members of the Committees, merchants or traders were the most numerous group consisting of 30. It means that this group was merely one-half of the total strength of the Corporation. The social or political workers came next with 10, the agriculturists and medicos with six each, lawyers with four, the well-off with some property with four, teachers with three and factory workers with one.

Among the 30 merchant-Corporators, 11 were engaged in political work, 13 had previous experience as Corporator and three had been legislators (two of these had also been Corporators). Among the lawyers, three had experience as Corporator, one had been legislator and three were engaged in active political work. Three from among the medico-Corporators were involved in active politics and one had been a Corporator. One teacher-Corporator had been in the Corporation before. Among the social workers, one was recently elected M.L.A., nobody had previous experience as Corporator, but two were involved in active politics. Among the political workers, one had been a Corporator and two legislators. The lone factory-worker member had been a Corporator and was also in active politics. From agriculturists, three were in Corporation before and four were in active politics. From among others, two had been in active politics but none had been a Corporator or a legislator.

Let us see the party composition of the different professional groups. Among the merchants, Congressman were 14, Nagari Sanghatana 11, Janasangh two and Independents three. It means that both the Congress as well as the Nagari Sanghatana had more influence over the merchants or trading community than any other group. Among the lawyer-group, the Congress commanded one Corporator, Nagari Sanghatana two and Janasangh one. In the group of Medico-Corporators the Congress had two, Nagari Sanghatana three and Janasangh one. The Nagari Sanghatana had one teacher Corporator while the Janasangh had two. Among the social workers, the Congressman were three, Nagari Sanghatana one and Independents two. From among the political workers, Nagari Sanghatana had a majority: Nagari Sanghatana had the following of three and Congress of one in this group. The lone factory worker was of Nagari Sanghatana persuasion. Among the agriculturists, the Congress and the Nagari Sanghatana had an equal following of three members. Among the others, the Congress two, was followed by Nagari Sanghatana one and Independent one.

The agriculturist-Corporators (except one, who was also a trader) were elected from some outlying rural constituencies. The merchant or trader Corporators, on the other hand, were dispersed in almost all constituencies of the city. The lawyer and teacher Corporators were, however, elected from constituencies in which educated voters were concentrated in sizeable numbers.

Experience

There were as many as 30 Corporators involved in active politics. Twenty-three had previous experience as Corporator, seven Corporators had been legislators (two of these had been Corporators also). This indicates that a considerable number of Committee members had experience of work in Corporation or in active politics and that a few had also experience of the work in legislature.

Of those who were involved in active politics, Congressmen were 10, Nagari Sanghatana 17, Janasangh two and Independent one. Those with previous experience as Corporator were Congress eight, Nagari Sanghatana 10, Janasangh four and Independent one. Among the legislators, there was only one Congressman and Nagari Sanghatana was followed by six. The breakdown shows that Nagari Sanghatana had a larger number of experienced Corporators than either the Congress or the Janasangh.

The members who were experienced as Corporators or active political workers were dispersed over almost all constituencies. But that was not the case with those who had legislative experience. Three out of seven legislator-Corporators were elected from Sadashiv Peth constituency while two from Bhawani Peth and one each from South-West and Budhwar constituencies. It was interesting to find that two legislator-Corporators belonged to the Bhawani constituency, a constituency not consisting of educated people.

Parties

The party-wise breakdown of the Committee members was Congress 26, Nagari Sanghatana 26, Janasangh six and Independents six. This party position might not have correspondence with the strength of the parties as revealed in the elections to the Committees. This break-up also does not take into account the frequent re-alignments after the elections. The membership of the Congress indicated here also included two or three Independent members, who closely followed the lead given by the Congress party.

Both the Congress as well as the Nagari Sanghatana commanded following, by and large, from the different parts of the city, but it was found that the Congress candidates were not elected at all from eight constituencies out of the total number of 20 constituencies. These were Rasta, Nagesh, Ganj-Ghorpadi, Budhwar, Narayan, Sadashiv (two constituencies) and Hadapsar, Nagari Sanghatana candidates were also not elected from four constituencies, viz., Somawar, Guruwar, Shaniwar and Yerawda. These constituencies could be considered as strongholds of the other parties or groups. The influence of the Janasangh was confined to four constituencies, viz., Sadashiv, Shaniwar, Budhwar and Narayan, where there was a concentration of Brahmin electorates. The influence of the Independents was restricted to six constituencies, viz., Ganj, Budhwar, Raviwar, Kasba, Sadashiv and Yerawda. These were pockets of influence of individual Independent candidates.

Constituencies

Members were elected from 20 ward constituencies. The provision of multi-member constituencies facilitated the election of minority groups located in different ward constituencies. The important reason for the election in considerable numbers of representatives of small castes or communities, like the Brahmins, the castes lower than Marathas, etc., was the prevalence of multi-member constituencies. Two-member constituencies were five in number, three-member constituencies nine, four-member constituencies four, five-member constituency one and six-member constituency one. It was really curious that such a wide variety of multi-member constituencies was laid down for the elections to the Municipal Corporation. Five seats had been reserved for the scheduled castes in different constituencies.

There were no reserved seats for the women. Nevertheless, in all, four women Corporators were elected. One of these was not a member of any Committee. This woman Corporator belonged to the Nagari Sanghatana. Three women Committee members belonged to Congress (one), Nagari Sanghatana (one) and Janasangh (one). One woman Committee member was under-matriculate while two others were graduates and secondary teachers. All the three were social and political workers. One was a Gujarati Bania while two others were Brahmins. The Congress Gujarati Bania Committee member was elected from the Raviwar Peth constituency where there was a sizeable electorate belonging to the Gujarati Bania Community. Two Brahmin women Committee members were elected from the Sadashiv Peth and Shivajinagar (South-West) constituencies. One woman Corporator, who was not a Committee member, had been elected from the Sadashiv Peth constituency. The three constituencies, from which these women Committee members were elected, were educationally advanced.

4

CO-ORDINATION COMMITTEE

RATIONALE AND COMPOSITION

Brief History

THE CO-ORDINATION Committee was set up in the Poona Municipal Corporation, in the first instance, in 1963. Records show that one meeting of the Committee was held on 5th October, 1963. There was a break in the meetings of the Committee which resumed regular work since 17th May, 1965; however, the Co-ordination Committee operated on an informal basis in 1963 as well as in 1965 and 1966. During 1965 and 1966, six and five meetings of the Co-ordination Committee were held, respectively. It was only in January 1967, that a formal resolution regarding the composition, sphere of business and procedures of the Co-ordination Committee was passed by the General Body of the Corporation. Actually, there was not much difference between the terms of reference and the procedures of working of the Co-ordination Committee before and after the formal resolution was passed by the General Body of the Corporation. During 1967, six meetings of the Co-ordination Committee were held. For the sake of uniformity of analysis in this chapter, all the 17 meetings of the Co-ordination Committee, since 1963 till 16th November, 1967, have been covered.

A Special Device

The Co-ordination Committee is a special device employed by the Poona Municipal Corporation to deal expeditiously with the business before it. No specific provision was made for the Co-ordination Committee in the Corporation's Act as well as in the rules under the Act framed by the Corporation itself. The Standing Committee, the General Body of the Corporation and the Municipal Commissioner were expected to operate as co-ordinating agencies in the Corporation according to the Corporation's Act and even today these authorities do operate as co-ordinating agencies in the Corporation. The functions of the Poona Municipal Corporation have multiplied during the last 15 years or so since its establishment. The functions of the Corporation have also grown in diversity. The population of the city has increased about four-fold and the area of operation of the Corporation has also expanded considerably. The conception regarding the functions of the Municipal Corporation has undergone a radical change. Today the Corporation is expected not merely to perform basic civic functions, like health and sanitation, but it is also desired that the Corporation should seek the promotion of the welfare of its citizens in all its varied implications. Consequently, the business of the Corporation has grown considerably, so the statutory authorities, prescribed by the Act and the rules, find it difficult to co-ordinate the execution of the varied functions by the Corporation. No uniform perspective can be discovered in the functioning of the Corporation. The city has expanded physically in different directions and the Corporation is trying to cover the various aspects of the citizens' lives, but the Corporation is not in a position to plan the City's development in a reasonable and systematic manner. The Corporation also finds it difficult to secure resources for the implementation of its various development schemes. This underlines the need for deliberate long-term planning of its functions. The Co-ordination Committee was conceived on account of this need for deliberate planning of city's development.

Experiment in Bombay City

The Bombay Municipal Corporation tried with the Co-ordination Committee and it is gathered that the Committee was working successfully there. There were also audible rumblings and grievances regarding the Co-ordination Committee in Bombay Municipal Corporation from some of the Corporators there. It was alleged that the Co-ordination Committee encroached upon the prescribed sphere of business of the respective statutory authorities of the Bombay Municipal Corporation. By and large, the experiment with the Co-ordination Committee in Bombay City had been a success. Moreover, the report of the Zakaria Committee on the changes in the Acts concerning Municipal Corporations outlined the need for the constitution of the Co-ordination Committee. These factors led the

Poona Municipal Corporation to form the Co-ordination Committee in 1963. The constitution of the Co-ordination Committee was put on a regular basis, as it has been noted above, in January 1967.

Functions

The terms of reference, as laid down in the resolution regarding the Co-ordination Committee, referred to four factors. First, the Committee sought to bring about uniformity and co-ordination among the different authorities and as between the officials and the elected Corporators. Secondly, the Committee would determine basic policies regarding different issues and subjects arising before the Corporation from time to time. Thirdly, the Committee would iron out the issues underlying important subjects to be discussed and decided upon by the General Body of the Corporation. In the events of urgency, the Co-ordination Committee could decide matters and its decisions would be laid before the General Body of the Corporation for final approval. Fourthly, the Co-ordination Committee would review the progress of different development schemes and works and also give broad guidelines for their speedier execution. The Co-ordination Committee thus would decide upon priorities and modalities regarding the implementation of development works as well as normal functions of the Corporation. The Committee would particularly focus its attention on the economic and financial implications of the functions of the Corporation.

Composition

The composition of the Co-ordination Committee as prescribed by the resolution sought to give representation to the important office-bearers of the Corporation as well as the leaders of the parties in the Corporation. The members of the Committee would be the Mayor, the Deputy Mayor, the Chairman of the Standing Committee, the Transport Committee, the School Board and the four Special Committees (Public works, Law, Medical and Improvement). The resolution mentioned seven representatives of parties in the Corporation to be the members of the Committee: two of the Nagari Sanghatana, two of the Congress party, one of the Janasangh and two from the remaining Corporators. The representatives of the parties were to be named by the Mayor. The term of the Co-ordination

Committee would be co-extensive with the term of the General Body of the Corporation, but it is obvious that the membership of the Committee would change almost every year with the annual re-elections of the office-bearers of the Corporation as well as of the leaders of the different parties in the Corporation.

Informality

The decisions of the Co-ordination Committee were informal and not binding on the different statutory authorities of the Corporation unless and until the latter adopted these informal decisions as their own. The resolution, therefore, rightly laid down that no wide publicity should be given to the informal decisions of the Co-ordination Committee. Such publicity would unnecessarily hamper free thinking and decisions by the statutory authorities. The resolution, however, mentioned that the informal decisions of the Co-ordination Committee should be recorded along with the items in the agenda of the different authorities of the Corporation. It also left a guideline that the agenda of the meetings of the Co-ordination Committee should be circulated among all the Corporators so that they might be able to think over the agenda and suggest their own additions. The Corporators concerned who raised items for discussion in the Co-ordination Committee would be invited to the meetings of the Committee in which their items would be discussed.

Meetings

The Mayor was authorised by the resolution to frame the agenda of the Co-ordination Committee meetings. He would consult the Municipal Commissioner before he framed the agenda of the Committee meetings. In fact, the agenda of the meetings of the Co-ordination Committee was the outcome of the proposals from the Mayor's Office and th Office of the Municipal Commissioner. The Mayor would act as the chairman of the meetings of the Co-ordination Committee. In the absence of the Mayor, the Deputy Mayor and, in the latter's absence, the Chairman of the Standing Committee would preside over the meetings of the Committee. The Secretary of the Municipal Corporation would also act as the Secretary of the Co-ordination Committee, so he would convene the meetings of the Committee, keep their proceedings and records and deal with its business in general. The

Municipal Commissioner and his officials would attend the meetings of the Committee and it is implicit that they would participate in the proceedings of the Committee. The resolution stipulates that the Co-ordination Committee should meet at least once in every month and on more occasions, if necessary.

SCOPE OF DISCUSSIONS

Issues

In all, 17 meetings of the Co-ordination Committee were held during the period 1963 to 1967. In these meetings, 179 items were raised. Out of these, on 37 items information was furnished by the Municipal Commissioner to the Committee and there was not much discussion on these items and no decision was expected to be taken on these items by the Committee. The remaining 142 items were discussed by the Committee. Out of these, 11 items pertained to administrative organisation including staff matters, 38 related to finance, 20 to major development schemes, 12 to functional administration, seven to building regulations, six to public grievances, eight to slums, 15 to Corporation proceedings and 25 to miscellaneous items including road-widening.

This would show that the Co-ordination Committee was seized of a variety of issues of long-term as well as short-term significance. The Co-ordination Committee, by virtue of the resolution regarding its scope, was expected to deal mainly with the policy issues, but it was found that the agenda for its meetings was studded with subsidiary items, like holding of receptions to dignitaries, exclusion of certain plots or lands from reservations or list for slum clearance, and so on. It seems, due care was not taken to rationalise the composition of the agenda for the meetings of the Committee. The Mayor as well as the Municipal Commissioner allowed Committee's berth to all the sundry items which they found inconvenient to deal with by themselves. This added to the weight of the agenda of the Committee's meetings. Naturally, this left little room for detailed discussion of important policy items which led to their postponement from time to time.

Information supplied by the Office

Items on which information was furnished to the Committee by the

Municipal Commissioner also concerned different subjects. Ten items were concerned with development works, such as loans for filtered water scheme and for other development works like Stadium, Theatre, etc. Eight items of information pertained to functional administration, as for example sanitary facilities at Corporation Employee's Colonies, etc. Three items were concerning the State Government communications regarding the Flood Protection Committee. Two items dealt with the Poona Municipal Transport (PMT), one item was regarding land acquisition in Poona Cantonment Area for the PMT, and the other was concerning report by the Municipal Commissioner on the accounts of the PMT which was a very delicate issue for the Commissioner to deal with. Three issues were regarding information related to the staff matters, like increase in the Dearness Allowance, B Area allowance, etc. Three issues were concerning Corporation proceedings, like finance for the reception to dignitaries, intimation of election of Corporators to the Standing Committee, and so on. The Commissioner also informed the Committee regarding the financial situation of the Corporation, arrears of rent owed to the Corporation in certain localities and the levy of octroi. Three issues of information pertained to dangerous houses, leasing of land to cane-crushers, etc. One item was concerning Chaphekar Memorial and another concerning the accommodation of persons displaced due to road-widening. Sometimes, a few suggestions were broached by Corporators after the Commissioner had furnished information, but these suggestions were *obiter dicta*. The purpose underlying the furnishing of information by the Commissioner was that the Co-ordination Committee should know the progress regarding important matters before the Corporation like development works, implementation of important functions like primary education, maintenance of roads, welfare of its own employees, progress of the P.M.T., the condition and safety of houses in the Corporation area and accommodation of persons displaced due to road-widening and other causes. The members of the Co-ordination Committee also felt that they were taken into confidence by the Commissioner who informed them in regard to the progress of the important activities of the Municipal Corporation. This also prevented discussion on certain items on which information was supplied by the Commissioner.

Issues regarding Administrative Organisation

In regard to administrative organisation, different issues were raised in the meetings of the Co-ordination Committee. The grant of Dearness Allowance at increased rates cropped up from time to time. As the State Government raised the rates of Dearness Allowance to keep pace with the rising cost of living, the Corporation employees voiced demand for increase in the rates of their own Dearness Allowance. So it was incumbent on the Committee to consider this issue from time to time. Improved scales for its key officials were discussed by the Committee. The Co-ordination Committee had to take decision in this matter because this affected the overall efficiency of the working of the Corporation. The issue, as to which officials should be included in the proposition, was also a vital one. The questions of the appointments of a Liaison Officer and Planning-cum-Rural Development Officer were also raised and discussed in the Co-ordination Committee. The Liaison Officer was to act as a bridge between administration and the public at large. He would also operate as a Public Relations and Press Officer of the Corporation. The Planning-cum-Rural Development Officer was to take care of the planning of the development functions as well as matters concerning rural development in the Corporation area. The Municipal Commissioner expected that the person for the post would be deputed from the office of the Divisional Commissioner. Similarly, the appointment of the Administrative Officer of the School Board was taken for discussion in the Co-ordination Committee. This appointment was a controversial matter and it was postponed on several occasions by the General Body of the Corporation. If unanimity could be reached in the Co-ordination Committee, it would have facilitated the final decision by the General Body of the Corporation. The absorption of the surplus staff of the Mangalwar Hospital taken over by the Corporation from a Missionary institution was also raised before the Co-ordination Committee.

Grants to Institutions

The proposals regarding grants to different institutions in the city and outside were also placed before the Co-ordination Committee. It should be noted here that not all the proposals regarding grants were put before the Co-ordination Committee. It was rather intriguing why certain proposals were pinpointed for discussion in the Committee. Proposals for grants to certain colleges in the city, to the Swami Vivekanand Shila Samiti and to the Lokamanya Tilak Memorial at London were placed before the Committee for decision.

Assortment of Issues

The question of heavy incidence of State Government charge of loans was also raised before the Committee. The State Government gave its guarantee to the loans raised by the Corporation from time to time in the open market, for which the Government charged a small percentage on the loans. But this charge was considered to be heavy by the Corporation, hence it was thought that the Government should be requested to drop this charge on loans. The acquisition of Mangalwar Hospital referred to above, subscription to a State Government loan, compensation to a family affected by a house collapse for which the Corporation was responsible, the cost of roads in private residential colonies, and so on; were some of the other issues pertaining to expenditure aspect. Among the items concerning revenue aspect were the octroi, the slabs in regard to house tax, grants from Government, etc.

Major Development Works

The most important issues which were discussed by the Co-ordination Committee were concerning the major development works in the city. One of the main objectives of the Co-ordination Committee was to speed up the execution of major development works in the city; and it must be said that the Co-ordination Committee was successful in giving an impetus to the implementation of major development works. This was also due to the leadership of administration by a competent and genial Municipal Commissioner during the years 1965 to 1967. The major development works that were discussed in the Committee were the construction of Nehru Stadium, the new Phule market building, hospitals, bridges across the river, the drama theatre, proposals regarding river site improvement and an idea of starting trolley bus in the city.

Other Works

The Committee was also seized of different aspects of functional administration. The roads in the city as well as in the new suburbs needed repairs. The number of students in primary schools was rising but the accommodation for them was scanty. There was an urgent need for the Corporation to construct more school buildings because the hired ones were inadequate and unsatisfactory. The primary school buildings suffered from lack of sanitary facilities. The new suburbs like Kothrud were without water supply. The Corporation had to think of a temporary water supply scheme pending completion of the scheme of water supply from Khadakwasla Dam. The city needed additional crematoria and there was also the question of erecting an electrically operated crematorium. All this and other aspects of functional administration were discussed by the Co-ordination Committee. On some of these, there were no clear-cut solutions because they were matters of routine administration, but the Committee expressed its concern over the important aspects of functional administration like school buildings, water supply, and so on.

Building Regulations

The building regulations prescribed by the Corporation were found to be inadequate in certain respects, e.g., repairs to dangerous houses, provision of sanitary facilities in rural parts of the city, constructions within the flood-line in the centre of the city, the provision of pumping-sets in the residential houses, provisions regarding pulling down of houses for road-widening purposes, etc. These matters involved consideration of different aspects to the questions, e.g., the claims of the private house-owners, the financial provisions involved and public purpose. The Committee, it must be said, could not discuss all these aspects in detail and so could not form guidelines to the statutory authorities in these matters.

Public Grievances

The grievances were voiced and ventilated by other individuals or different sections among the citizens. For example, roads in Vijayanagar Colony could not be constructed by the Corporation and the reason was that the residents of the colony had not remitted necessary money to the Corporation. Electric polls had fallen down but nothing was done about it for a long time. The Corporation regulations prevented setting of pumps to lift up water. There were a number of private wells in the city, but in times of scarcity of water supply people could not use the water from these wells, so they demanded that they should be allowed to set pumps on these private wells. At a number of places, repairs to roads were going on, but because intimations were not given to the people in the localities concerned they were put to a lot of inconvenience. Such public grievances also were tackled by the Co-ordination Committee. It could, of course, be realised that such public grievances, if allowed to be raised in the meetings of the Co-ordination Committee, would have swelled the agenda and made discussion of important policy issues well-nigh impossible.

Slums

Slums were growing in the city in all places with the growth of industries in the city. The twin issue of slum improvement and slum clearance was set before the Co-ordination Committee for discussion. Pending the clearance of the existing slums they had to be improved so that residents there were provided with minimum amenities, like, water supply, sanitation and electric lighting. The problem of slum clearance had huge dimensions but the problem of slum improvement also involved various intricate issues. The Co-ordination Committee tried to finalise a list of slums that were to be improved in course of years to come. The provision of alternative sites for the accommodation of the slum-dwellers was also under consideration of the Committee. Alternative sites were proposed in different extended parts of the city like Health Camp, Bibwewadi, Dhanakwadi, etc. The twin issues were too difficult and complex for the Co-ordination Committee to tackle.

Corporation's Proceedings

Pending before the Co-ordination Committee were also certain issues concerning Corporation's own proceedings. The meetings of the General Body of the Corporation were adjourned too frequently with the result that business mounted from time to time and important matters could not be disposed of by the Corporation. A reform of the procedures regarding the General Body meetings was to be thought of. The Corporation needed a publicity organ. Such a publication was issued out by the Corporation in the past, but it was discontinued. The question of resumption of the publication was to be discussed by the Co-ordination Committee. A Corporator had suggested that an independent vigilance commission to deal with cases of corruption should be set up in the Municipal Corporation on the lines of the Central Vigilance Commission. The Committee had to sort out the need for such an independent vigilance commission. An opportunity of establishing relations with a town in Norway presented itself before the Corporation. The Co-ordination Committee had to decide this issue. The office-bearers of the Corporation, including the Mayor, received communications from citizens on different matters. How to dispose of these communications was to be decided by the Co-ordination Committee. Whether a detailed note was to be expected from the Departments concerned or the Departments would be asked to take necessary action on these communications was to be discussed by the Committee. Whether allowances should also be granted to the Corporators for attendance at the meetings of different committees including the School Board, was also placed before the Committee. The Mayor of the Corporation was to be provided with residence. The site for locating this residence was for the Committee to decide. It was felt that the jurisdiction of the Corporation should be extended to Katraj Gaothan. This was also placed before the Committee.

Miscellaneous Issues

Miscellaneous issues, like alternative accommodation for persons displaced due to road-widening, removal of a temple in the city, memorials to personalities like Veer Chaphekar, Jijabai and others, renovation of the mosque at Karve Road-Sambhaji Bridge corner and so on, were also before the Committee for discussion.

Framing of Agenda

As noted earlier, the agenda for the meetings of the Co-ordination Committee was framed by putting together items from the Mayor's office and the office of the Municipal Commissioner. It was found that a large majority of the items in the agenda, viz., two-thirds, were proposed by the Administration. the Corporators, through written communications or oral suggestions, were responsible for 35 items included in the agenda. The office of the Mayor proposed seven items. Three items stemmed from public grievances. This, of course, did not mean that public grievances were completely excluded from the items proposed by the administration. Some public grievances were incorporated in certain proposed items from the administration. This break down did not include items on which information was furnished by the Municipal Commissioner. Some items proposed by the administration were based on communications from the allied organisations like the School Board or the State Government. A majority of the items were directed by the administration, because in the Poona Municipal Corporation set-up the administration headed by the Municipal Commissioner was responsible for the execution of policies adopted by the General Body of the Corporation. As such, the administration was a respository of the necessary information regarding different issues facing it. The Corporators, however, were free to propose certain grievances or issues for discussion by the Co-ordination Committee. For example, temporary accommodation to stall-holders in Phule Market, who were displaced on account of the construction of the new building, was raised by a Corporator. Discrimination regarding constructions within flood-line was also broached by a Corporator. The issue of setting up an independent vigilance commission noted above for the Corporation was raised by a Corporator through a written communication. The question of octroi pass refund, supply of flags to Corporators, raising of income limit from Rs. 200 to Rs. 300 per month for admission to Corporation primary schools, erecting statues of dignitaries and receptions to VIPs and such other questions, were raised by Corporators because they thought them to be important.

The desirability of rationalising the agenda of the Co-ordination Committee meetings has been referred to above. A few items were of little consequence and so ought not to have found place in the agenda of the Committee meetings. The issue of excluding particular slums from the list for clearance ought not to have been raised in the Co-ordination Committee. It should have been left for the relevant statutory Committees to decide. The construction of a platform for meetings at Shaniwar Wada was also not so important as to be posed before the Co-ordination Committee. The representation of the Corporation at the proposed Seminar on Town-Planning at Bombay was a matter to be sorted out by the Commissioner's office in consultation with the Mayor's office. Model of stands to hang balances in the new Phule Market was too trivial a matter for the Co-ordination Committee to tackle. The distribution of milk through vans donated by the CARE was also an issue to be left to the relevant Committee to grapple with. It need not be repeated that to make the Co-ordination Committee's work more meaningful, the framing of agenda for its meetings ought to have been given more careful attention than it had been given so far.

Decisiveness

How far were the deliberations of the Co-ordination Committee decisive? It was creditable to the Co-ordination Committee that on 112 out of 142 items discussed by it definite decisions were taken. Not all these decisions were the last word to be uttered by the Committee. Some decisions were to the effect that "the issues should be decided by the Municipal Commissioner or the Department concerned", or that "information should be collected by the Commissioner and placed before the Co-ordination Committee", or that "Government action is awaited". Nine items were postponed from time to time. Among the items postponed repeatedly were the issues of slum improvement and slum clearance, construction of school buildings and reform of procedures regarding the General Body meetings. On 17 items the Co-ordination Committee could not arrive at any decisions. Among these were again the issues of slum clearance, slab for the levy of house-tax, proposal to amend the Acts concerned to facilitate slum clearance, allowances for Corporators for attending Committee meetings, site for Mayor's residence, etc.

Issues on which definite decisions were taken by the Co-ordination Committee were various. It was decided to request the State Government to give grant for the development of rural areas. It was also decided by the Co-ordination Committee to approach the Central Government to remit the service tax on its buildings in the city. The question of provision of accommodation to the Corporation employees was tackled decisively by the Committee. But the Committee could not come to a firm decision regarding taking back of the site transferred to the Maharashtra Housing Board in Bibwewadi. The Committee decided to request Government to shift an industrial zone from the irrigated tract at Hadapsar. The pending claims of green belts in the city and industrial development were skilfully dealt with by the Corporation in this particular case. The Committee also took a decision to widen the Laxmi Road form one end to another although it knew that this was a very difficult task. The resumption of publication of *Nagari Jeevan*, the organ of the Municipal Corporation, was decided by the Committee. Willing approval was given by the Committee to different proposals regarding the completion of major development works like the stadium, theatre, hospitals, filtered water supply scheme, and so on. What could be done with regard to the unused land acquired for road-widening was a question raised before the

Committee. It was decided to follow the provisions in the given laws in this respect. The Committee gave a clear 'no' to a proposal from a Corporator regarding supply of flags to the Corporators. The Committee took a bold decision in deciding that no more exemptions in the matter of levy of octroi should be given to recent industries and that the Government be approached for compensation in lieu of octroi collection. The Committee also decided that the income limit of the guardians of pupils for admission to Corporation secondary schools should not raised from Rs. 200 to Rs. 300 per month. The reason given for the decision was that this would increase the number of prospective candidates for admission beyond the capacity of the schools. Instead, the Committee reiterated the policy of the Corporation to grant admissions to the children of all the Municipal employees irrespective of income limit. The issue of renovation of the mosque on Karve Road-Sambhaji Bridge corner was a very delicate one. It was also proposed to acquire the mosque for road-widening purpose. The Committee decided that both these issues of permission regarding renovation and acquisition of mosque for road-widening should be decided simultaneously. The Committee generally gave its approval to proposals regarding increase in the rates of Dearness Allowance as and when the financial position of the Corporation permitted. The question of re-appointments of retired personnel like the arbitrator, superintendent of octroi, were also decided sympathetically by the Committee. Similarly the question of raising the maximum slabs of scales of key officials was decided favourably with due consideration for the services of these officials. It was, however, surprising that the Secretary of the Municipal Corporation was excluded from the list of these key officials. The temporary water supply scheme for Kothrud was approved with no grudge by the Committee. So it solved an urgent problem before an expanded suburb. Taking on lease of Ganapati Mandir Hill at Sarasbag was decided upon without loss of time by the Committee. This facilitated the development of the garden at Sarasbag, a beauty spot in the city. The Committee showed courage in giving a decision that, instead of granting a portion of ground-rent to the Municipal Sports Club, the Club should request an increase in grant by the Corporation.

THE ROLE OF THE COMMITTEE

Execution of Decisions

About 50 per cent of the items, on which definite decisions were taken by the Co-ordination Committee, were followed up in execution. Twelve decisions of the Committee were not executed. Two were executed partially and in three cases execution did not start at all.

Decision to widen the Laxmi Road was shelved. Similarly nothing was done about the slum clearance decision. In matters regarding students' hostel at 'J' Road (which was to be transferred to a willing students' organisation), exemption from Stamp Duty required for refund of Octroi, shifting of Chiplunkar Statue, Jijamata Memorial, levy of a fine if repairs to drainage were not done, no follow-up action was taken by the relevant authorities of the Corporation. Of course, responsibility for this would not be that of the Co-ordination Committee. The Corporation did not receive from the State Government full grant claimed for the drama theatre and the stadium.

The important decisions of the Co-ordination Committee which were followed up in action included the removal of the Sati Temple from the widened road, the construction of a Municipal Employees' Colony at Health Camp, the allocation of blocks in Maharashtra Housing Board colonies to those affected by road-widening, the resumption of publication of *Nagari Jeevan* (the organ of the corporation), riverside improvement, the construction of major development works like the stadium, the drama theatre and the bridge across the river, the formal constitution for the Co-ordination Committee, the acquisition of the Mangalwar Hospital, repairs to privately owned school buildings by the Corporation, revised rules regarding the General Body Meetings, the inclusion of Kothrud Gaothan within Corporation limits, the lease of Ganapati Mandir Hill at Sarasbag, laying of water-line and drainage at Sahakar Nagar by the Corporation, and so on.

Acceleration in Execution of Major Development Works

It is very difficult to pronounce a definite judgement on the role of the Co-ordination Committee on the basis of the experience of its working so far. The Co-ordination Committee has worked for over two-and-half years. The association of an able and amiable Municipal Commissioner with the working of the Corporation in general and the Co-ordination Committee in particular could not be kept out of the picture while evaluating the role of the Co-ordination Committee. The main achievement of the Co-ordination Committee was the acceleration of execution of major development works in the city. The office-bearers of the Corporation as well as party leaders were taken into confidence by the Municipal Commissioner through the meetings of the Co-ordination Committee in regard to the undertaking and the completion of the major development works. These were points of prestige not only to the administration but also to the City Fathers. The Commissioner was successful in infusing a sense of urgency among the office-bearers and party leaders regarding the prompt execution of these development works.

Failures and Gains

But the Co-ordination Committee failed to deal with policy proposals, for example, slum clearance, building regulations, house-tax; and so on. These were matters which apparently were not of urgent consequences and so could be processed leisurely through different statutory Committees. Certain other issues, like sizable grants to certain institutions such as the Lokmanya Tilak Memorial at London, accommodation for Municipal employees, accommodation for persons affected by road-widening, salaries of key officials, were also tackled successfully by the Co-ordination Committee.

Much of the success of the Co-ordination Committee would depend upon the compactness of business before it. The temptation to swell the agenda of the Co-ordination Committee had to be got over by both the Mayor's office as well as the office of the Municipal Commissioner. The Co-ordination Committee should not be looked upon as a safe berth for inconvenient propositions and subjects. The Co-ordination Committee would better concentrate its attention on important policy matters, financial proposals, major development works, and questions pertaining to the development of the city in general. If the Co-ordination Committee frittered away its energies on insignificant matters or detailed operation of administration or issues affecting particular individuals or parties, its rationale would not be justified. A feeling existed among a few Corporators that the Co-ordination Committee sought to encroach on their own preserve. This feeling was manifested in a notable instance of resentment by a statutory Committee against a decision of the Co-ordination Committee. The Law Committee declined to approve of creating new staff posts for the proposed journal *Nagari Jeevan*. Later, this feeling was got over by persuading, in a meeting of the Co-ordination Committee, the Chairman of the Law Committee to secure the approval of his

Committee to the proposed new posts. The essence of the success of the Co-ordination Committee lay in its informal working. It had the role to create a cordial atmosphere among important constituents of the Corporation and thus pave the way for a speedier execution of important tasks confronting it.

5

AD-HOC COMMITTEES

THE RATIONALE

THE 'AD-HOC' Committees are a special device provided for in the Act to facilitate the policy-making and administrative functions of the Corporation. They are not designed to operate as substitutes for the permanent statutory committees, viz. the Standing Committee, the Transport Committee or the Special Committees. The Ad-hoc Committees seek to provide the Corporation with guidelines in chalking out a new policy or a change in the given policy in regard to its obligatory or optional functions. They also review decisions of permanent committees which they think are wrong on account of defect of omission or commission. Besides, they would not hesitate to scrutinise irregular or improper administrative actions in particular cases or matters. Sometimes matters affecting subjects within the competence of more than one permanent Committee or authority have necessarily to be referred to the Ad-hoc Committees for elucidation. All in all, the Ad-hoc Committees are meant to be used by the Corporation as an instrument when other authorities are not helpful or in the wrong in regard to policy or administrative decisions.

Not a Daily Recipe

But this would not imply that the Ad-hoc Committees are a daily recipe. They are to be used sparingly, otherwise their edge would be blunted and not be serviceable. The permanent statutory committees have, as far as possible, to be utilised to work out details of a policy or a change in an accepted policy or to deliberate on the administrative implications of different matters. Similarly, the executive authorities, viz. the Municipal Commissioner and the Transport Manager, are to be allowed discretion, within the framework of the prescribed rules, bye-laws, etc., in implementing decisions of the Corporation, the

Standing Committee and the Transport Committee. The investigatory or interrogatory power of the Ad-hoc Committees is intended to be applied to the Administration of the Corporation on infrequent occasions. The type of cases or matters and the frequency for using the device of the Ad-hoc Committees is to be judged by the Corporation itself. No rigid yardstick is available for deciding the use of the Ad-hoc Committees. But broad indications could be given as to when the use is not called for or would be infructuous.

FREQUENCY AND TERMS OF REFERENCE

The Tally

The total number of Ad-hoc Committees appointed by the Corporation during the five years, (1962 to 67), was 27. Out of these 27 Ad-hoc Committees, 24 were Ad-hoc Committees proper and three were delegations to wait on the State Government to secure redress of certain inconveniences or grievances. The delegations were also designated as Ad-hoc Committees perhaps because the Act had not provided for them and as Ad-hoc Committees they could undertake travelling to places outside Poona for their work at the expense of the Corporation.

The year 1964 witnessed the appointment of the highest number of Ad-hoc Committees, viz. 11, including two delegations. In 1963 the next highest number, viz. seven was set up. Both these years, 1963 and 1964, were post-Panshet flood years and as such confronted such problems as rehabilitation of the flood-affected and the accentuated growth of slums. The tempo of the activity of the Corporation also rose during the middle period, 1963-64, after the fresh general elections to the Corporation in 1962. The next two succeeding years, 1965 and 1966, saw the setting up of five (inclusive of one delegation) and three Ad-hoc Committees, respectively. 1962 was the least active year for only one Ad-hoc Committee and that too the annually recurring Grant-in-Aid Committee was set up.

Committees of Long-term and Short-term Significance

The Ad-hoc Committees could be classified as having long-term and short-term significance. The number of Committees bearing long-term significance was five, two of these involved amendments to the Act.

The number of Committees having short-term significance was 19, 13 of which involved adoption of new policies or administrative measures and six review of decisions or actions already taken. The year-wise break-up of the two categories as well as delegations is shown Table 5.1

TABLE 5.1 Ad-hoc Committees, Long-term and Short-term: Year-wise Break-up.

Year	Long-term			Short-term			Total	Dele-gation	Total
	Involv-ing Am-endmets to Act	Others	Total	New Policy/ Admi-nistra-tive Measure	Review of Ad-mn. De-cisions Actions	Total			
	(a)	(b)	(c)	(a)	(b)	(c)			
1	2	3	4	5	6	7	8	9	10
1962	—	—	—	1	—	1	1	—	1
1963	1	2	3	3	1	4	7	—	7
1964	—	—	—	5	4	9	9	2	11
1965	1	—	1	2	1	3	4	1	5
1966	—	1	1	2	—	2	3	—	3
1967	—	—	—	—	—	—	—	—	—
Total	2	3	5	13	6	19	24	3	27

Out of the five Ad-hoc Committees dealing with long-term changes, two concerned changes in the Act, one each secondary education, housing (public works) and miscellaneous subjects (such as water supply, industry, transport facilities). Among the 13 Committees of short-term bearing involving consideration of new policies or administrative measures, five pertained to public works, five annual grants-in-aid to public institutions, two primary education and one Corporation proceedings. Six Committees of short-run significance involving review of decisions or actions already taken could be distributed among the following subjects: two transport undertaking, three public works and one administrative organisation of the Corporation. The three delegations were concerned with water-rates charged by the State Government, vacant State Government lands in the city and public grievances regarding the Government Sassoon Hospital. This reveals that the Corporation sought to handle through its Ad-hoc Committees a variety of subjects regarding constitutional matters pertaining to Corporation, public works, transport, education, its own proceedings, and so on.

Subject-wise Break-up

Table 5.2 indicates the subjectwise annual break-up of the *Ad hoc* Committees and delegations.

Committees on Constitution of Corporation

Two of the long-term problems tackled by Ad-hoc Committees concerned the constitution of the Corporation. One related to the report of the State Government Committee on Municipal Corporations, popularly known as Zakaria Committee (Zakaria, the State Minister for Urban Development, being its Chairman), submitted in 1965. The Corporation did not favour the important recommendations of the Zakaria Committee, viz., those bearing on the relationship between the Mayor and the Commissioner. It thought that the Mayor was not given his due authority and powers by the Zakaria Committee. In the local government of some of the Western countries, the Mayor occupied a pivotal position. In some of the States in the country, particularly in the North, the Mayor enjoyed significant authority, being the representative of the citizenry. Nearer home also, in the State of Maharashtra itself, the President and other elected office-bearers of the *Zilla Parishads*, the reformed rural district councils, exercised weighty functions and powers. As compared to the functions and powers of the elected heads of local governments mentioned above, those vested in the Mayor by the Zakaria Committee were insignificant. The Mayor was offered the Chairmanship of the newly proposed Co-ordination Committee by the Zakaria Committee. His sumptuary allowance was increased by the Committee. To remove the recurring bottlenecks in the Poona Municipal Corporation, provision was made in the Committee's report for the attendance of the Municipal Commissioner at the Corporation meetings as also for the suspension of the Transport Manager. But these were palliative measures which did not meet the aspirations of the Corporators. In opposition to the appointment of an Ad-hoc Committee at that juncture, a few Corporators argued that the

TABLE 5.2 Ad-hoc Committees: Subject-wise Annual break-up

Year	Long-Term						Short-Term								Committees	Delegations			
	Involving Amendment to Act		Others			Total	New Policy/Administrative measures			Review of Admn. Decisions				Total	Total	Pub. works		Other matters	Total
	Constitution of Corporation	Transport	Housing	Sec. Edn.	Municipalisation of Industries etc.		Grants-in-Aid	Pub. works	Prim. Edn.	Corp. proceeds	Transport	Bldg. permissions	Report on Admn. organ.			Municipal	Non-Muni.	Non-Muni.	
1962	—	—	—	—	—	—	1	—	—	—	—	—	—	1	1	—	—	—	—
1963	—	1	—	1	1	3	1	2	—	—	—	1	—	4	7	—	—	—	—
1964	—	—	—	—	—	—	1	2	1	1	2	1	1	9	9	—	1	1	2
1965	1	—	—	—	—	1	1	—	1	—	—	1	—	3	4	1	—	—	1
1966	—	—	1	—	—	1	1	1	—	—	—	—	—	2	3	—	—	—	—
1967	—	—	—	—	—	—	—	—	—	—	—	—	—	—		—	—	—	-
Total	1	1	1	1	1	5	5	5	2	1	2	3	1	19	24	1	1	1	3

report would take time to be put in the shape of a Bill during which the Corporation would have ample opportunity to ventilate its views on the report. Corporators had not received, let alone read, copies of the report. But the most important objection to the setting up of the Committee was that the point of view of the Corporation had already been represented to the Committee being embodied in the minute of dissent to the report signed by two of its members who were the Mayor and a Corporator of the Poona Municipal Corporation. A more appropriate course of action for the Corporation, according to another Corporator, was to sound a consensus among the representatives of the Municipal Corporations in the State. But these lone voices of caution did not deter the Corporation from setting up the Committee. The appointment of the Committee was not only opportune, being made just on the issue of the State Government Zakaria Committee's report, but it also had an intimate bearing on a matter of great concern to the Corporation, the constitution and functions of the Municipal Corporation itself.

The second Ad-hoc Committee (set up in 1963) bearing on the constitution of the Corporation related to the stature and tenure of the Transport Manager of the Corporation who looked after the operation of the Poona Municipal Bus Transport. The gravamen of the indictment by the Corporation was that the qualifications required of the Transport Manager were too low for the efficient conduct of the operations of the Municipal Bus Transport and that his tenure was permanent resulting in lack of Corporation's control over him. The size of the operations of the Municipal Bus Transport had by 1963 grown more than three-fold since its inception in 1950. The fleet of buses had gone up from 57 to 186, while its income had risen from Rs. 20 lakhs to Rs. 58 lakhs. A majority of the Corporators thought that the sizable Transport Undertaking needed to be managed by an administrator of the cadre of the IAS to be an efficient proposition. They also felt that the permanent Transport Manager who did not possess the requisite qualifications for the post was a liability on the Corporation since he could manage the undertaking in any way he liked. The supervision of the Transport Committee was too slack and the Corporation's control was too remote and infrequent to be effective. It was alleged that the then Transport Manager had become too powerful having built up support in the dominant political party and trade union and that his management was ridden with improper practices. Once before, in 1958, the then ruling Samyukta Maharashtra Samiti group in the

Corporation had tried to deal with the matter. On the other hand, the opponents of the move for the appointment of the Ad-hoc Committee pointed out that the expansion of the undertaking was due to the efficient administration of the Transport Manager, that his appointment was regular and that, further, experience of the trade rather than formal qualifications or general administrative experience was required for the post. It was natural that certain concomitant factors and incidents in the situation created a suspicious atmosphere in regard to the management by the then Transport Manager which led to the setting up of the Ad-hoc Committee. But the reasoning underlying the setting up of the Committee betrayed an inadequate understanding of the implications of the provisions regarding the Transport Undertaking contained in the Municipal Corporations Act. As pointed out in Chapter 2, the Transport Manager, whose stipulated qualifications were decidedly lower than those of the Municipal Commissioner, ought to have been placed under him as far as the overall administrative control over the Transport Undertaking was concerned. Or, else, the Transport Manager ought to have been, in qualifications and status, nearly equal to the Municipal Commissioner. If the appointment of the Ad-hoc Committee on the report of the Zakaria Committee showed up the discontent among the Corporators regarding the existing relationship between the deliberative and executive wings of the Corporation as embodied in the Act, the institution of this Committee disclosed the inherent anomaly about the administrative pattern of the Transport Undertaking laid down in the Act.

Committees on Secondary Schools, Housing for Low-income Groups and Municipalisation of Industries, etc.

The three remaining Ad-hoc Committees bearing long-term significance pertained to the administration of Corporation's secondary schools (1963), the preparation of the housing schemes for the low-income groups in the city (1966) and consideration of municipalisation of industries, business and trade, of sources of water-supply, low-income group-housing, cheap transport facilities, reservations for roads, etc. (1963). The first Committee sought to tackle problems that arose out of the increase in the number of the secondary schools (including the technical school and technical classes) conducted by the Corporation and could not be solved in the normal course of administration. The second Committee dealt with an issue (viz. housing for low-income groups) the nature and dimensions of which were fairly well-known to the Corporation and its administration. It was not going to reveal anything new to the Corporation. It was true, as pointed out by the mover of the resolution on the Committee, that the need of housing for the low-income groups was not emphasised so much as the need for housing for the slum-dwellers. Housing as such, for any class of citizens, was considered beyond the pale of the Municipal Corporation. The need in this regard was for bold action for finding financial resources as well as lands for building houses. The third Committee sought to put its hands on a number of diverse and complex problems and grasp them in one sweep. It was bound to fail in the realisation of its objective. The mover of the resolution regarding the Committee had himself proposed in the terms of reference three varied subjects. The amendment added yet more subjects still wider and more varied in scope, like provision of new roads, traffic regulation, creation of cheap transport facilities, reservations of locations of industries, residential areas, etc. The Committee ought to have confined its coverage only to one subject, like, municipalisation of industries, business and trade, as it was crucial for increasing the income of the Municipal Corporation.

Secondary education was an optional function of the Municipal Corporation, but even then the Poona Municipal Corporation had established five secondary schools by 1963. Besides, it conducted a technical school which was an old institution. It also ran the regional library on behalf of the State Government and granted aid to public libraries in the city. It spent as much as Rs. 7 lakhs on secondary education. The first secondary high school was set up by the Corporation immediately after its inception to enable the poor guardians to educate their wards in high school without payment of fees. The free secondary education was facilitated on account of the initiative of a few retired secondary teachers who offered their voluntary services to the Corporation. Later on, four more high schools including one for girls, were instituted by the Corporation. The original idealistic spirit underlying the first Corporation high school evaporated and secondary education in Corporation's high schools became the concern of departmental routine as with other Municipal subjects. In order to secure grants-in-aid from the State Government, the Corporation had to apply government approved pay scales to the teachers in their high schools; this nullified the idea of voluntary service by retired teachers. With the growth in the number of teachers and students, complaints by teachers and students flowed in, but neither the Corporation nor the Commissioner had devised any special administrative cell to look after the overall supervision and direction over these high schools. The Assistant Commissioner incharge of the subject was overburdened with other administrative responsibilities. In the beginning of the first high school an Ad-hoc advisory committee was set up but it was never brought into the focus of the administration of these high schools. The Law, Revenue and General Purposes Committee dealt with the matters concerning the high schools as well as the regional library. The Standing Committee took care of financial and more important personnel matters. But these bodies could not provide overall guidance and detailed administrative supervision to the high schools. While the administrative supervision could be provided only by a special division under the Commissioner, the overall guidance, the Corporators felt, could be given only by a new Special Committee for secondary education and the related subjects like the regional library.

Grants-in-aid Committee

Of all the Ad-hoc Committees having short-term significance, the Committee to consider the applications of institutions and associations for grants-in-aid was the only annually recurring Committee as grants-in-aid were to be disbursed for every year. Another Committee of short-term bearing, appointed to report on the naming of roads and other public places (1963), continued its deliberations even after it had presented its first report after one year (1964) and made its supplementary reports available later intermittently. Giving grants-in-aid to public institutions and associations promoting care and training of handicapped children, museums, technical and industrial schools, libraries, sports, social service, relief to the destitute and delinquent persons, medical relief, public safety, health and convenience or instruction was a discretionary function of the Corporation. It was not obligatory on the Corporation to set up annually the Grants-in-Aid Committee, but the consideration of applications involved visits to the institutions and associations concerned as well as examination of their credentials on the basis of the documentary material like the annual reports and accounts, and these could be done by the Ad-hoc Committees in a better way and more quickly than by the whole body of the Corporation.

Besides the five Committees to determine the allotment of grant-in-aid to public institutions and associations, eight Ad-hoc Committees grappled with short-term issues concerning new policies or administrative measures or changes in them. Of these eight Committees, five dealt with public works, two with primary education and one with the Corporation proceedings.

Committees on Works

The five Ad-hoc Committees on public works pertained to the formulation of the proposal regarding the Nehru Stadium (1964), the framing of a priority list of roads to be widened and whose corners had to be rounded off (1966), the naming of roads and other public places (1963), consideration of measures for the safety of the riverside buildings and residents (1964), and devising ways for the improvement of the conditions in the Corporation housing colonies (1963). Out of these five subjects, the last two, dealing with consideration of measures for the safety of the riverside buildings and residents and devising ways for the improvement of the conditions in the Corporation housing colonies, were appropriate for deliberation by the Ad-hoc Committees. The first three subjects (viz., the formulation of the proposal regarding the Nehru Stadium, the framing of a priority list of roads to be widened and whose corners had to be rounded off, and the naming of roads and other public places) could have been discussed by the concerned permanent Committees, as, for example, the Public Works Committee in the case of the first subject. The proposal for the construction of a sports stadium had already been accepted by the Corporation; that the stadium should be entitled Nehru Stadium to commemorate the departed sports-loving leader was readily agreed to by the Corporation while discussing the motion on the setting up of the Ad-hoc Committee. The Public Works Committee could have worked out the financial and administrative implications of the proposal, as usual, in consultation with the Administration. The second subject was urgent in the sense that the convenience of the house-owners whose houses were affected by road widening had also to be taken into account while executing the programme. But this as well as the naming of roads and other public places could have been taken care of by the respective permanent Committees. The Corporation, it seems, was keen to associate itself directly with these three prestigious issues.

This was not the case with the two issues concerning the safety of the riverside buildings and residents and the improvement in the conditions of the Corporation housing colonies. The first issue came to the forefront as a result of the flood of the Mutha river due to the bursting of the Panshet and Khadakwasla dams in July 1961. The question was discussed now and then by the Corporation even before the devastating 1961 flood. As long as in 1945 a suggestion was broached to construct a protective wall on the river banks as also to make it obligatory on the house-owners on the riverside to lay out plinths of minimum height as foundation of houses. In the wake of the flood in 1958 also certain proposals were mooted in this regard. After the July 1962 flood, the State Government, at the instance of the Municipal Corporation, had fixed, by a statute, the flood-line within which no constructions were to be permitted. As a result of the pressure from the affected vacant land-owners and house-owners, the Municipal Corporation relented. The Corporation was also taken aback by the enormous expenditure involved in the rehabilitation of the flood-affected people; it was not prepared for more expenditure on the accommodation of those affected by the demarcation of the flood-line. But the cancellation of the flood-line by the State Government, again at the instance of the Municipal Corporation, did not absolve the Corporation of the responsibility concerning the security of the riverside buildings and residents. On the other hand, this task of the Corporation became more arduous. The proposed Ad-hoc Committee would suggest measures to promote this objective. A few members opposed the setting up of the Committee on the plea that the cancellation of the flood-line by the State Government had solved the issue for good. On the other hand, those who pressed for the appointment of the Committee urged the importance of adopting measures for the security of the riverside buildings and residents from the point of view of the overall planning of the whole city. The need for securing the co-operation of the State Government to facilitate the realisation of the objective was also stressed by a few other Corporators. Without substantial financial support from the State Government, it was pointed out, those dishoused as a result of these security measures would not be accommodated elsewhere in the city. It was also urged that Government should not de-requisition lands urgently required by the Corporation for housing persons who would be affected by these security measures. Besides, Government was expected to help by way of throwing open their own vacant lands for raising constructions to house the affected persons.

The other appropriate issue for consideration by an Ad-hoc Committee was concerning the improvement of the conditions of the Corporation housing colonies. These colonies fetched the Corporation about Rs. 3 lakhs by way of rent per year. The residents of the colonies did not feel secure from thefts and such other acts. They lacked certain basic amenities. The problem of unauthorised sub-tenancies had assumed a serious proportion. The issue could have been handled by the Public Works Committee, but the Corporation felt a special responsibility towards the Municipal employee-residents of these colonies.

Committees on Primary Education

Similarly, two other issues of immediate importance having policy or administrative implications, viz., problems facing primary education (1964) and continuation of teachers on the roll of *Zilla Parishads* by the Corporation (1965), could have been sorted out in the first instance by the Corporation School Board. In the case of the first issue concerning its important obligatory function, the Corporation thought it better to confront it by itself through an Ad-hoc Committee. The Corporation's primary schools suffered from the shortage of buildings, paucity of qualified teachers, deteriorating standard of students and other serious difficulties. It could be appreciated that the Corporation felt so keenly about these problems facing its primary schools and finding out ways and means to solve them. The second issue, viz. continuation of teachers on the roll of *Zilla Parishads*, however, could have been well left out to the care of the School Board.

Committee on Corporation Proceedings

The remaining issue of short-term policy significance pertained to the Corporation proceedings (1964). This, of course, the Corporation alone could tackle. And it was proper that it entrusted the preliminary consideration of the issue to an Ad-hoc Committee. The existing rules governing the supplementary questions, adjournment motions, etc. were loose and came in the way of more efficient despatch of business by the Corporation in its meetings.

Committees on Errors of Administration

If the Corporation's authority to get various broad issues involving policy or administrative implications discussed through Ad-hoc Committees was indisputable, its competence to examine through Ad-hoc Committees the errors of omission or commission on the part of the Administration in specific individual cases or types of cases was questionable. Six such instances occurred during 1962-67. Three instances impinged directly on the sphere of the administrative jurisdiction of the Commissioner: violation of building regulations by the Shirin Talkies (1963), infringement of the conditions of temporary construction on leased land by the Poonam Restaurant (1964), and public complaints concerning grant of building permissions by Administration (1965). The fourth case did not involve interference in administration but arose out of curiosity of the Corporation to know the contents of a shelved report on the organisation of certain administrative departments and to intimate the Administration its views on the report (1964). The two remaining cases not merely sought to criticise certain shortcomings of the administration of the Transport Manager but also reflected on the working of the Transport Committee. These were concerning the letter written by the Chairman of the Transport Committee to the District Collector, who was the land acquisition authority, regarding the de-requisitioning of a plot previously requisitioned for the P.M.T. (1964) and audit reports by the Municipal Chief Auditor on the P.M.T. stores and the failure of the Transport Manager to take action on them (1964).

The appointment of the Ad-hoc Committees in these cases was consistent with the Corporation's final responsibility regarding the implementation of policies adopted by it as well as the instruments for implementation, viz., the given statutory provisions, bye-laws, regulations etc. The Corporation was also authorised by the Act to secure access to the necessary information with the Administration. The point at issue was whether such cases reviewing Administrative actions were occasional or too frequent. That during a five-year period only six such instances occurred was as much creditable to the Corporation as to the Municipal Administration. This clarified the intention of the Corporation underlying the setting up of these Ad-hoc Committees, viz., to apply correctives to the actions of Administration rather than to act as its substitute.

The proprietor of the Shirin Talkies had violated building regulations on account of construction beyond the set-back line on the north, on the undemarcated corridor across Municipal land on the west and above the *nallah* (drainage water course) on the east. The officials concerned had cleared the construction. In respect of the Poonam Restaurant also the officials had not only approved the plan and estimates but also issued the completion certificate to a semi-permanent construction which had infringed the permission for temporary structure on a leased Municipal land granted by the Corporation. The propriety of the action of the Corporation in setting up the Ad-hoc Committee was questioned by a few members who pointed to the inconclusive action by the Public Works Committee that was the competent authority to deal with the case at that stage. In regard to building permissions by the Administration in general public complaints were widespread. These formed a majority among the public grievances ventilated with the Corporators. Administrative decisions varied from case to case and from official to official dealing with the cases. In some cases house-owners also might have been in the wrong. But the Corporators took up cudgels on behalf of the complaining house-owners. A prominent Corporator as well as the official on the spot at the meeting advocated that the matter fell within the competence of the Commissioner. The former also tried to prevail on the Corporators that the relevant permanent Committee (viz. the Public Works Committee) ought to deal with the particular grievances regarding building permissions. But the trend of opinion among the Corporators favouring the institution of the Committee was too strong to be reversed by this lone dissenting voice.

The Commissioner had appointed two consultants, Messers Beacons & Co. and Bhamburkar, to report on the administrative organisation of the P.M.T. Workshop and Supervision Department and certain (the Pubic Works and Stores) departments of the Corporation. Nothing was heard about the reports of the consultants and action on them by the Corporation. Attempts by individual Corporators to extract the information about the contents of the reports of the consultants from the Administration had failed. It was puzzling why the Administration was so reticent about the contents of the reports. An insignificant excuse that copies of the reports were not available with the Administration was held out by the official at the meeting, but to no effect.

The audit reports on the P.M.T. Stores by the Municipal Chief Auditor had revealed a loss of about 14 per cent of the stores worth Rs. 2 lakhs out of the total stores value of Rs. 14 lakhs. In the State Transport the loss in stores was limited to 0.37 per cent. The Corporators were rightly worried over this loss which reflected adversely not only on the administration of the Transport Manager but also on the overall supervision by the Transport Committee. The Corporation had full authority under the Act to take action on the audit reports through the appointment of an Ad-hoc Committee in the matter. In the other matter, the Chairman of the Transport Committee had written a letter to the District Collector (the land acquisition authority) communicating the decision of the Transport Committee to request him to de-requisition a plot requisitioned earlier to accommodate the expanding bus-stand at the Deccan Gymkhana. According to rules the Transport Manager, the administrative head of the P.M.T., ought to have written the letter. The whole affair was shady and even the leader of the dominant Congress party had earlier (10-1-1964) moved an adjournment motion on the subject. It was in the air that the resolution was adopted at the meeting held just on the eve of the periodical election of the Committee and that, further, the meeting was ordered by the Chairman even before some members who were late by a few minutes were present at the meeting. It was also surprising that the Transport Manager did not point out to the Chairman that he (the Chairman) was not authorised to communicate the resolution to the District Collector. It was further intriguing how the Collector's office which usually consumed considerable time in acting on such resolutions hurried through the action within two weeks. Most of the Corporators who participated in the discussion on the subject desired that action ought to be taken against the Chairman for his illegal communication. But a few members referred to the litigation on the plot pending in the court of law as well as to the Chairman ceasing to be not only member of the Transport Committee but also member of the Corporation. But the Corporation decided to go ahead in the matter with delegation of its deliberation to an Ad-hoc Committee.

COMPOSITION

Size

The size of the Ad-hoc Committees was, except in a single case, large. The deliberative function of the Ad-hoc Committees, in fact, called for small, compact size of membership. But the Corporation in general favoured large-sized Ad-hoc Committees. Corporators were keen to include their own favourite colleagues in the Ad-hoc Committees with the result that the size of the Ad-hoc Committees swelled beyond proportion. And this occurred in spite of the recognition by the Corporators that a large number of them did not show keenness to attend the meetings of the Ad-hoc Committees. In cases of a few (two) Committees, proposd members of the Committees, on their own initiative, withdrew their names from the lists, but later additions more than compensated for the slimming of the size of these Committees. In as many as nine cases, Corporators pressed for substantial additions to the membership of the Committees.

A majority, viz. 15, of the 27 Ad-hoc Committees had been six and 10 members, while only one Committee (viz. on priority among roads to be widened) was compact having five members, i.e., eight per cent of the total membership (65). Six Committees possessed between 11 and 15 members, these included two delegations. Five Committees had more than 15 members. The Committee on safety of riverside buildings included the highest number of 21. Probably they thought that the wards affected by the 1961-flood should be accorded representation in the Committee. The Grants-in-Aid Committee for 1966-67 had 20 members, that for 1962-63 – 18 and that for 1964-65 – 16. These Committees gave representation to different wards of the city so that the claims to grants of institutions located there were not lost sight of. It was beyond comprehension as to why the size of the Ad-hoc Committee on the Zakaria Committee Report was as large as 16. After all, the report concerned policy matters and a few knowledgeable Corporators alone could have contributed to the discussion in the Committee and produced a meaningful report.

The question of the compact size of the Ad-hoc Committees did not engage the attention of the Corporation at all. Perhaps the Corporators thought that a sizable number of absentees at their meetings would make for the desirable optimum size. It was left to the mover of the resolution regarding a Committee or somebody else later to propose the name of members of the Committee and still later to the movers of amendments to make additions. At no stage of the discussion on any Ad-hoc Committee was any inkling given out of the conception underlying the relationship between the size of its membership and its subject-matter or its very rationale.

Party Considerations

It does not seem that the elections of the members of the Ad-hoc Committees were held mainly on the basis of party considerations. No party or group enjoyed a clear absolute majority in the Corporation during the period of study (1962-67), though the balance tilted in favour of the Congress or the Nagari Sanghatana (the Civic Front) on this or that issue or at election of this or that office-bearer. On a few controversial Committees, like the one on Shirin Talkies or Poonam Restaurant, Corporators who knew either of the two sides of the issue were placed. The Congress, the Nagari Sanghatana and the Independents were represented on all the Committees. The Janasangh, however, was not represented on two Committees only out of the total of 27 Committees. These were the Committees to consider housing for the low-income groups and the delegation to wait on the State Government in the matter of vacant government plots. On the delegation, however, a Janasangh Corporator was appointed a member in the capacity of the then Chairman of the Standing Committee. The Committee on housing for the low-income groups had a small size of six members, so the Janasangh might not have found representation on it. On a few Committees the Independents secured a much larger representation than their strength called for. A few active Independent Corporators were given membership of a number of Committees. The opinions expressed in the discussions in the Ad-hoc Committees or in the Corporation meetings on the resolutions to set up the Committees or on the reports of the Committees, were not marked by cleavages on party lines. Sometimes members belonging to the same political parties gave out opposite views on some subjects. So there was no question of the Independents voicing views dissonant from those ventilated by party representatives. On this aspect, the discussions in the Ad-hoc Committees followed the general trend of discussions in the Corporation and permanent Committees.

The Congress had a majority on two Ad-hoc Committees while the Nagari Sanghatana on one Committee. On two others the Congress enjoyed half the representation, while on another one the Nagari Sanghatana had this privilege. But these majorities, as pointed out above, were not going to fashion the decisions of the Committees in the fixed mould of party views.

Ex-officio membership was accorded to the Mayor, the Deputy Mayor, or the Chairman of permanent Committees, like the Standing Committee, the Law Committee, the Public Works or Improvement Committee on Ad-hoc Committees dealing with subjects on which their presence was considered to be desirable. These were the Stadium Committee, the Committee on the change in the Act regarding the

P.M.T. organisation, the Zakaria Report Committee, the safety of riverside buildings Committee and the delegation regarding vacant government plots. On the P.M.T. organisation Committee the Corporation deliberately did not give representation to the concerned Transport Committee as it was bound to have a bias in favour of the existing P.M.T. management pattern.

In as many 12 out of the total of 27 Ad-hoc Committees movers of the resolutions on the institution of Committees were included. In two of these, both the mover as well as the seconder of the resolutions were given place. The purpose underlying the inclusion of the mover seemed to ensure the fructification of the object behind the appointment of the Committee. It does not, however, mean that the non-inclusion of the movers in the case of the remaining 15 Committees did not lead to substantial results.

Active Members

Seventeen Corporators out of the total of 65 participated in more than five Ad-hoc Committees. Out of these, four belonged to more than 10 Committees. These four included the leader of the Janasangh group, a Congress Corporator and two Independents. The break-up of the group of the former 17 Corporators was: five Congress, six Nagari Sanghatana, two Janasangh and four Independents. The Independents were proportionately more numerous than their strength in the Corporation in both these groups. The leaders of the Congress and the Janasangh groups belonged to the group of 17. It would be worthwhile to tally whether these 17 Corporators were very active in the Corporation as well as permanent Committee meetings. The extent of the participation of the latter group of four most active members in the Corporation and the permanent Committees also would need a probe. The leaders of the Congress and the Janasangh groups, so also two S.S.P. Corporators in the Nagari Sanghatana, were included in Committees on important controversial subjects like the Poonam Restaurant and the safety of riverside buildings. The leaders of both the Congress and the Janasangh groups secured place in all the three delegations to wait on the State Government. Each of the two abovementioned S.S.P. Corporators was, however, given place only on one delegation.

CONTENTS OF COMMITTEES' REPORTS

Of the three main types of Ad-hoc Committees those dealing with short-term policies or administrative measures were most constructive and fruitful in their reporting. The Ad-hoc Committees reviewing administrative actions failed in making reports or making substantial reports. The Committees that sought to tackle long-term policies did not cut much ice in exposing the relevant issues or hinting at their solutions.

The short-term issues were urgent, their implications were easily understandable by the members and their solution was mostly within the reach of the Corporation. There were no major vested interests which blocked the sorting out of these issues. The Administration did not evince an attitude of non-cooperation in either making available the supporting material for facilitating the deliberations of the Committees or opposing in any other way the working of the Committees. In the review of administrative actions, the officials not only disfavoured the appointment of Committees but also stood in the way of their speedier deliberations by withholding relevant records, remaining absent at their meetings and so on. The blame for the ineffectual reporting of these Committees did not solely lie on the Administration. On some of these administrative actions, Corporators and Committees' members were divided sympathising or opposing those responsible for the administrative actions. The Committees dealing with long-term policies failed to do justice to the issues involved in their solution. The reports were either scrappy jumping at conclusions without delving into their implications or trod beaten tracks. The solutions of most of these problems were beyond the ken of the Corporation, this must have overweighed the thinking of the Committees' members and made them reserved in making reports. On these problems of long-term significance the Committees ought not to have been appointed, but once they were set up they ought to have deliberated on them exhaustively and produced worthwhile reports and made meaningful and significant suggestions.

Committees on Corporation Constitution

Out of the two Ad-hoc Committees concerned with long-term constitutional problems the Committee dealing with the Poona Municipal Transport organisation produced a very disappointing report. The problem of the role and position of the Transport Manager *vis-a-vis* the Municipal Commissioner and of the Transport Committee *vis-a-vis* the Standing Committee and Corporation was very vital to the working of the Poona Municipal Transport as well as the Municipal Corporation. But the report of the Committee merely directed the reference of the problem to the Zakaria Committee appointed by the Maharashtra Government to study the constitution of the Municipal Corporations and consoled itself that the problem would receive due attention of the Zakaria Committee since the Poona Municipal Corporation was represented on it by three persons associated with it, viz. the Mayor, another Corporator and the Municipal Commissioner. The second of these two Ad-hoc Committees, dealing with the Zakaria Committee's report itself, recommended sweeping changes in the constitution of the Municipal Corporations without explaining the rationale behind them or examining their political and administrative implications. The Committee proposed the Cabinet form of government for the Municipal Corporations. The leader of the majority party or group in the Corporation would act as the Chief Executive Councillor and he would choose from his colleagues – Executive Councillors – to be in charge of different administrative departments of the Corporation. While the Municipal Commissioner would act as the Secretary of the Executive Council, the Departmental Heads would be Secretaries to the respective Departmental Executive Councillors. The Corporators not belonging to the majority group would operate as the party-in-opposition. The Mayor would be directly elected by the citizen-voters. The report neglected to bring out the implications of these proposals affecting the Administration, relationship between the Mayor and the Chief Executive Councillor and the working of political parties. This omission was significant and accounted for the unconvincing nature of the report.

Committees on Municipalisation of Trades, Sites Reservation and Housing

Two of the three Ad-hoc Committees bearing on long-term problems of functional importance covered beaten tracks. These were the Committees set up to analyse the issue of municipalisation of trades, reservation of sites, transport, etc., and the problem of housing for low-income groups. The first Committee, instead of grappling with the crucial issue of municipalisation of trades, sought to deal with the problem of housing referred to the other Ad-hoc Committee. It contented itself merely by concluding that vacant lands in the city, including those belonging to government, should be acquired, developed, divided into plots and sold out to the needy proposed house-builders by the Municipal Corporation on no-profit-no-loss basis. The conclusion was not very much different from the main proposal of the other Committee on Housing for low-income groups. The main proposal of the latter Committee was that the Municipal Corporation should acquire sites in Koregaon Park in the city, develop them at own expense and lease them for a period of 99 years to group co-operative housing societies or to individuals at rent equal to the interest on invested capital. The Committee recommended that Government should extend to these co-operative societies all the facilities granted to the Maharashtra State Housing Board or the backward classes' housing societies. Though the main recommendation of the Committee did not break any new ground the analysis of the problem by the Committee was admirable.

For the upper classes, housing presented no problem because they could afford to build their own houses or hire them at even exorbitant rents. The lower classes could take advantage of the government schemes for slum-dwellers, backward classes, etc., but the extent of the schemes was limited. The housing problem stared in the face of the middle classes alone. There were not enough houses being built for hire since the rent did not tally even with the interest from banks on the same amounts as invested in construction. Nor did people construct houses for their own hiring on account of the difficulties of securing lands as sites for housing, rising construction costs and so on. The way out proposed by the Committee was to lease out Corporation sites to co-operative societies or even to individuals. The Committee calculated that each individual block-owner in three-storeyed buildings consisting of 12 blocks each would be required to bear about Rs. 60 per month towards the payment of arrears of loan on account of construction of the house. This much expenditure, the Committee thought, would be within the financial capacity of the persons belonging to middle classes.

Committees on Secondary Education, Technical Schools and Regional Library

The third of the Ad-hoc Committees of long-term policy significance pertained to the secondary schools, technical schools and regional library conducted by the Corporation. The conclusion of the Committee's report was reasonable. It was that since the administration of secondary schools and related matters had grown, its consideration should be entrusted to a fifth permanent Special Committee which should be created by the Corporation with the sanction of the government. At the time of reporting by the Committee decisions in these matters were taken by respective Special Committees whereas no independent department existed in the Commissioner's office to take care of the administration of these matters. The Committee, however, failed to examine the administration of secondary schools, technical schools and regional library in detail. Such an examination would have made the Committee's conclusion appear more logical.

As compared to the Ad-hoc Committees on long-term issues, the Ad-hoc Committees on short-term policy or administrative matters (not involving review of administrative actions) produced fruitful results in the form of solid constructive reports followed by positive administrative actions.

Committee on Grants-in-aid

For every financial year, by the close of the third quarter, an Ad-hoc Committee was formed to advise on the allotment of grants-in-aid totalling Rs. 50,000 to registered public institutions engaged in welfare activities in the city. The applicant-institutions had to fulfil certain conditions such as furnishing the Corporation of annual report and audited annual accounts and balance-sheet. Not all the institutions fulfilling these conditions were necessarily included in the list of grantees by the Committee. Those institutions which received grants or allocations from some other authorities, if the Committee so thought, might be excluded from the list. Institutions which were not registered or did not submit annual reports and audited accounts were obviously not held eligible for grants by the Committee. If, by oversight, such institutions were included in the list, the Auditor excluded them at the time of actual disbursal of grants.

The Ad-hoc Committees appointed to consider distribution of grants-in-aid to public institutions differed from other Ad-hoc Committees dealing with both long-term and short-term problems. They were set up every year to consider a matter that was, so to say, a normal routine function of the Municipal Corporation. The consideration involved detailed scrutiny of the applications for grants-in-aid in the light of the given rules in the matter. In one sense, the Committees were not commissioned to probe a new problem or discover a new solution to an existing problem. They were asked to discharge a routine function. But the discharge of this routine function also involved careful examination as to the genuineness of the activities of the applicant-institutions and their public character through personal visits to the institutions. The number of applications received by the Committee every year were above 100 while those which were admitted for grants were between 60 and about 100.

Committees on Road Widening, naming of Roads, Public Places and Stadium

Three other Ad-hoc Committees that dealt with short-term administrative matters, viz. the list of roads to be widened, naming of roads and other public places and the sports stadium, did not require serious thought or very hard work. The first Committee picked up six roads to be accorded priority in road-widening. Another conclusion of the Committee that the widening of roads in the city was generally not possible due to heavy compensation involved was as much hackneyed as disturbing. The remaining recommendation that town-planning schemes should be applied to extended suburbs and that amenities, including wide roads, should be provided for in them was not new, in that the existing or proposed town-planning schemes had provided for these.

The Committee on the naming of roads and other public places did a fine job in preparing by March 1967 five such lists. Names of well-known deceased persons were given without disturbing existing names of living big persons. Before preparing lists letters from individual citizens as well as official suggestions were taken into account.

The work of the Sports Stadium Committee had become easier as the decision to construct the Stadium had already been taken in 1962 by the Corporation. The Committee opined that the construction would have to be executed in stages and that during the year of report by the Committee (1964) the Corporation should provide Rs. 5 lakhs in the budget pending grants from the Central and State Governments. The Committee expected the Stadium to be up-to-date and self-sufficient in amenities to be provided for various kinds of sports including Indian.

The Committee also wanted on the roadside outskirts of the ground the construction of a building for hire for commercial shopping purposes. the Committee's directive that the office should be ready with detailed plans and estimates for the work was just an implication of the main proposal for the Stadium building including stands.

Committee on Safety of Riverside Buildings and Residents

The problem of the safety of riverside buildings and residents was the most vital among the short-term problems tackled by the Ad-hoc Committees. It became important because of the recent abolition of the flood-line laid out in the wake of the Panshet flood. The Committee chalked out two sets of recommendations, one to prevent devastation and damage due to floods in future and the other to facilitate rehabilitation of the persons affected by the Panshet flood. The first set of recommendations included those regarding removal of obstacles in the Mutha river to obviate overflowing of flood water and construction of retaining walls along the riversides. A few subsidiary proposals in this set were mooted to ease flow of traffic on the riverside or across the river. These were to construct a 100 feet wide road on the eastern riverside, to widen the Sambhaji Bridge and to lay out a slab on the Nagzari Nala downstream the Sambhaji Bridge. The second set of recommendations covered such points as provision of alternative plots to those whose lands were acquired for reconstruction, seeking financial assistance from the Governments – State and Central – for rehabilitation, getting loans sanctioned by the Collector for housing, and stay of pulling down of unauthorized constructions just close the river, built after the flood. The last proposal was short-sighted. But, all in all, the Committee did justice to its defined terms of reference.

Committee on Facilities in Municipal Housing Colonies for Employees

Along with the Committee on the safety of riverside buildings the other Committee on short-term issues relating to public works that produced a substantial report was pertaining the facilities in the Municipal Corporation residential colonies. Out of 15 suggestions broached by the Committee 11 had a bearing on amenities and conveniences to be provided and four on miscellaneous matters. Increase in the total accommodation through construction of more *chawls* as well as more attention to repairs and maintenance of the existing *chawls* and more water-supply and sanitary facilities were asked for by the Committee. Provision of playgrounds and creation of recreation centres to be conducted by an association of residents would relieve the humdrum life in the colonies. Planting of trees in the colonies would beautify their environs. Compound walls ought to be raised to protect the colonies from small nuisances as well as thefts and tar-roads laid out within and outside the colonies. Miscellaneous issues like dealing with undesirable sub-tenancies, need for allocation of tenements to genuine low-income groups among the Corporation employees, prevention of development of slums round the colonies and arrangement for receiving complaints of the residents, were also dealt with by the Committee and suitable proposals made.

Committee on Primary Education

The third Committee dealing with short-term issues that did justice to the terms of reference in its report was that appointed to review primary education imparted in the Municipal schools. The extent of available school accommodation was limited, so the Committee suggested that a plan for the construction of school buildings should be outlined. There was also a need for more playgrounds for schools. A majority of the students in the Municipal primary schools evinced a poor quality; they also displayed a low standard of orderliness and cleanliness. This was mainly because most of these students belonged to backward sections. To remove the first defect, it was essential to keep limit on the total strength of students in the schools so also to keep a record of the progress of the students. To tackle the latter defect, campaigns among students to inculcate habits of cleanliness and orderliness were called for. Another handicap of these schools was in regard to the low quality of teachers employed by them. Their scales were low; very few of these had training in English-teaching. The remedies proposed by the Committee were to recruit retired trained teachers as well as secondary teachers to train the existing untrained staff in teaching English and Grammar, to seek to close double shift (an impossible task due to the paucity of school-buildings) and to set up an association of parents in order to create amity between teachers and parents for fostering proper spirit among the students. The improvement in the quality of primary education imparted in the Corporation schools was indeed an uphill task.

The Ad-hoc Committee set up to consider ways of removing the anomaly of continuation of teachers who had not resigned their posts in the *Zilla Parishad* on appointment in the Corporation had a limited term of reference. The Committee viewed the appointment of these teachers as not being wrong since they had later resigned their posts in the *Zilla Parishad.* The punishment of stoppage of increments for two years of all these teachers was considered adequate by the Committee. No further action was proposed by the Committee.

Committee on Corporation Proceedings

The Ad-hoc Committee on new rules regarding the Corporation proceedings also did its job satisfactorily within the terms referred to it for consideration. The Corporation used to discuss many a time issues extraneous to its own jurisdiction and relevance and waste its valuable time. The Committee directed that only subjects relating to Municipal affairs should be included in the agenda for a meeting. Similarly, it suggested that adjournment motions also should have a bearing on Municipal matters and that to introduce order in the proceedings half an hour's notice before the meeting be given. Again, with the same objective in view, the Committee desired two changes in the proceedings, one change suggested was that the Mayor should move a condolence resolution and only party leaders or their nominees should speak on it. The other change proposed was that in a meeting at the most five questions and five supplementaries for each question may be asked and that each question be allotted five minutes at the most.

Committees to Review Administrative Actions

The reports of the Ad-hoc Committees set up to review administrative actions were the most infructuous of all types of Ad-hoc Committees. Three of the six Ad-hoc Committees of this type could not produce any reports. These were the Committees on audit objections on the administration of the Transport Undertaking, the violation of the building regulations by the Poonam Restaurant and the public grievances regarding the execution of the building regulations in general. The first and the third Committees could not make any dent into the problems referred to them on account of the reluctance of the Administration to show records and to co-operate in general with the work of the Committees. The second Committee held about two scores of meetings but with no concrete result. The Corporation had to give a new lease of life to the Committees on the Poonam Restaurant as well as the building regulations in general. Nor did all the members of the Committees pull together against the Administration. The reports of the three remaining Ad-hoc Committees reviewing administrative actions also were not fruitful because they were merely denunciatory and did not recommend any positive remedial actions. The Committee on the communication by the Chairman of the Transport Committee to the Collector regarding de-requisitioning of a plot disapproved of inaction by the Transport Committee, its Chairman, the Transport Manager, so also quick action by the Collector's office. Similarly, the violation of the building regulations by the Shirin Talkies provoked the Committee's resentment against the building permission issued by the Administration, but the Committee at the end of its report contented itself by exhorting the Administration not to commit such mistake in future. In both the cases the Committees thought it fit not to resort to any disciplinary actions on the officials concerned because they did not desire that relations between the Corporation and the officials should be strained beyond repair. The Committee that sought to follow the recommendations of the two consultants, the Ibcon-Beacons and Bhamburkar, and the actions by the Corporation on these, secured its objective as the Administration furnished the required information.

Delegations

Out of the three delegations only one, viz. on grievances regarding the Sassoon Hospital, was successful in securing a promise from the State Government that some of the grievances would be removed. The report of this Delegation-Committee was very brief and matter-of-fact.

Absence of Keenness to Attend Meetings

A majority of members of the Ad-hoc Committees did not evince keenness to attend the meetings of the Committees. One obvious reason, as given out at a number of times at the Corporation meetings, was that the attendance at the meetings of the Ad-hoc Committees, as in the case of those of the Special and the Standing Committees, did not fetch any allowance. Secondly, few of the members of the Ad-hoc Committees were genuinely interested in the work of these Committees which demanded study of the issues concerned and bit of hard work involved in collecting relevant information from the office and elsewhere. The least number of meetings, viz. one, was held by the Ad-hoc Committee on the Sports Stadium and the largest, viz. above two scores, by that on the Poonam Restaurant. The general grievance was that even though a large number of meetings were convened, very few actually transacted serious business. Actually, because attendance at meetings was very thin, they did not conduct serious business and this called for the convening of more meetings. Some other Ad-hoc Committees which convened meetings above 10 were those on building permissions (12), Corporation proceedings (12), Ibcon, etc. (11), and Shirin Talkies (11). It is worth recalling that in the case of two of these Committees, viz., on building permissions and Shirin Talkies, the Administration had withheld the required information from them.

Chairmen

The Corporation had appointed chairman in case of only one Ad-hoc Committee. So, it is presumed that it was left to the Committees to elect their own chairmen. It was not that these chairmen themselves moved the reports of their Committees in the Corporation meetings for adoption; sometimes some other members of the Committees undertook this responsibility. This meant that the procedures regarding this aspect of the Committees' proceedings were informal. Except in the cases of the short-term Committees reviewing administrative actions the Administration extended cooperation to the Committees by supplying the necessary information, giving oral explanations, accompanying the Committees on visits to the institutions or field establishments or sites. In a few cases (e.g., the safety of riverside buildings) the Committees made use of the notes prepared by other institutions like the Gokhale Institute and the Institute of Engineers.

Time taken to Submit Reports

The Committee on Sports Stadium was most quick in submitting report to the Corporation, it took only one week. The annual Grant-in-Aid Committees were next in completing their work early within about two months since they were time-bound to submit reports before the close of the budget-year. Besides, three Committees on long-term issues (including two pertaining to changes in the Municipal Corporations

Act) and three on short-term ones (on naming of roads, teachers' appointment and Corporation colonies) completed work within a year. As many as 10 Committees took more than a year for their work. Those on reports of Ibcon, etc., and Shirin Talkies spent three years while two other Committees on Secondary Education and Municipalisation of Trades required four years to complete their reports. No particular reasoning could be traced as to the time taken for completion of reports by the different Ad-hoc Committees except the convenience and pre-occupations of the members of the respective Committees. The Committees reviewing administrative actions, as mentioned above, were handicapped due to the non-cooperative attitude of the Administration.

It took two to eight months for the consideration of the reports by the Corporation of 18 Committees after they were submitted to it. Reports of four Committees were considered by the Corporation after more than eight months since they were forwarded to it, one of these took 18 months. The Grants-in-Aid Committees were the only Committees which were time-bound in this respect. The slow despatch of business by the General Body of the Corporation due to pre-occupation with extraneous business and limited time-span of meetings was also responsible for this.

Discussion of Committees' Reports in the Corporation

It is worth noting that the reports of only two Ad-hoc Committees were discussed as such in the Corporation meeting. These were the reports of the Committees on naming of roads and other public places and safety of riverside buildings. In the case of the former, a small hint was dropped that suggestions be invited from the people at large by publicising the matter in newspapers. But on the just ground that this would unnecessarily delay the Committee's report, the hint was shelved. The latter Committee's report (on safety of riverside buildings) evoked a considerable discussion in the Coporation meeting. The proposal of the Committee to lay out a road close to the eastern bank of the Mutha river from the Sambhaji Bridge to the Sangam Bridge was opposed by the Janasangh Corporators some of whom represented the constituencies incorporating the location of the proposed road. Their main argument was that the proposed road would displace residents in the area of its location and that the new road was unnecessary since the existing roads in the area were adequate to cope with the traffic. But on heated debate, the objection to the proposal was defeated and the Committee's report was adopted by the Corporation.

The main reason for the unanimity in the General Body of the Corporation regarding the adoption of the reports of the Ad-hoc Committees was the due regard for the labours put in by the Committees. The Corporation welcomed the reports of the Committees which in general sought to broaden or streamline the Corporation's existing functions. Sometimes a ground was pleaded for not adopting the report, viz., that it was not signed by all the members of the Committee. But the objection was answered by pointing to the absence of these non-signatory members and their non-opposition to the report. The report of one Committee, viz. on the Corporation proceedings, contained a note of dissent by the minority but in the Corporation meeting no mention of this note of dissent was made and the majority report was adopted unanimously.

CORPORATION'S ACTION ON REPORTS

The report of the Ad-hoc Committees on long-term issues, so also on short-term issues, involving review of administrative actions, proved to be infructuous in respect of the follow-up action.

Report of Committee on State Government's Zakaria Committee Report

The implementation of the proposals of the Ad-hoc Committees on long-term issues lay with the State Government which did not act upon them. The State Government did not like to disturb the Zakaria Committee's main recommendation regarding the continuance of the existing pattern of separation between the deliberative and executive wings of the Municipal Corporations. Nor was the new legislation embodying the Zakaria Committee's recommendations enacted immediately after the submission of the report. The Ad-hoc Committee on the administrative organisation of the Poona Municipal Transport itself was mute on any change in it and wanted the Corporation to wait for the Zakaria Committee's report for decision on the matter. The Zakaria Committee's recommendations, as mentioned above, were not translated into legislation immediately after the submission of the report.

State Government's Action not Forthcoming on Secondary School Committee Report

The proposal of the Ad-hoc Committee on secondary schools to institute a fifth Special Committee on the subject was also not acted upon by the State Government immediately. So also with the proposals of the Ad-hoc Committees on housing and municipalisation of trades, regarding transfer of vacant Government lands to the Corporation and assistance towards construction of houses by the Corporation. The reports of the Ad-hoc Committees on short-term issues involving review of administrative action were in the main denunciatory, not embodying any positive remedial actions. So, no question of the follow-up of their recommendations arose.

The follow-up action by the Corporation, however, assumed importance in the case of the reports of the Ad-hoc Committees on short-term policy or administrative problems (not involving review of administrative action). Not that all the recommendations of these Committees were executed by the Corporation. Some of the recommendations which involved large financial outlay or State Government action were not put into action.

Report on Annual Grants-in-Aid

The recommendation of the Annual Grants-in-Aid Committees, except those which were not followed by fulfilment of the prescribed rules regarding registration, audit, etc., were executed. Similarly, the reports of the Sports Stadium Committee and the Naming of Roads Committee were acted upon. Action even on the priority roads mentioned by the Road-widening Committee could not be taken in full by the Corporation because of the delaying legal procedures concerning land right in general and land acquisition in particular. The priority roads could be widened at places and not over the entire stipulated lengths.

Report on Riverside Buildings

The recommendations of the Ad-hoc Committee on riverside buildings were partly implemented. The recommendation regarding removal of obstacles in the Mutha river was concretised in the form of a river improvement scheme awaiting approval and financial assistance from the State Government. Construction of retaining walls on the riversides was undertaken by the Corporation. Similarly, work on the 100 feet wide road from the Sambhaji Bridge to the Sangam Bridge on the eastern riverside as well as on the slab on the Nagzari Nala was begun. The proposal for widening the Sambhaji Bridge was, however, dropped since it was very costly and would have entailed inconvenience to the traffic on the bridge. Moreover, a few more bridges for pedestrians were proposed to be laid on the river. For the rehabilitation of the flood-affected, the Corporation was doing whatever was possible for it. It built a few more *chawls* for its own employees. The main responsibility in this regard was of the State Government which it partially fulfilled. As far as the stay of pulling down of unauthorised constructions close to the river was concerned, the Corporation accepted the plea but was not willing to permit new constructions.

Report on Corporation Colonies

In regard to the improvements suggested by the Ad-hoc Committee on the Corporation colonies it was heartening to find that they were being effected, but not to the extent desired by the Committee. Budgetary allocations were made for construction of more *chawls* as well as for repairs and maintenance of the existing ones. Similarly, arrangements for more water-supply and sanitary facilities to the colonies were being made. An association of the residents of the colonies was formed and a social worker appointed to educate the residents in hygiene, but in regard to provision of playgrounds and planting of trees in and around the colonies progress could not be registered. Compound walls were being raised around some of the colonies, but they did not ensure the security of belongings of the residents. Better roads also were being laid out improving communications within and without the colonies. Allotment of tenements in the colonies was made to the employees below the salary of Rs. 175 per month. But not much could be done in regard to abolition of sub-tenancies and prevention of development of slums round the colonies. Complaints of the residents were registered in the office in the colonies as well as the Corporation headquarters.

Committee on Primary Education

The same trend as in the case of the above committee was discerned in the case of the action on the report of the Committee on primary education. In some respects definite action was being taken, in others financial scarcity and built-in handicaps (as in the case of the low standards of students) stood in the way of visible progress. In regard to the expansion of physical accommodation for schools, though a ten-year plan was framed, its execution was slow. Hired premises for schools playgrounds were not available. Unless extensive sites for schools were provided no progress was possible in the matter. Quick improvement in the quality of education in the primary schools could not be expected as the pre-requisite for this was improvement in the quality of students, and as long as the existing standards of education continued the level of students could not rise. Increased inputs of better teachers, improved equipment, more spacious accommodation and stricter discipline over years alone could yield substantial results in course of time. Restriction on the strength of the schools was one way out, but the Corporation could not think of this since to provide educational opportunity to those who could not be accommodated in private schools was the rationale underlying the educational efforts of the Corporation. The Committee's proposal, in the same context, to maintain a record of the progress of the students was implemented. Campaigns to spread cleanliness among the students were undertaken by the staff; special health units for the examination of the students were also set up. To tone up the quality of teachers, they were deputed in batches to the State Institute of Education and training colleges for training in English and other subjects. Attempts were also being made to induct retired secondary teachers. The closing of the double shift to lighten the burden on the teachers was not possible so long as more physical accommodation was not available. So also the existing work-load on teachers could not be reduced because the difficult financial situation of the Corporation did not allow it to employ more teachers. An association of parents to inculcate a proper spirit among their wards was set up. This account would create an impression that everything possible to improve the quality of primary schools was being done by the Corporation. Even in the existing set-up, with stricter supervision over the teachers and better utilisation of the existing facilities the quality of primary education could be raised to some extent. But the Corporation failed to attend to this alternative.

The report of the other Ad-hoc Committee on primary education regarding the appointment of teachers on the roll of *Zilla Parishads* was meant for record only.

Report on Corporation Proceedings

That the Corporation did not want to be bound by some of the recommendations of the Committee on its own proceedings that were already accepted by it was clear from the fact that only two of its recommendations were followed by it. These were concerning the condolence resolutions and the maximum number of questions and supplementaries to be asked in a meeting.

CONCLUSION

Broadly speaking, the use of the device of Ad-hoc Committees was fruitful in respect of short-term policies or administrative issues in the sense that it led to concrete results in administrative action. This did not imply that the Corporation executed all the proposals containing in the reports of these Committees. Compared to these, the Ad-hoc Committees on long-term issues and those reviewing administrative actions did not lead to fruitful results. From this it would be unreasonable to infer that the setting up of the Ad-hoc Committees on long-term problems or for review of administrative actions was not justified at all. The Corporation should have bestowed more care on the setting up on Ad-hoc Committees on these types of subjects. It ought to include knowledgeable Corporators in the Ad-hoc Committees on long-range problems to ensure quality reports. It must also make sure of official co-operation in the conduct of inquiries on administrative actions before it appointed Ad-hoc Committees on these. The Corporation was within its rights in the setting up of Ad-hoc Committees to review administrative actions. But it had to take care that their efficacy was ensured, otherwise belief in the Corporation's competence to deal with matters within its own sphere of jurisdiction might be impaired.

Apart from this pragmatic aspect, the Ad-hoc Committees had a great educative value. The members of these Committees came face-to-face confronting various inter-departmental issues of great significance for the welfare of the citizens or the efficiency of the Corporation. Their intellect would get sharpened and the horizons of their experience would be widened in the process of their participation in these Committees. One wished that all of them evinced a seriousness of purpose the tasks of the Ad-hoc Committees demanded.

6

DECISION-MAKING IN THE STATUTORY COMMITTEES

THE STANDING COMMITTEE

THE STANDING COMMITTEE has primary authority in financial and personnel matters. In these matters it overrides the Special Committees. Over a certain financial limit and in regard to certain higher posts, the Corporation (General Body) has overriding authority over and above the Standing Committee (vide Chapter 2 'The Structure'). Only decisions of the Standing Committee which evoked discussion in Committee meetings have been covered for analysis here. The other decisions are not covered for our purposes, these were insignificant though in the Municipal administration they would be substantial.

The decision-making process in the Standing Committee was more authoritative than that in the Special Committees which was advisory in character. The Standing Committee comprised four components: the elected members including the Chairman, the official elements consisting of the Municipal Commissioner and the Assistant Commissioners, the specialist officers — heads of functional departments like engineering, medicine and health, octroi, auditor, etc., — and the Municipal Secretary. In theory, the elected members decided all matters before the Standing Committee. But, in actual practice, the Municipal Commissioner and the Heads of Departments, in their consultative presence in the Committee's meetings, influenced the decisions of the Committee. The information furnished by the officials to the Committee formed the basis of the discussions and decisions to be taken by the Committee. But in a large number of items placed before the Committee for consideration and decision-making this information was not thorough or even adequate enough to enable the members of the Committee to form their own judgement by reflecting on the matters before it, precedent to decision. On the other hand, the Municipal Commissioner and the Heads of the Departments were well equipped to defend their stand in the 'dockets' *vis-a-vis* the criticisms offered by the members and the stand they had taken. The personalities of the Commissioner and the officials, particularly the former, and their relations with the members of the Committee also influenced the decision-making by the members. The Municipal Secretary, in comparison with the Municipal Commissioner and the Department Heads, did not figure in the decision-making process in the Standing Committee except in regard to the items pertaining to his own Secretariat. But, in the matters pertaining the Municipal Secretariat, the members of the Standing Committee exercised influence.

The changing membership of the Standing Committee every year also hampered members acquiring an indepth knowledge of the subject-matter before the Committee, and hence their influencing its decisions substantially.

Thirty meetings of the Standing Committee were observed by us during the period December 1966–April 1967.

A. Personel Matters

Decisions with Policy Implications

During four to five months' period, spreading over December 1966 — April 1967, important policy or decisional matters that came up before the Standing Committee in regard to Personnel were few.

Enrolment of Municipal Corporation Personnel as Members of Political Parties

A member belonging to the S.S.P. mooted a suggestion to allow the employees of the Municipal Corporation to enrol as members of political parties. The member cited the situation in the Western countries such as the U.K., the U.S.A., to support his suggestion that Municipal employees should enjoy the right of the citizens to play their legitimate role as members of political parties. The Municipal Commissioner, like a true civil servant, opposed the member's suggestion on the ground that, if accepted, it might politicise the administration, affecting its efficiency and impartiality. The Commissioner also pointed out that while the Masterman Committee in

Britain had recommended the grant of political rights to the subordinate employees only, the mover had included both the superior and subordinate categories of Municipal employees in his proposal. It is interesting to note a member had supported the proposal in the General Body but he expressed opposition to it in the Standing Committee. The matter was rushed through the General Body without referring it to the Municipal Commissioner for his opinion. It was also raised in the Committee whether the Commissioner had offended the General Body by expressing his opinion against its resolution in the Standing Committee. The mover's arguments seemed to persuade the Chairman of the Standing Committee and some other members to his point of view. The Municipal Commissioner further argued that the issue being political and pervading all the local bodies deserved to be decided by the State Government. But the Chairman and the members of his persuasion rightly thought that the Municipal Corporation was an autonomous local government and as such could take its own policy decision. On this the Municipal Commissioner averred that an all-India body like the Mayors' Conference should deliberate over it and give its recommendations on the issue. The mover, however, differed from him to air the view that the Mayors' Conference was not a useful forum for this purpose. The feeling among the Committee members in favour of the mover's suggestion was so strong that in the end a Sub-Committee was appointed to consider the issue in detail. But the Sub-Committee met rarely.

Conversion of Post of Labour Legal Officer as Labour Welfare Officer

A matter, though it should have emanated from the Public Works Committee, was considered by the Standing Committee without the consultation with the Public Works Committee. The matter concerned a proposal from a few members that the post of Labour Legal Officer be converted to Labour Welfare Officer on the ground that the officer did not look after the welfare of the workers employed by the Corporation minding only the legal issues of their employment. On the Municipal Commissioner pointing out that the implementation of the matter would call for an amendment of the Municipal Corporation Act and that the present incumbent was being deputed to the labour welfare officers training course at Calcutta, the proposal was withdrawn.

Preference to Freedom-fighters in Municipal Service

A proposal that came from some members in the General Body wanted a preference to be given to the freedom-fighters in the service of the Municipal Corporation. The Standing Committee was in favour of the proposal and so referred it to the Municipal Commissioner for framing the necessary amendment in the Municipal service rules. The members had feared that the Commissioner would oppose the proposal, but he was all in its favour.

Appointment of a Lady Doctor as Medical Superintendent of Hospital

The appointment of a lady doctor to an officer's post of a medical superintendent of a newly acquired private hospital, at a salary of Rs. 800 p.m., evoked a good deal of discussion in the Standing Committee. The lady doctor was a senior staff member in the private hospital when it was taken over by the Municipal Corporation. It was pointed out by a member that earlier the Medical Officer of Health (MOH) had opined that the existing staff should not be absorbed in the private hospitals being taken over by the Municipal Corporation. But the M.O.H. denied having made the statement. A doubt was expressed whether a good doctor — which the selected lady doctor was according to the opinion of the Corporator member of the Committee in the area of the hospital — would prove to be a competent medical superintendent of the hospital. A fear was expressed by a member that under the lady doctor's stewardship the hospital would become a female patients hospital. Objection was also aired to the additional increments being given to the selected doctor. The M.O.H. replied that the additional increments given were in lieu of the private practice being denied to the lady doctor. At long last, the Standing Committee approved of the appointment.

Extension of Retirement Age of Secondary School Teachers from 58 to 60 Years of age

A policy issue discussed in the Standing Committee was about the extension of the age of retirement of the teachers in the secondary schools conducted by the Municipal Corporation. The amendment to the existing rules in favour of the extension from the age of 58 to 60 years was moved by a member. Such extension was granted in the privately managed secondary schools. The Municipal Commissioner raised a query whether the Grant-in-Code applied to the private secondary schools, under which the extension could be granted by the private managements, was applicable to the government (and by implication the municipal) secondary schools. At the next meeting, the mover himself furnished the information that the Grant-in-Code applied to the private secondary schools was not applicable to the government (and municipal) schools. The mover pointed out that the Municipal Corporation authorities chose to adopt whichever practice suited them. In the case of a medical staff member on loan from the government, though the Municipal Corporation's rule permitted the extension up to 58 years, the government rule of 55 years was applied to the employee. It was finally decided that the Municipal Commissioner should put up proposals on the merit of each case.

Merger of D.A. for Pension, Pushing Back of Year of Application

An issue relating to the date of including a part of the Dearness Allowance of the Corporation employees for the determination of their pension was also raised by a member in his proposal. The State Government had stipulated 1961 as this year while the mover had proposed 1958. Varied opinions were aired on the proposal. The matter was advised for reference to the State Government, which the Committee did.

Extension of Tenure

The Standing Committee was generally in favour of the extension of tenure to the staff. The Committee acted in these matters on the recommendation of the Municipal Commissioner. Extension was granted by the Committee to the temporary posts of Electrical Supervisors. The members expressed resentment over the lack of full information in the docket on the post, furnished by the office. Some members entertained a fear that unqualified persons may get extended tenure or relatives of the incumbents may get in. Items proposed by the office to grant extension to the staff on loan from the State Government's Town-Planning Department for town-planning work and from other Departments for land acquisition work were discussed. The members were hesitant to grant extension. In respect of the State Government's town-planning staff the Committee members complained that information about the quality of their work in the Municipal Corporation had not been supplied by the office. But the Municipal Commissioner prevailed upon them by pointing out that the government town-planning staff inducted in the Corporation was intelligent and that the Municipal Corporation would suffer if the Government withdrew the staff. In regard to the State Government personnel inducted for the land acquisition work, members criticised that their work was slow; the Municipal Commissioner had conveyed the anticipated criticism to the Divisional Commissioner in whose office and/or under his control the staff might have served earlier.

Increments, Leave and Allowances

Increments and allowances to the staff also figured for discussion and decision on the agenda of the meetings of the Standing Committee. An SSP member proposed an allowance of Rs. 20 p.m. to the employees who had passed the Local Self-Government Diploma examination conducted by the All-India Local Self-Government (L.S.G.) Institute at Bombay. The Diploma imparted the holders knowledge of the local governments in India and abroad and also gave them preliminary factual information of the basic functional areas of Municipal administration. The member's plea was well-justified. The Municipal Commissioner, however, opined that University graduates were superior in knowledge to the L.S.G. Diploma-holders. In Nagpur and Sholapur Municipal Corporations no such allowance was paid, while in Bombay Municipal Corporation it was paid subject to some conditions. The response to the Diploma in the State was also poor as evident from the number of those who passed it. Due to the mover's insistence that the Diploma imparted knowledge useful to the employees of the Municipal Corporation, the payment of an allowance of Rs. 10 p.m. to the Diploma-holders was resolved.

It was usual in the Municipal Corporation for officers of the Corporation to avail of the facility of accumulated privilege leave after retirement. This practice was advantageous to both the officers and the Municipal Corporation. The officers enjoyed full-salaried privilege leave after their retirement and the Municipal Corporation availed of the extended services of experienced officers after their retirement. In the case before a meeting of the Standing Committee, observed by us, the Octroi Superintendent was allowed by the Committee to avail of the privilege leave of four months after his retirement.

On another item before the Standing Committee, a special disability allowance was granted to an employee in the Medical Department, who worked on refuse carriage. The refuse carriages did not have a proper cover and so were at time injurious to the employees who worked on them. The Medical Officer of Health promised the Committee to look into the matter. A halting allowance to the drivers and *havaldars* accompanying the Corporators and the Office-bearers was also agreed upon. Such an allowance was paid to the staff of the Municipal Commissioner. The necessary change in the service conditions and rules was approved to be effected by the Municipal Commissioner.

The Municipal Commissioner's proposal to grant overtime allowance of Rs. 40 p.m. to the employees working on the road electrification programme was agreed to by the members after initial hesitation. Some members pointed out that this was the usual work expected of the employees for which no overtime allowance needed to be paid. The Municipal Secretary added that the staff in his Secretariat worked overtime but were not paid any overtime allowance. The Municipal Commissioner cited the instance of an engineer who supervised during overtime hours the construction of the Municipal Corporation building, for which he was paid Rs. 100 p.m. as overtime allowance. The Committee was persuaded by this instance in favour of the proposal of the Municipal Commissioner.

Sometimes, Corporators took keen interest in certain employees and placed before the Standing Committee proposals for extra benefits to them. The grant of a bicycle allowance of Rs. 5 p.m. was proposed by a member to a senior clerk in the office of the Municipal Secretary, doing outdoor duties for the Mayor. It was surprising that the proposal was not routed through the Municipal Secretary and so did not carry his remarks. But the proposal being reasonable and implying a very modest additional financial commitment, was adopted by the Committee.

Deputing Officials to Courses and Conferences

The Municipal Corporation officials, on their own or on being encouraged or prodded by the superior officers, were deputed to various training courses or conferences. The further training in their own area of specialisation or an allied area equipped the officials better for the performance of functions and also improved their qualification to hold higher posts in due course. Deputation at conferences exposed the officials to discourses and deliberations on their subjects of specialisation or allied subjects in which more learned and experienced persons participated. It also gave them an opportunity to articulate their own views based on self-experiences and to benefit from interactions with other participants. The Standing Committee considered the deputation of the officials to various training courses and conferences.

The deputation of the officials to the higher diploma course in local government at the All-India Institute of Local Self-Government at Bombay was considered by the Standing Committee. Though it was given out in a meeting of the Committee that the training in the course would not be of much use to the officials from the Municipal Secretary's office, some of them were also deputed on the Committee's resolution along with those from the office of the Municipal Commissioner. The deputation of a Deputy City Engineer to a refresher course at the Central Highway Research Institute at Delhi was also resolved. Members were keen to know whether and how the knowledge gained at such courses was applied on resuming duties at the Municipal Corporation. The Municipal Commissioner rightly replied that every time the application of the knowledge obtained at these courses was not possible either because the resources were lacking or there was no scope for such application. The real object underlying these courses was to facilitate the coming together of the officials and their discussing the common problems. Even the qualifications of the concerned official to be deputed to the course were questioned in the meeting. The Municipal Commissioner defended his choice by pointing out that the official possessed higher than the requisite qualification and that he had not been deputed so far to a course held at a distant place like Delhi. The members were desirous to know the content of knowledge obtained by the deputationists and how it would be applied in the Municipal Corporation. On the Municipal Commissioner assuring the Committee the furnishing of such information in future, it approved the deputation of the official to the course.

B. Proposals from Special Committees

Levying or revising the rates or fees for the services or amenities provided by the Municipal Corporation was within the purview of the powers of the Standing Committee even though the items emanated from the Special Committees which devoted special consideration to these from the point of view of the subjects of their concern. An item from the Medical Relief and Public Health Committee proposed rise in the fees of the anaesthesist. A question was raised by members as to why the fee charged for call at night was higher. The Medical Officer of Health replied that at night anaesthesists were not willing to respond. Another proposal from the same Special Committee to increase the rates of cots and surgery at the Municipal maternity homes due to the rise in overall costs was before the Standing Committee. Yet another item pertaining the medical subject proposed the rate for X-ray. It was much lower, viz. Re. 1 per X-ray, then prevailing in private hospitals and clinics. Members enquired why only two to three X-ray photos a day were taken in the Municipal hospitals. This cheap facility in the Municipal hospitals was not advertised adequately. Further, patients from outside medical doctors were not allowed the facility. The Medical Officer of Health promised to look into the matter. All the three proposals were adopted by the Standing Committee.

C. Purchase and Sale

Several items regarding purchase and sale came up before the Standing Committee during the period of our observation. No definite policies or attitudes were in evidence in the decisions taken by the Standing Committee in these matters. *Ad hocism* seemed to influence these decisions. The opinion of the Municipal Commissioner seemed to prevail in the end when majority of members were not inclined. But not so weighty were the views of other officials on occasions when the Municipal Commissioner was absent or he chose to remain silent. On the items in regard to which the official proposals were weak, members voiced differences. But, in general, the attitudes of the members were inclined to allow the benefit of doubt to the official stand. The personalities of the opposing members also counted in carrying the Committee with their point of view. Except in construction matters members were not prepared for thorough discussions as they were not armed with facts relating to the matters and with the knowledge of the functional area concerned.

Proposals Accepted

On an item of the purchase of an oil painting to be fixed at a Municipal hospital, the Standing Committee correctly decided to delegate the authority to the Municipal Commissioner. In such items of purchase of objects of art, choice by inviting tenders was not the appropriate method. In a number of items discretion was granted to be exercised by the Municipal Commissioner over the choice of a tender, even with the lowest price/cost. For the purchase of an operation table and other instruments, it was the opinion of the Standing Committee that the lowest tender did not necessarily indicate quality goods. In the purchase of four road asphalt mixers, the Company, approved by the Municipal Commissioner even with the highest price among the tenders received, was approved by the Standing Committee. The Committee accepted the view of the Commissioner that the experience and reputation of the tenderers as well as the quality of goods and their suitability for the given purpose had to be taken into account. The objection raised to the purchase of four machines at a time was answered by the Commissioner by pointing out that the area of the Municipal Corporation had expanded recently and four asphalt mixers could repair the roads at increased speed.

Sometimes wiser counsels of the Committee members were not liked by the officials. For example, their suggestion to go in for the purchase of an air-compressor at Bombay, where a good quality would be available at a cheaper price, was not found acceptable by the officials. The tenders received for advertisements in newspapers were passed by the Standing Committee, but with a rider that important public notices should be publicised in all leading newspapers though a particular newspaper was not in the approved list.

A tender with a higher than the market rate for the construction of a medical store with an R.C.C. slab was accepted on its pleading by the Medical Officer of Health. Some members preferred a tin shade to the R.C.C. slab. The M.O.H. favoured the R.C.C. slab in preference to the tin shade on more than one ground. Costly equipment had to be stored, R.C.C. slab would protect it better than the tin shade. Tin shade would not protect it from heavy rains. Upper floors could not be constructed on a tin shade. Moreover, the difference between the cost of an R.C.C. slab and a tin shade was not marked. There was, however, not much discussion on the rate of construction of an R.C.C. slab and a tin shade. The extension to the tenure of hire of a transformer of the Maharashtra State Electricity Board for six months instead of one year proposed by the office was approved by the Standing Committee. The Chairman of the Committee desired that the Municipal Corporation should install its own transformer to which the Municipal Commissioner responded that this could not be done due to the strike.

The tender for washing clothes of the Municipal employees was accepted after some discussion. Some members querried as to why the Corporation itself should not have its own washing machine. The Municipal Commissioner responded that it would be costlier. Then members put in another query as to why the medical department gave its clothes for washing outside even though it had its own machine. The M.O.H. replied that the machine was not in working condition and would be got repaired.

The tenders for the construction of a watchman's quarter in a Municipal open space, a water storage tank and a compound wall were accepted by the Standing Committee. Members, however, expressed the view that the Municipal Corporation itself ought to undertake these constructions. The Municipal Commissioner replied that this would be costlier than the contract. Members entered a rejoinder that the quality of the work constructed on contract was low. An additional work in a school building was approved on the recommendation of the school Head-master whose opinion was valued by the Committee. The necessity of an iron grill attached to the school building was realised by the Committee despite initial opposition from a few members.

Proposals Negatived

Some proposals by the office were not adopted by the Standing Committee due to the higher cost involved or their unreasonableness otherwise. The demand for an X-ray tube at Rs. 14,278, for which a tender was passed a year-and-half ago, was revived. The price had increased in the meantime. In the meanwhile, another machine had been installed. The Medical Officer of Health explained the need of the additional X-ray machine by referring to a long time taken by the Corporation in processing a fresh proposal for another X-ray machine when required. The demand was considered unreasonable by the Committee and so withdrawn by the Municipal Commissioner.

The Chairman of the Standing Committee showed exemplary courage, of course within his own right, when he asked an intruder trader seeking to influence the decision of the Committee on purchase of timber to leave the meeting.

The office proposal for the purchase of a truck chassis of a certain company's make, at a higher price than the tenders of other companies was rejected by the Standing Committee. It was a rare instance of forthrightness on the part of the Standing Committee. The storekeeper argued that for the sake of standardisation the truck chassis of the particular company was preferred as the chassis purchased earlier belonged to that company. Members averred that the recommended company's chassis were not of a good quality. They also questioned the propriety of recommending the chassis of that company at a higher price when tenders at lower price had been received. The storekeeper's assurance to purchase the chassis of other companies in future did not assuage the resentment of the Committee members over the office proposal.

The Standing Committee members evinced interest in debating the variations in tender agreements and changes in the rates approved earlier. This interest was, however, not evident in several cases of purchase and sale.

In an item of the sale of timber in Corporation's stock, the members questioned its propriety when timber was being purchased as firewood. They suggested the use of timber to be sold as firewood instead of purchasing it. The Municipal Commissioner pointed out that the timber offered for sale had to be cut according to specifications, which would be costlier than the purchase of timber. But due to members' opposition the Municipal Commissioner did not press his proposal.

D. Land Acquisition Proposals

It was sensed that the vested interests brought pressure on some members in some of the land acquisition proposals. The proposals moved by the Municipal Commissioner were agreed to by the Standing Committee. This indicated the influence he carried with the members of the Standing Committee.

Municipal Commissioner's Proposals Accepted

The official proposal to acquire certain buildings in certain localities for road widening was accepted by the Standing Committee. The members agreed to include in the proposal a square that needed to be widened. The Municipal Commissioner had put up a proposal to acquire a vacant land by negotiation with the land-owner. The land was wrongly acquired by the engineering department of the Corporation; the land-owner took objection to it. The proposal was accepted. No member, however, cared to know who was the official responsible for the wrong acquisition. There was a proposal of the Municipal Commissioner to hire a place for a Municipal pumping station for 20 years. Members instead suggested the acquisition of the place as the amount of compensation was not large. But the Municipal Commissioner persisted in his proposal for hiring the place as the acquisition would take a long time. However, he agreed to the member's suggestion to reduce the period of hire to five years.

Members' Proposals/Suggestions Negatived

A member moved a proposal to acquire a place for road widening. The place where a three-storeyed building stood belonged to a Congress member. At the first meeting in which the item appeared, the Chairman, a Congressman and a friend of the member having vested interest, were absent. The Municipal Commissioner shrewdly hinted that the arguments for and against should be heard by the Chairman who was absent at the meeting. The item was, therefore, postponed to the next meeting. The Chairman opposed the member's proposal on the ground that the compensation for land acquisition would be costly as it had to take into account the three-storeyed building on it. The member heeding this point withdrew the proposal.

A letter to exclude a certain area from acquisition was placed before a meeting of the Standing Committee. A nationalised bank in the area had complained that its business was suffering due to the blockage of traffic occurring on account of the non-execution of the road widening in the absence of land acquisition at issue. The Chairman refused to yield to the pressure exerted by the vested interests. So the letter under discussion was put aside. This instance brought out that next to the Municipal Commissioner it was the Chairman of the Standing Committee who was influential in the process of decision-making in it.

A suggestion was considered by the Standing Committee to return to a property-owner a portion of an acquired place not required by the Corporation. But the Municipal Commissioner brought to the notice of the Committee that a large compensation had been paid due to a building on it. The suggestion was defeated in deference to the Commissioner's plea.

The suggestion of a member was to allot alternative accommodation to the persons affected by road widening. The

Municipal Commissioner argued against the suggestion as in his view it would entail a heavy and impracticable commitment for the Municipal Corporation. The Commissioner stated that he had accepted moral responsibility in the matter and acted upon it in the past, but legal responsibility in this behalf would be difficult to fulfil in practice. Some members aired views favourable to the mover's suggestion. But in the end the Commissioner's view prevailed and the suggestion was not accepted.

The same member who had moved the above suggestion broached another suggestion in a meeting of the Standing Committee. It was that at the beginning of each year how much land would be acquired should be estimated and in keeping with this estimate land should be asked to be vacated for road widening.

E. Budget Estimates

It was surprising that small budget estimates were picked up by the members for criticism and large ones were left untouched. This might indicate their regard for the Municipal Commissioner's budget proposals in general or their lack of mastery over the facts and the subject-matter of the budget estimates involving large amounts.

Estimates Criticised but Agreed to

The motor-cycle allowance of Rs. 60 p.m. proposed to be paid to the Sanitary Inspectors, though opposed initially, was agreed to in view of the large area of the field duties covered by them. Similarly, the vehicle allowance for doctors visiting *mofussil* and urban centres frequently was passed.

The new posts in the Medical Department were opposed by a member who was personally not inclined to the Medical Officer of Health. The member even suggested an alternative pattern of the administrative set-up. But the Standing Committee did not follow the member's negative stand. The additional staff, so also the new post of Public Relations Officer, were approved of without discussion. The members did not even broach the nature of duties of the proposed new staff.

The health needs of the children drew concern by the Standing Committee. More money was asked for in the section on eye glasses for the school children, though the amount for the current year was not exhausted. The reasons cited for the larger estimate than for the current year were the rising costs and the increase in the number of students to be served. More amount for the children's health unit than sanctioned was also approved by the Committee.

The amount proposed for building new funeral grounds was approved by the Standing Committee. The members offered the criticism that in the past the implementation of similar proposals took longer time than expected. The greater expenditure for a Corporation hospital than for the current year asked for was agreed to, though members elicited information on the expenditure on food, tonics and medical charges.

The amount of Rs. 65,000 for the repair of the main hall in the Municipal Corporation was approved. Some members on their own suggested the construction of a new hall, an item not on the agenda of the Committee's meeting. Similarly, the estimates for the Public Works Department were passed by the Committee without much debate.

The discretionary grant at the disposal of the Municipal Commissioner was raised from Rs. 1,800 to Rs. 2,000. This also indicated the regard the Committee members had for the Municipal Commissioner.

Proposals not Approved

The official proposal of a new post for catching stray dogs was opposed as there was not enough work for the new post. Instead, an additional allowance to the employees doing the work was agreed to be continued. Similarly, a motor-cycle to the four Senior Inspectors in the Anti-Milk-Adulteration Department was not agreed to due to the opposition of a member and the insistence of the Chairman on consensus. The estimate for the maintenance Section was reduced by Rs. 2,000.

F. Miscellaneous

Loans from L.I.C.

An amount of Rs. 50 lakhs was sanctioned by the Life Insurance Corporation of India with the State Government's approval for the filtered water supply scheme of the Municipal Corporation. An additional loan of Rs. 40 lakhs was proposed by the Municipal Commissioner in a meeting of the Standing Committee to complete the works. The Committee approved the Corporation entering into agreement with the L.I.C. In anticipation of the approval of the General Body of the Municipal Corporation, the Standing Committee allowed the Municipal Commissioner to enter into the necessary agreement with the L.I.C. This instance again brought out how influential the Municipal Commissioner was in carrying the Standing Committee with him even in prestigious and important projects like the filtered water supply to Pune city.

Sale of Corporation's Land

A land of the Corporation was unutilised. The issue before the Standing Committee was whether to give it on rent or to sell it. The Committee favoured its sale. The next issue for decision was whether to sell it to neighbouring land-owners or stall-holders offering a higher price. The alternative modes of sale for consideration before the Committee were negotiation, inviting tenders or public auction. The Standing Committee decided to sell the land by public auction.

Grievances

Grievances on certain issues were aired by members in the Standing Committee meetings. A grievance related to the tenements of the Corporation. Some of them were alleged to have been sub-let. The Municipal Commissioner promised to look into the grievances. The criticism that the rent of the tenements was high was not heeded by the majority of the Committee's members. A Corporator aired a grievance that the Dearness Allowance cases of the Municipal employees were not disposed of expeditiously. The Municipal Commissioner agreed to do the needful in the matter. The Chairman of the Standing Committee offered to write to the Chairmen of the Standing Committees of the Sholapur and Nagpur Municipal Corporations regarding the rate of D.A. being paid by them.

G. Prime Factors in Decision-Making[2]

The weighty influence carried by the Municipal Commissioner and the Heads of the Departments in decision-making by the Standing

Committee was noticeable in most of the matters before the Committee. The trust of the Committee the Commissioner enjoyed was amply seen in the authority for entering into an agreement with the L.I.C. it delegated him in anticipation of a formal vote of the Corporation. In some matters the Committee registered disagreement with the official stand, as the official view was not in the financial interest of the Municipal Corporation or obviously unreasonable. The Heads of the Departments also influenced the decision-making in the Committee as they possessed thorough knowledge of the subjects under consideration. This was seen even in those few matters in which this or that member evinced his personal bias against the head of the department. The creation of a few major posts evoked discussion in the Committee while minor posts eluded its attention. Members were keen to discuss matters about few particular employees than the policies or the principles involved.

Excepting a few members, the elected personnel of the Standing Committee did not possess adequate information about the subjects considered by the Committee. This was also a reason why they were influenced by the official stand in various matters. The rule of consensus upheld by the Chairman of the Standing Committee might have to an extent hindered the pressing of views by individual members to the point of decision. But it could not have hampered the free expression of views by them on several matters open to being viewed from different angles. The members' silence on budget estimates with sizeable financial import was conspicuous and exemplified their lack of knowledge in the matters.

The Chairman's resisting and thwarting the influence by outside vested interests in matters regarding land acquisition and purchase was noteworthy. The Chairman should also be given credit for maintaining a cordial atmosphere during the discussions in the meetings of the Committee. On most of the items which evoked some discussion, officials' answers to the queries raised quietened them. A very few items elicited longer discussions in which more than one or two members participated and officials had to respond.

The discussions and decisions in the Standing Committee did not bring out much comprehensive thinking on the part of the members on lines of certain policies to be realised over years, say, a decade or so. These were marked by *ad-hocism.* The multi-political-party affiliation of the members of the Committee also partly accounted for this *ad-hocism*, along with the changing personnel in the annual elections to the Committee.

The co-option of personnel and financial experts in the Standing Committee is, therefore, advisable. An amendment to the Municipal Corporations Act would be necessary for the purpose.

A few observations on the modalities and atmosphere at the meetings would be in order.

Din and noise marked the meetings. Besides the members and the Municipal Commissioner and the Municipal Secretary, a large number of assisting staff were present at the meetings. It was problematic whether the presence of such a large number of staff was necessary. Mutual private conversations between members and officials marred the peace at the meetings and disturbed the concentration of the actors on their proceedings. The Chairman was found helpless in preventing the diversion of the discussions away from the items on the agenda and so could not dispose of much of the business.

At a few meetings observed, more than two-thirds of the total members were present. A few members joined late and one or two left before the meetings closed.

Members showed reluctance to hold the meetings on Sunday. With the consent of the members, in deference to the wishes of the Municipal Commissioner and other officials, particular pressing items were advanced for consideration or order of priorities changed.

THE TRANSPORT COMMITTEE

In the Committee system of the Poona Municipal Corporation, next tc the Standing Committee, the Transport Committee ranks in order of importance. In fact, in the State Municipal Corporations Act governing the Poona Municipal Corporation, it is laid down that in the context of the Municipal Transport, wherever the term 'Municipal Commissioner' occurs it should be substituted by the term 'Transport Manager'(TM). The Transport Manager has the same authority and powers over the Poona Municipal (Bus) Transport Undertaking as the Municipal Commissioner possesses over the Poona Municipal Corporation. Except in financial matters, in regard to the final moving of the Transport budget, the Transport Committee has the same powers as the Standing Committee over the Municipal Corporation matters. So, the Municipal Transport Undertaking enjoys and exercises an internal autonomy both in its operations as well as powers of oversight and policy approval by Committee. In regard to the Poona Municipal

Transport (P.M.T.) budget after it is approved by the Transport Committee it is transmitted to the Standing Committee for its approval and then it is placed before the Corporation (General Body) for adoption like the Municipal Corporation budget. The Municipal Corporation (General Body) has the same powers *vis-a-vis* the Transport Committee and the Transport Manager and his staff as in relation to the Standing Committee and the Municipal Commissioner and his personnel.

In all, 25 meetings of the Transport Committee were observed during the first half of 1967. The items considered and decided upon by the Transport Committee do not exhibit that much variety as those before the Standing Committee, obviously because financial and personnel matters considered earlier by the Special Committees in their functional aspect have to be again considered and finally approved by the Standing Committee. The Transport Committee, on the other hand, considers and decides upon only matters in regard to the Municipal Transport. But the financial and operational stakes involved in the matters decided by the Transport Committee have greater importance and urgency than those approved by any other Committee. The capital invested in the Municipal Transport runs into crores of rupees, and is more visible than that invested in other municipal functions. The Municipal Transport plays a vital role in the physical movements of the citizens and their dependants. It provides the cheapest mode of urban and also rurban mechanised transport to the population living in the metropolitan and surrounding rural areas.

A. Operational Matters: Official Items

Guides in Luxury Buses

The P.M.T. operated luxury buses everyday for the city sight-seeing. A letter from the Publicity Department of the State Government placed before a meeting of the Transport Committee by the Transport Manager pointed out that the information on the different places, monuments and other sights provided by the conductors of the P.M.T. was not thorough and, so, satisfying to the passengers, mostly from outside the city. The letter had suggested two alternatives to improve the situation. Either the guides from the State Publicity Department who were more proficient in the skill of giving out information should be placed in the luxury buses of the P.M.T. or the P.M.T. conductors should be got trained by the State Publicity Department. Both the suggestions were not acceptable to the Transport Manager. It seemed that the fact of unsatisfactory information given by the P.M.T. conductors mentioned in the State Publicity Department's letter was not palatable to the Transport Manager. He instead proposed that the members of the Transport Committee be taken (in the luxury bus) to the different places by the State Publicity Department, obviously to demonstrate the better performance by the State Department guide on the job of providing information on the sights in the city. The proposal was approved by the Transport Committee. However, it was found later that the *status quo* continued.

Need of Large Size Buses

Earlier, some 20 buses of a certain description had been ordered by the P.M.T. The Transport Manager later intended to have these 20 buses, but of a larger size, to accommodate more passengers. The item was placed before a meeting of the Transport Committee for approval. A member asked reasons for the intended change. The meeting was informed by the Manager that the larger size of the ordered buses would yield more income to the P.M.T. from the passenger fare and the buses could also be used for traffic to the outlying suburban areas. Further, it would not entail a higher cost per bus ordered. The members satisfied with the Manager's explanation approved of his suggestion.

Child's Death Compensation to His Father

A child had died in an accident with a P.M.T. bus. The father of the deceased child asked the Transport Manager to pay him compensation of Rs. 5,000 for the loss of his child. The item was there at a meeting of the Transport Committee for consideration. The Transport Manager placed two points at the meeting. He informed the Committee that the police authorities had filed a criminal case against the P.M.T. driver of the bus which had met with the accident. He also pointed out that even if a certain sum as a compensation was granted by the P.M.T., the father of the deceased child could take recourse to the law court. He, however, expressed the opinion that the sum of Rs. 5,000 asked for by the deceased child's father be paid. A member assured the Committee that the said father was known to him and if paid the asked for compensation he would not approach the court of law. But the other members prevailed upon the Transport Manager to enter into an agreement with the said father in regard to the payment of compensation of Rs. 5,000 to him and an assurance on his part not to go to the court of law after the payment.

Non-official Items

In operational matters, besides the official items moved by the Transport Manager, members mooted their own proposals. In these items also it was found that out of five types of proposals, in majority of three the opinion of the Transport Manager prevailed and in one the proposal was accepted by the Transport Committee *in toto*, while in another, which was a bunch of separate proposals by different members, the varied opinions of the Transport Manager on them were accepted by the Committee. The financial costs and administrative implications of the proposals were the main considerations that weighed with the Committee in these matters.

Provision of Air-conditioners in Luxury Buses

A proposal moved by a member was regarding the provision of air-conditioners in the luxury buses with the P.M.T. The Transport Manager expressed adverse opinion on the proposal. In the first place, he pointed out, the cost of the new equipment would come to a lakh of rupees. Secondly, the luxury buses would remain idle during the period of execution of repairs. Further, he reasoned, the Poona climate did not call for the air-conditioning of the luxury buses. Only the mover of the proposal favoured it. The Chairman of the Standing Committee, an *ex-officio* member of the Transport Committee, desired that the proposal be put to vote, but the Chairman of the Transport Committee got it postponed to be finally defeated in another succeeding meeting.

Monthly Passes for Industrial Workers

Another proposal of a member which attracted adverse opinion of the Transport Manager was concerning the issue of monthly passes on the P.M.T. buses to the industrial workers. Industries had developed in the suburbs of the Poona City and its environs. Industrial workers plied in the P.M.T. buses between the main city and the suburbs and also between the suburbs. The proposal was reasonable and would have brought in a convenient facility to them. The Transport Manager was opposed to the proposal on more than one ground. It would have increased the work of the P.M.T. administrative staff by way of issue of passes, custody of money collected, etc. The conductors would have been goaded to slackness, was another ground cited by the Transport Manager. Fake passes might come into vogue, was still another ground advanced by him against the proposal. The Committee relied on the views expressed by the Transport Manager and negatived a reasonable proposal of a member that would have meant a convenient facility to the industrial workers of the city and the suburbs.

Exhibition of Family Planning Advertisement at Concessional Rate

Still another proposal of a member negatived by the Transport Committee on account of the Transport Manager's adverse remark related to the exhibition in P.M.T. buses of an advertisement of the Family Planning Association at concessional rate. The Transport Manager's argument dwelt on the infectious nature of the proposal if implemented and the consequent loss of revenue to the P.M.T. This was not correct as very few advertisements appeared in the P.M.T. buses, most of the advertisement space in the buses remaining vacant. And, further, an advertisement relating to family planning would have promoted a national cause and also would have conduced to the interests and welfare of the people, particularly the poor who travelled in the P.M.T. buses.

Free Travel Passes to Disabled Persons

One of the two proposals of members considered favourably by the Transport Manager related to the issue of free travel passes to the disabled persons. Already the blind persons had been given this facility by the P.M.T. A member wanted the Transport Manager to outline a classification of the disabled persons and to opine to the Committee as to which of these classes deserved free travel passes in P.M.T. buses. But the Transport Manager himself expressed a favourble opinion on the proposal. So it was agreed to by the Committee.

The other proposal or rather a bunch of proposals, on some of which the Transport Manager expressed favourably, concerned new bus routes, extension of existing routes and changes in them. The Transport Committee accepted the opinions reported by the Transport

Manager.

Thus, even in most of the matters moved by the members of the Transport Committee, it went by the views of the Transport Manager. This indicated the predominant position of the Transport Manager in the decision-making process of the Transport Committee which stood next to the Standing Committee in the important role it performed in the decisions of the Poona Municipal Corporation.

B. Personnel Matters

The efficiency of the P.M.T. depended as much on the efficiency of its personnel as — nay more than — on the efficiency of the buses and the accessory materials used in its workshop.

The meetings of the Transport Committee were a scene of the display of the assertiveness of the Transport Manager so as to overshadow, or if such attempts failed, to take away the initiative from, or in the last resort to persuade the Transport Committee. This predominant position the Transport Manager strove to wrest from the Transport Committee by dint of his forceful personality as well as on account of the absence of full, nay adequate, knowledge of the P.M.T. operations and management on the part of the members of the Transport Committee. The Transport Manager on occasions did not furnish full information on some items in the agenda of the Committee's meetings. Sometimes members had not read the dockets supplied by the Transport Manager in full with the result that they leaned heavily on him for even the factual information relating to the items to be discussed.

Advertisement Contents for Works Manager's Post

An item in regard to personnel matters discussed by the Transport Committee concerned the contents of an advertisement for the post of Works Manager in the P.M.T. In an earlier advertisement for the post special qualification of degree or diploma in Automobile Engineering was not included. The members belonging to all political parties then realised that to attract persons competent for the job of Works Manager the possession of a degree or diploma in Automobile Engineering had to be inserted as a necessary qualification for the post in the advertisement. The Transport Manager opined in the meeting of the Committee that there was no need to re-advertise the post as in the earlier advertisement mention was made that the applicant possessing degree or diploma in Automobile Engineering would be preferred and the experienced applicant would be granted suitable increments. But the members insisted on the stipulation, in the fresh advertisement, of the qualification of a degree or diploma in Automobile Engineering as well as of experience being rewarded with suitable increments. On this insistence, the Transport Manager relented in his persistent adherence to the contents of the earlier advertisement. He however did not agree to a higher scale on par with that in the Ahmedabad City Bus Transport which had a much large bus fleet. But the Chairman of the Transport Committee was specially cautious pressing for the inclusion, in the Committee's resolution for reference to T.M., of a direction to him not to act on the earlier advertisement.

Appointments to Three Posts

The appointments to the three posts of Default Enquiry Officer, Chief Traffic Inspector and Chief Time-keeper were discussed by the Transport Committee. The Transport Manager had proposed the appointment of three employees in P.M.T. to these three posts. One member opposed the appointment of the employees in P.M.T. to the two posts of Default Enquiry Officer and Chief Time-keeper on the ground that the Transport Manager had not placed the seniority lists relating to the posts before the Committee. The member told the Committee that some other employees had approached him with the grievance that they were by-passed in respect of seniority by the T.M. in his proposals to the Committee. But the T.M. replied that the seniority lists for the posts had been placed by him before the Committee. The other members tried to persuade the dissenting member to keep up the convention of the Transport Committee to adopt the resolutions on appointments with unanimity and to co-operate with the Committee in the same way as they had done during the term of his Chairmanship of the Committee. It was astonishing why the members did not raise the question of the revival of the post of Chief Time-Keeper that was abolished by the former Transport Manager.

Confirmation of Chief Time-Keeper

On the recommendation of the Transport Manager the employee

temporarily appointed as Chief Time-keeper was confirmed by the Transport Committee. The employee was officiating in the post for the last twelve years. A member of the Committee objected to the method of placing cases of incumbents of different posts separately for approval of the Committee. The Transport Manager pointed to the difficulty that the posts could be placed before the Committee for confirmation or substantive appointment only after the schedule of the posts was sanctioned by the General Body of the Municipal Corporation. This item also indicated the dominant position occupied by the Transport Manager in the decision-making process in the P.M.T. in general and in the personnel matters in particular.

Additional Pay to the Asstt. Works Manager Officiating as Works Manager

Another item, however, pointed to the influence of members who had vested interests in certain employees for whom the Transport Manager had a soft corner. The item concerned approval of additional pay to the Assistant Works Manager who was looking after the duties of the Works Manager in addition to his own work. The Transport Committee was agreeable to the grant of 20 per cent special pay on the basis of the salary of the post of Works Manager. A member of the Committee suggested the payment, in addition, of Rs. 50. No objection was raised to this special suggestion of a member by the Chairman or other members. The Transport Manager, therefore, promised to bring before the next meeting of the Committee the proposal for granting two increments to the employee in addition to the special pay.

Court Case Against the Suspended Works Manager

The Works Manager had been suspended on the charge of misappropriation of an electric generator. He served a notice on the P.M.T. through a solicitor in Bombay. The legal department of the Municipal Corporation advised the P.M.T. would lose the case against the suspended Works Manager. The Chairman and some members of the Transport Committee also opined that a compromise be brought about with the Works Manager, the case be withdrawn from the court and pay during suspension period be remitted to him. But another member was frank to tell the Committee that until the court disposed of the case exonerating the Works Manager of the alleged charge, he

to the Congress Party, the Committee approved of the INTUC union demands by a majority of votes. The Chairman of S.S.P. persuasion, however, recorded the lone dissenting vote. Before the voting took place the Chairman rightly asked the Transport Manager to leave the meeting for the time being to enable the representatives of the two trade unions to discuss their demands with the members of the Committee.

Deputation of 11th Batch of Worker Trainees to CBWE Course

An item on which unanimity was evoked between the Transport Committee members and the Transport Manager and among the members related to the deputation of 22 P.M.T. employees to a training course conducted by the Central Board of Workers' Education (CBWE) of the Central Government. This was the 11th batch of trainees deputed by the P.M.T. to such courses. On query by the members, the T.M. informed that the different categories of workers such as the conductors, checkers, drivers, etc., were included in the batch. Caste was no consideration in the selection of the trainees, according to the Transport Manager. The trainees deputed at the last two courses had earned success at the examination held at the termination of the courses. On these elucidations by the T.M., the Committee resolved unanimously to depute the workers in the 11th trainees' batch.

At the instance of a suggestion from a member, the Transport Committee also agreed unanimously to give preference in the employment in the P.M.T. to the freedom-fighters. This was in keeping with the policy followed by the Poona Municipal Corporation in other municipal departments.

C. Purchase, Sale and Contracts

The Transport Committee considered various proposals for the purchase, sale and other contract matters. Except in two matters, in other matters the Committee agreed to the proposals of the Transport Manager. In one matter, a commitment given to a bus-body builder in Bombay by his predecessor during his suspension was decided to be honoured by the Transport Committee though this was opposed by the Transport Manager in office. In another matter, a proposal of two members for bus body building by a particular concern was rejected by the Committee as it would have taken away the concerned authority of the Transport Manager to initiate proposals in this behalf.

Commitment of Predecessor Chairman to Conversion of Buses with more Seats

In an item of an oral agreement to which the Transport Manager in office was not inclined, the previous Chairman of the Transport Committee in the presence of another member of the Committee had committed to the conversion of 28-seated into 37-seated buses by the same company which had built the buses. The standard buses having 28 seats were not found suitable as the complete space for standby passengers was not used by them with the result that an optimum number of passengers were not accommodated resulting in loss of income by the P.M.T. Technically the previous Chairman (T.C.) ought to have got the oral commitment with the bus-body-building company approved of by the Transport Committee. But a member of the Committee, who was an eye-witness to the commitment by the then Chairman to the bus-body-building company proprietor, vouched for the commitment to the members and the Chairman in office. The Transport Manager in office who was reluctant to accept the commitment had to consent to it. Full facts obtained from the previous Chairman with a note by the Transport Manager in office were placed before the Committee at its next meeting. The payment of difference between the cost earlier agreed to and the one demanded later by the bus-body-building company was approved of by the Committee.

Payment of 80 per cent of Cost of Luxury Buses as Advance instead of 50 per cent

The Transport Manager's proposal in another item was accepted by the Transport Committee. The Company manufacturing two luxury buses for the P.M.T. asked for 80 per cent of the cost as advance instead of 50 per cent already paid (the contract had provided for payment of 80 per cent of cost as advance). The T.M. suggested to the Committee that a rebate in the cost of the two luxury buses at the rate of 4 per cent on the advance be asked for from the company, which the Committee accepted.

Proposal for Bus Body-building by a Company without Following Legal Procedure

An unsavoury proposal was brought in by two members of the Transport Committee. The proposal was to get the bus bodies built by a particular company. Another member insisted that the proper method was to consider the tenders invited by the Transport Manager through a proper administrative action. The Committee agreed that such favouritism would raise unnecessary doubts and suspicions in the public. The two members' proposal was, therefore, rejected by the Committee.

Some other Contracts

Proposals by the Transport Manager for contracts for (i) washing the uniforms of drivers, conductors, etc., (ii) remoulding of tyres and (iii) stitching of clothes were agreed to by the Transport Committee. The proposal (i) was recommended by the T.M. in view of satisfactory work by a tenderer though the cost was higher than that quoted by another tenderer. In proposal (ii) the tenderer recommended by T.M. had offered the lowest cost, so there was no question of the T.M. asking for a special consideration, which item (i) involved. Members, however, asked queries about the number of tenders, the quality of the materials to be used and the possibility of their adulteration. In regard to proposal (iii), the T.M. explained that the performance of the recommended tenderer was satisfactory.

Two Suggestions not Accepted

Two suggestions of members, regarding the disposal of non-usable empty barrels to co-operatives and the purchase of an oil purification plant, were not approved of by the Committee. In the first case, the T.M. clarified that preference to the co-operatives in the sale of confiscated goods laid down by the Central Government did not apply to materials to be disposed of. The suggestion to purchase an oil purification plant was broached by a member so that much of the oil that was being wasted would be utilised. The Chairman desired the T.M. to explore the type of plant needed and its availability before any decision was taken. At the next meeting the T.M. gave the advice for not accepting the proposal as it would be costly. The T.M.'s advice was accepted by the Committee.

D. Miscellaneous

The three miscellaneous items discussed by the Transport Committee were concerning the ban on the use of the car at the disposal of the Transport Manager outside the limits of the Municipal Corporation, ban on the practice of the repair of private cars of the Corporators at the P.M.T. Workshop, and the resignation of an S.S.P. member of the Transport Committee due to permission not being given to the State Government to sue the Transport Manager for the sale of machines imported with the permit of the Central Government. The third item directly affected the Transport Manager, but the first two did not.

Financial Provision for Petrol for Chairman's Car during November-March

The car at the disposal of the Transport Manager was often used by the Chairman of the Transport Committee even to visit areas outside the Municipal Corporation limits. Members brought forward a suggestion to place ban on the use of the car at the disposal of the Transport Manager outside the municipal limits. The related matter under discussion and for decision by the Committee was the supplementary budgetary provision up to 31st March during the current financial year for petrol to be used in Chairman's car. The difficulty arose because the previous Chairman's term for one year ended in October during the year, while the financial provision for petrol for the present Chairman's car was up to 31st March of the next calendar year. The outgoing Chairman had exhausted most of the annual budgetary provision for petrol for Chairman's car by the end of his term in October in the middle of the financial year, the result being the next Chairman elected anew finding himself without financial provision for petrol for use in his car from November to March next. Members did not favour the supplementary grant. A suggestion was mooted for a monthly ration of petrol for the Chairman's car. The Chairman explained that he used the sanctioned petrol for official purposes, using petrol for private visits from his own funds. At long last the supplementary budgetary provision was approved of by the Committee out of deference to the Chairman and concern for the dire need of petrol for his official use.

Ban on use of P.M.T. Workshop for Repair of Private Cars of Members

Private cars of the Corporators and the members of the Municipal Committees would be repaired at the P.M.T. Workshop, of course, on payment of the necessary cost. But the use of this public facility for private purposes was resented by some members of the Transport Committee who brought in a letter to stop such use. Only cars of the Transport department of the Municipal Corporation and buses of the Municipal School Board, according to this letter, would be repaired at the P.M.T. Workshop. It was alleged by some other members that the letter was aimed at certain members and Corporators. On being asked, the Transport Manager supplied the Committee information on the number of private cars repaired at the P.M.T. Workshop. It seemed the Transport Committee was divided on the issue, the Chairman of the Standing Committee opposing the use of the P.M.T. Workshop for repairing of private cars. Finally, the letter concerned was agreed to be filed, reflecting the Committee's reluctance to take a decision on an awkward issue embarrassing to the members as it would spoil the inter-personal relationships among them.

S.S.P. Member's Resignation and Chairman not Signing the Minutes

Still another controversial issue was considered and discussed by the Transport Committee. One S.S.P. member of the Committee tendered resignation from the membership of the Committee due to permission not being granted to the State Government to sue the Transport Manager, who was alleged to have been involved in the sale of equipments imported with the permit of the Central Government. The Committee, while accepting the resignation of the S.S.P. Member, disapproved of his remarks in his letter of resignation. But the Chairman declined to approve of the minutes of the preceding meeting in the course of which the S.S.P. member had tendered resignation from the membership of the Committee and the Committee had adopted the resolution resenting the remarks in the S.S.P. member's resignation letter. The fact that was contended by the Chairman and majority of the Committee's members was whether the Chairman had opposed the Committee's resolution. The majority of the Committee's members stuck to the view that the Chairman was present at the meeting when this resolution was passed and that the resolution was in order as it had been moved and seconded by a member each. The

Chairman's signature to the resolution was not required, the majority pointed out. The Assistant Municipal Secretary, who was present when this transpired, also corroborated the above version pressed for acceptance by the majority of members of the Committee. So far the Chairman had withheld his signature on the minutes of the preceding meeting. The Congress members held out a threat that, if the Chairman belonging to the S.S.P. did not sign the minutes of the last meeting of the Committee, this would be treated as a contempt of the whole Committee. Finally, a member moved that the meeting should be dissolved until the Chairman signed the proceedings of the last meeting including the resolution protesting the remark of the S.S.P. member who resigned. At the next meeting of the Committee, the Chairman signed the minutes of the meeting at issue without further hesitation. All this indicated the confidence of the majority of the membership of the Transport Committee enjoyed by the Transport Manager.

E. Factors in Decision-making

The Transport Manager was the most influential factor in the decision-making process in the Transport Committee. In the Standing Committee also, the Municipal Commissioner as the official head of the Municipal administration influenced the decision-making process in the Committee. But two differences were noticed between the role of the Municipal Commissioner and that of the Transport Manager in the decision-making processes in the Standing and the Transport Committees, respectively. The Municipal Commissioner allowed the heads of various administrative departments in the Municipal Corporation to put across and defend the respective official items in the Standing Committee. Sometimes the Municipal Commissioner would take up the side of members when he found the stand of the heads of departments untenable. In the Transport Committee no other official intervened between the Transport Committee and the Transport Manager. This was essentially because the Transport Manager was the source of the unified command in the Poona Municipal (Bus) Transport Undertaking, while in actual practice in the Municipal administration (excluding the bus transport undertaking) power and authority had been delegated to the heads of the various departments from the office of the Municipal Commissioner though in the Municipal Corporations Act the Municipal Commissioner represented the statutory headship of the Municipal administration. In the second place, the Transport Manager would seek to assert his authority as the official head of the Municipal bus undertaking every now and then in regard to each item before the Transport Committee, unlike the Municipal Commissioner whose final authority as head of the whole Municipal administration was implicitly accepted by the members of at Standing Committee and the Commissioner would not show it off on each juncture of the discussion of different items in the Standing Committee.

The Chairman of the Transport Committee supported the aggrieved employees — the suspended and dismissed workers — even though some cases were not justifiable. As he was in a hopeless minority — he with another member formed the two – some S.S.P. group — in the Transport Committee, he did not carry the Committee with him. The Chairman of the Standing Committee, who was an *ex-officio* member of the Transport Committee, did not assert his views except on one or two items. One or two members — these were in a minority — sought to further their vested interests by suggesting the choice of their favourite companies for contract without observing the legal procedure or the promotion/appointment and/or special monetary gain in favour of certain employees. Another member was a stickler of the prescribed procedure in the appointment/promotion of employees to higher posts. The rest of the members did not have fixed views on different items before the Committee, mostly being influenced by the Transport Manager's opinions, on rare occasions siding with other member's views that were different from those of the Transport Manager.

Matters regarding personnel evoked much discussion in the Transport Committee, as in the Standing Committee. But in financial and operational matters most of the members were reticent, mainly because of their lack of knowledge of the facts of the cases. They were not particular even in reading the information supplied in the dockets furnished by the Transport Manager.

THE PUBLIC WORKS COMMITTEE

The Public Works Committee (PWC) was one of the four Special Committees of the Poona Municipal Corporation. The Public Works Committee as a Special Committee was to be consulted on construction works of the Municipal Corporation. It also exercised the power of approval of expenditure proposals up to a certain limit, the next authority exercising such proposals with higher ceiling being the

Standing Committee, and the highest body having the last word in all policy and budget matters, including those executive matters with a large outlay, being the General Body of the Municipal Corporation.

The subjects that came before the Public Works Committee for consultation included the making and repairing of the roads, setting of lights on roads, giving public water connections and accepting the terms of various tenders and administrative budget allocations for individual public works of the Municipal Corporation submitted through the Municipal Commissioner.

During the observation period in 1967, 18 meetings of the Public Works Committee from January to October 1967, were attended by us.

A. Construction and Repair of Roads

A sizeable number of items on the agenda of the meetings of the Public Works Committee related to the construction of new roads or repairs of the existing roads. Most of the times the tendered amounts or firm administrative estimates of the proposed items were approved by the Committee without discussion. On a few items members of the Committee raised queries and asked for the inspection of the sites of the roads. The site inspection was asked when the road was a long or prominent one or it was aligned on a controversial site or there was some difficulty involved, such as the acquisition of a privately owned site. On the budget estimate for making a tar road in a public garden some members questioned the necessity of the proposal as they were afraid the natural sight of a garden would be lost due to the vision of a tar road. The explanation of the City Engineer, that the tar road would help keep both the garden and the road clean and mud would not remain there, persuaded them to agree to the proposal.

Sometimes the members did not care to go in depth into the proposals. This facilitated their adoption. A road proposal showed a small amount of expenditure on it. On a query, an official clarified that the expenditure was for only a *kuccha* road and that later a *pucca* road would be laid out. No member asked as to why the exercise would be repeated, finally resulting in a greater expenditure.

A new road proposal with the firm expenditure of more than Rs. 2.5 lakhs which had been provided for in the budget was unnecessarily stalled in a Committee meeting due to the opposition of a member from that area. A few members indicated their support to the proposal on the grounds that (i) the proposal had been pending for long and (ii) slums might develop on the site if the road did not come about. But the Chairman did not provide guidance to the meeting, though the officials had indicated their keenness about the proposal. Earlier, a small provision of Rs. 18,000 for the purpose had also lapsed. Finally, the consideration of the item was postponed to a meeting of the Committee to be held in November, i.e., the following month. At the next and fifth time of a meeting of the P.W.C. the item was adopted.

The relationship between the Municipal Corporation and a promoter-builder was discussed in the course of the consideration of an item before the Public Works Committee. The Co-ordination Committee of the Poona Municipal Corporation (P.M.C.) had accorded its approval to the Municipal Corporation sharing the cost of the land for the road and the road for the development of a residential area in four survey numbers in a suburb, that was a part of the approved development plan of the city. An administrative proposal for the approval of the P.M.C's share of a little more than Rs. 1 lakh along with an equal amount of expenditure by the applicant promoter-builder was discussed by the P.W. Committee. A 60 feet Municipal road went through the locality. Members of the Committee had inspected the site. The Committee was by and large opposed to the P.M.C. sharing the development expenditure urged by the applicant promoter-builder as it was going to financially benefit him alone. The item was, therefore, postponed 10 to 12 times by the P.W. Committee, though the Municipal Commissioner and the Chairman were in favour of the Co-ordination Committee's resolution for the Corporation and the promoter-builder equally sharing the cost of development. The Committee was in favour of waiting for a few years to let the plots in the whole area develop.

Many a times the proposals for the repair of roads were moved by the members of the Committee belonging to different political parties represented in the Municipal Corporation. An annual plan for the construction and repair of roads should have been outlined and adopted by the P.M.C. But proposals for road construction and repairs were entertained and discussed in the P.W. Committee on an *ad hoc* basis. Administrative exigencies and members' insistence were accommodated within the available budget. In this process, the needs of the newly affiliated suburbs, though urgent, were side-tracked.

The sporadic digging and disfiguring of the roads due to the works of the State Electricity Board, the Central Telephone Department and the water supply and drainage sections of the engineering department of the P.M.C. itself, caused repairs to the same roads in the city on multiple occasions. This also cut into the budget of the P.M.C. The members' insistence on conversion of metalled into tar roads also aggravated the financial difficulties of the P.M.C. on roads account.

B. Mercury Lamps in Place of Shade Lamps

A member had suggested that mercury lamps (tubes) should replace the shade lamps on all the roads and in public squares in the municipal area. The Municipal Commissioner in his note of remark on the proposal had observed that the execution of the proposal would cost Rs. 20 lakhs which was not within the financial competence of the Municipal Corporation. The M.C. in his note had instead suggested that on important roads and in large public squares only the mercury lamps should be installed in place of shade lamps. A member pointed out a technical difficulty that due to the low voltage in Poona there would not be uniform lighting throughout the city despite the setting of mercury lamps and on the other hand it would result in the failure of electricity. The members were keen to have the facility of mercury lamps on important roads and in large public squares instead of not having it at all. So the Committee accepted the Municipal Commissioner's amendment to the mover member's proposal.

C. Water Taps

The proposals by members for setting new public water taps or increasing their number at particular places or increasing the number of outlets to the existing water taps were the most recurring items among the different types of items before the Public Works Committee. The members of the P.W.C. would put up proposals from their own constituency sometimes associating their colleague members with the proposals, reciprocating their friendly gesture by seconding their similar proposals. The officials resisted some of these proposals pleading the reason of the low pressure of water in the city. Members expressed doubts about the veracity of this ground pleaded by the officials for disfavouring most of these proposals. Other members realised the Corporation's difficulty, so they did not mind accepting the official noting on the members' proposals. The water connections to slum localities was a more difficult issue. The Co-ordination Committee had resolved to grant water connections to the slum localities included in the list agreed upon by Co-ordination Committee. Complaints were aired in the Public Works Committee regarding the genuineness of this list of slum localities agreed upon by the Co-ordination Committee. The aspersions were cast on the acceptability of the list of slums agreed upon by the Co-ordination Committee on account of the unrepresentative character of the Co-ordination Committee, different political parties and also Independents elected in the Municipal Corporation not being included in the Co-ordination Committee.

Sometimes unrealistic difficulties were pleaded by the officials in opposition to the members' suggestions for new public water taps. In an instance, the Department had responded unfavourably that earlier eight outlets had already been set in a nearby locality and that the existing water line was not large enough to bear additional supply of water. The Chairman of the Committee did not believe in the official statement. He even hinted that members had to resort to agitation to compel the Department to concede their suggestions. A member asked what would be the Department's response to a similar demand by a private houseowner. The official replied in the affirmative in case a water line was already existing in the locality. The member pressed the official to grant the suggestion for a public water tap being discussed in the Committee on the same analogy. The member's proposal could get through in the Committee.

D. Vested Interests

Behind certain proposals by members their vested interests lurked prominently. The construction of a protection wall behind a *nallah* (foul waste water open drain) adjoining the location of a co-operative housing society was proposed by a member who was a member of the co-operative housing society. The Municipal Commissioner did not agree to the proposal due to its high cost. The member argued that the colony affected by the intruding waste water drain was co-operative and did not belong to private persons. Moreover, he urged for the construction of only a part of the protective wall adjoining the boundary of the housing co-operative location. Another member suggested site inspection. The suggestion was reasonable. But the Chairman sided with the mover member's proposal. The officials responded that instead of a part of the wall the whole wall should be built so as to afford protection to the whole area affected by the *nallah*.

Finally, the department's suggestion prevailed. The Committee agreed to include the proposal in the next year's budget.

E. Irregularities

Sometimes procedures prescribed by the Municipal Corporations Act and the rules were not strictly followed by the Office and the P.W. Committee was not vigilant enough to see through these irregularities and to obviate them. The P.W.C. was authorised to sanction expenditure involving less than Rs. 50,000 on an item, which did not then require the sanction of the Municipal Corporation. Two separate budget estimates amounting to Rs. 50,000 and Rs. 40,000, respectively, were placed before the P.W.C. for the construction of a school compound wall. Some members pointed out as to why for the same work two separate estimates were put up. The officials were frank to admit that it was done to bypass the Corporation. Why the officials were afraid to put across the consolidated proposal of Rs. 90,000 to the Corporation for its sanction was beyond reason. In another instance, the construction of a godown for the stock of cement was almost completed when the item of the tender for it was placed before the P.W.C. in anticipation of its sanction. The official action clearly violated the legal provision. Except a member, the Committee acquiesced in the explanation of the City Engineer regarding the urgency of the work.

F. Expenditures for Works in Charitable Institutions

Generally the Public Works Committee was considerate in granting expenditures for the works required by Charitable institutions, whether social or religious. A Corporator brought forward a proposal for the construction of roads in the premises of a college at its cost. He suggested that this expenditure be donated to the institution. The Municipal Commissioner agreed to this suggestion of the member. So it was adopted unanimously by the P.W.C. Another proposal related to the construction of a temple on an alternative location and the construction of a hall on its premises was mooted by two corporators. The Municipal Commissioner referred to a resolution of the Co-ordination Committee which had agreed to the construction of the temple and of the hall. The budget estimate of Rs. 15,000 was, therefore, provided for from the residuary funds.

G. Novel Suggestions of Corporators not Accepted

In the Public Works Committee, as in other Committees, the Department did not show inclination to accept the novel suggestions of the Committee members. A woman Corporator moved a suggestion to fix a large binocular at a hill frequently visited by people which would afford them a full glimpse of the city. The corporator had proposed the charging of a small fee for the facility. The Department pointed out the difficulty that it would require the attendance of two persons to look after the binocular. The Municipal Commissioner appreciated the Corporator's suggestion, but expressed inability to implement it. He brought to the notice of the Committee that the hill on which the binocular was proposed to be set did not belong to the Municipal Corporation, hence the permission of the trustees who controlled it would be required. A shed would be required to be built over the binocular, which would cost about Rs. 3,000. The cost of maintenance of the facility would be higher than the possible income from it. Further, the foreign tourists had their own binoculars, so they would not need the help of the proposed binocular. The local visitors would initially show enthusiasm to use the binocular for a better sight of the city, but their enthusiasm would later taper off. The difficulties mentioned by the Municipal Commissioner and the officials were not insurmountable. The Municipal bureaucracy's apathy nullified a novel suggestion of a Corporator.

Another novel suggestion of another Corporator was also nipped in the bud by the Municipal bureaucracy. The Corporator had suggested to set water tanks in prominent parts of the city suffering from immediate water supply, so as to assuage fires as and when they occurred. The Municipal Commissioner's observation was negative. He remarked that the suggestion was not practicable. In the first place, the city was fast developing and the locations of water tanks would be required to be shifted to suit the new habitations due to the development of the city. The pumping arrangement would be required to be kept in order. Further, no such facility existed in other cities, including Bombay and Nagpur. In such circumstances the citizens had to bear the botheration. Members of the Committee in general agreed with the Commissioner's remark and did not accept the Corporator's suggestion.

H. School Buildings Plan

The 10-year plan of the construction of buildings for Municipal primary schools in the city, prepared by the Poona Municipal School Board, was considered by the Public Works Committee and referred back with its own suggestions. The P.W.C. also desired the School Board to indicate the priorities in the construction of the primary school buildings taking into account particularly the educational needs of the children of the backward classes and poorer families. The discussion of the item was the only one among the discussions in the Public Works Committee held in the course of its 18 meetings observed by us during January-October 1967, with long-term policy implications. For the proper imparting of instructions in the Municipal schools, as in schools elsewhere or conducted by private managements, their having sheltered accommodation was essential. The Primary Education Act of the Maharashtra Government had devolved the responsibility of universal primary education in Poona city on the Poona Municipal Corporation. Out of 139 Municipal primary schools only five imparted instructions during 11 a.m. to 5 p.m., i.e. full-time, the rest engaged the pupils in two shifts in mornings and afternoons for not more than four hours in each shift. Fifty-one of the Poona Municipal primary school buildings, most of which were located in the rural suburbs, had been hired from private owners. The rent being low the private owners neglected the repairs, white-washing and painting of the school buildings. The Sub-Committee of four members appointed by the P.W.C. to consider the issue in detail, which met nine times, had suggested the take-over of these privately owned school buildings by the Municipal Corporation. The growth of the city had necessitated the increase in the number of Municipal primary schools. The Sub-Committee had recommended their location within the distance of one-half of mile from any of the habitations of the families of the pupils. The spaces reserved for school purposes in the development plan of the city should also be acquired during the next 10 years, was another suggestion of the Sub-Committee. The quantum of the grants-in-aid for primary education received from the State Government according to its Grant-in-Code was inadequate, so the Sub-Committee had urged that the State Government should meet 50 per cent of the expenditure incurred by the Municipal Corporation on the acquisition of lands for schools and the construction of school buildings. The draft 10-year plan outlined by the School Board had not indicated the priorities of the construction of Municipal primary school buildings on the basis of the type of construction and the need for it. The Sub-Committee's suggestions were approved by the P.W.C. and remitted to the School Board for necessary action.

I. The Decision-making Process in the P.W. Committee

The opinions of the officials of the Engineering Department, who were mostly concerned with the items in the agenda of the meetings of the Committee, by and large, influenced most of the decisions regarding members' suggestions for new water taps or increase in the outlets of the existing water taps in public places and also regarding the making or repair of roads. But at times when the members were insistent and marshalled facts impressively, they carried the day over and above the opinions expressed by the officials.[3] The Municipal Commissioner would not remain present at the meetings of the P.W.C. unless certain items called for his presence. In one item, moved by a woman Corporator the Commissioner's negative opinion was accepted by the Committee, but in another item implying the discussion on the relationship of the Corporation with a private promoter-builder his opinion was not accepted by the Committee. The Municipal Commissioner who played a crucial role in the discussions and decisions of the Co-ordination Committee represented its final point of view in the Public Works Committee. But the decisions of the Co-ordination Committee as on the agreed list of slums for water supply and the equal sharing of the cost of the construction of roads in an area proposed to be developed by a promoter-builder, were contested in the P.W.C. and in the latter case rejected by it.

The items of pleas for new or increase in the number of water taps or increase in the number of outlets of the existing water taps in public places, or for the construction of new roads or repairs to the existing roads in bad shape, helped the Corporators to satisfy the demands of the people in their respective constituencies. They might not obtain the satisfaction of most of these demands being realised, via favourable notings by the officials, but on at least a few of these on which the movers of the concerned proposals could muster support of favourably inclined members — even though few in number — they could get their demands fulfilled.

Majority of the Committee members were not found receptive to innovative proposals by their colleague members. They shared with the bureaucracy the inclination to resent innovative proposals, like, the setting up of a large binocular at a prominent hill frequented by visitors, local and from outside, or laying of water tanks in different crowded localities to assuage fires.

The Public Works Committee lacked expertise in engineering. A provision exists in the Municipal Corporations Act for the co-option in the Committees of experts from outside the membership of the Municipal Corporation. But only once, till 1967, was this provision availed of. A few Corporators suggested to us that even in the general body of the Municipal Corporation experts should be co-opted and through it in the Committees of the Corporation.

Members were keen to fix inspections of sites of proposed works being considered by the P.W.C. But some of them did not spare time for these inspections. Most of those who were present at sites' inspections would not put in queries to the officials.

The meetings of the Public Works Committee were held for an hour prior to the meetings of the general body. Even the slim agenda before the meetings was not disposed of. Officials would be late in their presence at the meetings. At one meeting an item regarding an extension to the existing school accommodation in privately owned premises could have been decided more judiciously in favour of extension of the Municipality's own school building in a nearby place if the City Engineer were present a little earlier at the meeting. A meeting of the Committee started 15 minutes later than the appointed time and ended within 10 minutes. In all the agenda of the meeting had six items. The Chairman of the Committee did not attend. No discussion whatsoever was held. The Assistant Municipal Secretary, who attended the meeting on behalf of the Corporation's Secretariat, was himself in a hurry to speed up the proceeding and so eager to finish the business of the meeting as early as possible. The City Engineer and the Assistant City Engineer were absent at the beginning and appeared by the close of the meeting.

It seemed a majority of the decisions on the items on the agenda were taken before hand. Some members would ask the officials to do their own private work in the Corporation office, so these officials would not be attentive to the meeting. Sometimes the official communication regarding the agenda of the meetings of the Committee did not reach even the members, particularly in rural suburbs, a day in advance. At a meeting of the Committee a member got ruffled and rebuked the Secretariat office for not being punctual in this matter in spite of reminders in the past. Then a Secretariat official assured to see that the notice of the agenda of the meetings of the Committee reached the members at least a day in advance.

An allowance to attend the meetings of the general body of the Municipal Corporation was paid to the Corporators, but no such allowance was paid to the members of the various Committees to attend their meetings. If such an allowance was paid, the members would be enthused to attend the meetings of the Committees. The timing of the meetings of the Committees could also be changed to suit the convenience of the members. The total duration of the meetings should be long enough for the members to have meaningful and adequately exhaustive discussions on the items, at least the important ones, on the agenda.

Inherently, most of the items on the agenda of the meetings of the Public Works Committee lacked substance to elicit considerable discussion. Some items with sizeable expenditure were placed directly before the Standing Committee, which had the decisive authority in these matters. Works relating to medicine and public health and city improvements were primarily considered by the respective Committees and, if these involved large expenditures, they were sometimes placed directly before the Standing Committee. The induction in the Public Works Committee of at least one expert in engineering from outside the Municipal Corporation would instil some liveliness in the discussions of the Committee.

THE MEDICAL AND RELIEF AND PUBLIC HEALTH COMMITTEE

The Medical Relief and Public Health (M.R.P.H.) Committee was another Special Committee of the Poona Municipal Corporation. All public health and medical aid and relief matters had to be referred to it for consultation. But in personnel and financial matters the Standing Committee was the sanctioning authority and up to certain limits even in public health and medical matters, though in such matters as certain posts and those involving expenditures above certain ceilings the General Body of the Municipal Corporation possessed the deciding authority. In regard to the public works and purchase of health and medical equipments, appliances and accessories involving expenditures up to a certain ceiling, the M.R.P.H. Committee had the sanctioning authority.

The matters that came before the M.R.P.H. Committee included the setting up and construction or repairs of buildings for Municipal hospitals and dispensaries, purchase of equipments, appliances and accessories for these, creation and upgradation of the posts for these and other functions, like maintenance of sanitation in the city, fees chargeable at Municipal dispensaries and hospitals, construction of public lavatories and sanitary blocks, looking after crematoria and cemeteries, abatement of nuisance to public health and maintenance of public health and sanitation in general. These matters, except the setting up of hospitals, creation and upgradation of posts to man them, were routine, humdrum not requiring much room for discussions in the Committee.

The total number of the meetings of the Medical Relief and Public Health Committee observed by us for research purposes during January-September, 1967 were 12.

A. Official Items

Payment of Non-practising allowance to the M.O.H.

An official proposal of the Municipal Commissioner to provide for the payment of the arrears of the non-practising allowance to the Medical Officer of Health (M.O.H.) as per the State Government's communication, from the unspent balance in the current year's budget, created an unsavoury situation of an insult to the M.O.H. by a member. The M.O.H. rightly pointed out that this was not a new proposal and as such it ought to have been placed directly before the Standing Committee for onward transmission to the General Body of the Corporation. The Municipal Secretary's mistaken action in putting the item before the M.R.P.H. Committee caused an insulting situation for the M.O.H. A member then uttered an uncalled for remark that the payment of non-practising allowance itself was wrong though the item was placed before the wrong committee. The M.O.H. angrily averred that he had not made any comment, right or wrong. The same member questioned the propriety of the M.O.H. to intervene in the middle of the discussion. The M.O.H. replied that he had merely expressed his opinion. The member then flung an insulting remark that the value he attached to the opinion of the M.O.H. was "zero". Another member objected to the member's insulting remark and called upon the Chairman to take its cognisance. The M.O.H. threatened to leave the meeting, but another (lady) member dissuaded him. The Chairman ought to have set right the insulting member, but he kept passive. The matter was left then and there only. The proceedings of this committee as well as of the Standing Committee brought out the uncongenial relationship between some of their members and the Medical Officer of Health.

Increase in Charges for Anaesthesist at Operations at Night

On the other hand, another item was a smooth affair for the M.O.H. to pilot. The item placed by the Municipal Commissioner concerned the increase in the charges for the anaesthesists called to the hospitals and maternity homes to help in the surgical operations. It was proposed to increase the charges from the prevailing rate of Rs. 10 per operation at night to Rs. 25, the charge during day-time remaining the same. According to the M.O.H., the services of only four anaesthesists could be availed of by the Municipal Corporation. A scarcity was felt in regard to the availability of the anaesthesists in the city due to their small number and the pressure of demands from both the private and the public hospitals. An alternative proposal was mooted by some members for the appointment of two full-time anaesthesists, but, again, their availability was the obstacle indicated. A medical member, however, proposed an amendment to the increased rate officially proposed reducing it to Rs. 20 per operation at night. The medico member's amendment was accepted by the Committee. This indicated the weight the medico member's opinion carried on other members in the M.R.P.H. Committee.

Reduction in Fee for Medical Check-up

The members of the M.R.P.H. Committee, it was found, were, in general, disinclined to accept higher fees for medical aid rendered in the Municipal hospitals, dispensaries and maternity homes, but were keen to have lower fees. This proclivity was obviously the outcome of their concern for their poor constituents. The Municipal Corporation had commissioned a few months ago a scheme of complete medical check-up at a reasonable fee of Rs. 40. The response to the scheme was very poor. Hence the official proposal was mooted to reduce the fee to Rs. 25. It might be that due to absence of adequate publicity to the scheme the response to it was poor. No member brought in the point of stepping up the publicity for the scheme. On the other hand, a member suggested the scaling down of the fee for a medical check-up from the officially proposed rate of Rs. 25 to Rs. 20 to reach it to the poorer sections of the population of the city.

On one of the above three items unanimity of opinion essentially prevailed between the officials and the non-officials except that the latter desired still more leniency in the rate charged for medical check-up in a Municipal hospital. On another item members did not want the higher charge to be paid to the anaesthesists for night service, but their scarcity compelled the non-officials to concede the main official plea modified by a little lower charge to the satisfaction of the non-officials.

The third official item was in fact a non-consequential item in that it had emanated from the State Government and should really not have been placed before the M.R.P.H. Committee. But the mistake of the Municipal Secretariat resulted in an unhappy episode of insult to the Medical Officer of Health due to the rough attitude of a member and the inaction of the Chairman.

B. Items originated in Government Communications

Continuation of Family Planning Centres

Two official proposals before the meetings of the M.R.P.H. Committee observed by us resulted from the communications from the State Government. One Government communication had issued notices of termination of the services to its family planning personnel working for the time being under the jurisdiction of the Poona Municipal Corporation but whose salaries were met by the Government through a 100 per cent grant to it. The M.O.H. expressed difficulty about running the family planning centres without a Government grant but shared his view with the Committee members that for the promotion of family planning the Municipal Corporation ought to incur some expenditure on these family planning centres. These centres were to be conducted with government grant up to next February. The members were prepared to foot the bill of salaries of the personnel for one month, i.e. March. The alternative was the 'promoter' scheme suggested by the Government, under which a commission for each case would be paid to the promoters, but the follow-up measures were not assured in the scheme. The family planning centres collected data about those who underwent the family planning operation which helped them in the follow-up measures. The M.O.H. intended to put up a proposal for a budget provision for the continuation of the family planning centres up to the end of the current budget year, which the members promised to support.

Conversion of Refuse into Compost

Another State Government communication asking the local bodies to convert refuse into compost fertiliser instead of burning it resulted in the second official proposal. Compost-fertiliser would fetch an income to the Municipal Corporation saving at the same time the expenditure to be incurred on the purchase of the machinery for burning the refuse. The official proposal before the M.R.P.H. Committee was to request the Standing Committee to abolish the previous resolution approving of the financial provision for the purchase of the refuse burning machinery. The Committee did not evince any inclination to enquire about the quantity of the fertiliser that would be turned out and the financial implications involved in terms of the expenditure and the possible income.

The first official proposal conduced to the promotion of the autonomy of the Municipal Corporation while the second implied the unquestioned acceptance of the substance of the Government communication without examining its exact implications for the Municipal Corporation.

C. Non-Official Proposals

Several proposals were mooted by the members in the M.R.P.H. Committee. These related to setting up of sanitary blocks of public bathrooms, establishment of mobile and cottage hospitals and of children's clinic, institution of vegetable markets and other health, sanitation and medical matters.

Removal of Ashes and Bones from Crematorium

An official item before the Committee was regarding the removal of ashes and bones from a crematorium into the river close to it. The ashes and bones that remained at the burning place after the funeral not only created difficulties for the funerals of the corpses brought later to the crematorium but also led to insanitation. Among the Hindus a practice is followed to collect ashes of the burnt body from the crematorium on different days after the funeral according to the varying customs among different castes and families. The official difficulties were about preserving the ashes for the number of days depending upon the custom referred to above. As the members could not find the solution to a delicate issue affecting the sentiments of the citizens they decided to refer the matter to the Municipal Commissioner for remarks.

Public Urinals and Sanitary Blocks

Proposals for public urinals and sanitary blocks were mooted by the members to meet the needs in the respective localities. Generally, on these matters, the advice recorded by the Municipal Commissioner was accepted by the Committee. His advice in the majority of cases was negative. The major difficulty was that suitable places were not available. Sites indicated by members were owned by private individuals. In a case, on being pressed by members on a certain site owned privately, it was pointed out by the Municipal Commissioner that a Court's injunction against encroachment by the Municipal Corporation would be brought. In cases on which negative opinion was expressed by the Municipal Commissioner, members did not seem to be satisfied with it. Private owners of plots and buildings on these, who did not construct lavatories for the use of the tenants, it was also pointed out, would be too willing to let the Municipal Corporation construct sanitary blocks on their plots so that they would not be required to spend on the construction of sanitary blocks that was their legal responsibility.

Public Baths

A proposal for public baths moved a year ago was still pending with the office without the remark on it being remitted to the Committee. The Medical Officer of Health called upon the member to send in another proposal. Innovative proposals like, public baths tended to be put in cold storage by the officials.

Closing an Open Drainage

In another instance of an open drainage causing nuisance, however, the members pressed the officials to agree to take action. The officials pleaded that the location of the open drainage belonged to the government, on which it was pointed by the non-officials that in a similar case the open drainage was closed by the Municipal Corporation though the place belonged to the government as the former had the requisite legal power.

Entrance Gate to a Municipal School

As in the case of the family planning centres broached in above, in the item of the construction of an entrance gate to a Municipal school to prevent the use of the sanitary blocks inside by outsiders and the consequent insanitation, the spirit of co-operation between the officials and the non-officials was evinced. The official pleading that the school was within the jurisdiction of the Municipal School Board did not cut ice due to the retort by members that the school building and the plot belonged to the Municipal Corporation while the School Board was a mere tenant. It was found that at that juncture it was difficult for the School Board to incur the necessary expenditure, so it was suggested by members that the Health Department would be able to meet it from the unspent balance of its budget for the current year. This was accepted by the Committee unanimously.

Stopping Carrying Night-soil Baskets on Head in a Government Jail

The State Government issued directives to the Municipal Corporation much more frequently than the Municipal Corporation asking the State Government to comply with its rules. The Yerawda Central Jail authorities still allowed the carrying of night-soil baskets on heads. The matter was pointed out to the State Home Minister earlier, but his promise to discontinue the unhealthy and inhuman practice was not kept up. The Medical Officer of Health observed that though the Municipal Corporation had no jurisdiction over the State property of the Yerawda Jail the matter had been drawn to the attention of the State Government. Even then the Chairman suggested the site inspection of the Yerawda Jail which, he said, he was interested in seeing through. The suggestion was carried.

A Mobile Dispensary, a Cottage Hospital and a Children's Clinic

Three cognate proposals for additional medical facilities were considered by the Committee at the instance of some members. The idea of a mobile dispensary was suggested by a member whose constituency lacked the medical facility. According to the M.O.H., the suggestion had earlier been implemented, but the people in the locality where the facility was made available had not responded satisfactorily. The suggestion by some members that the mobile dispensary should be sent twice a week in every locality was also not acceptable to the M.O.H. Neither the original proposal nor the alternative was approved by the Committee. The proposal for a cottage hospital, which had been already accepted by the Committee two years ago, was revived in the Committee. The difficulty in its implementation, mentioned by the M.O.H., was the lack of proper site for the cottage hospital. The proposal was again referred to the Municipal Commissioner for his remark. No one cared to enquire about the budget provision that had been made without deciding the site for the construction, though the construction had already been agreed upon earlier in principle. It was surprising why the Committee had not gone in for site inspection when the site had not yet been finalised. Similarly, in another proposal for a children's clinic and care centre, accepted already, the issue of site fixation should have been clinched by the Committee. Instead, it was transmitted to the Municipal Commissioner for his remark about the suitability of the site of existing Municipal dispensary in the locality suggested by a Corporator living in the same locality and about the financial implications. The Committee did not delve into the issue of the inordinately long delay in the processing of and final decision on these two proposals.

Retaining Earlier Fees for Surgical Operations and Outdoor Patients

It has been stated above that the members of the M.R.P.H. Committee were keen on rendering the medical facilities to the people in the city at lowest possible fees. But, in view of the rising costs of medical equipments and services of medical doctors, the municipal administration was constrained to raise these fees moderately. Even then the raised fees for surgical operations in Municipal hospitals, maternity service in maternity homes and for outdoor patients in hospitals and dispensaries were lower than those prevailing in private clinics, maternity homes and dispensaries. Along with the poor, citizens from higher income groups also availed of the services offered by the Municipal medical units. Members, on the other hand, argued that the medical fees were not a source of revenue to the Municipal Corporation. Though the members were reluctant to increase the medical fees, they were not prepared for the confrontation with the Standing Committee which had recently resolved to increase the medical fees. So the resolution was shelved by the Committee.

Holding Annual Competition among Hotels and Award of Prizes for Standards of Sanitation

The municipal bureaucracy was not prepared to entertain innovative suggestions from the members of the Committee. A suggestion mooted was to hold an annual competition among hotels in maintaining better sanitary conditions and to award prizes to the higher rank-holders. The Municipal Commissioner did not favour the suggestion as the Municipal Corporation had already instituted a system of grading of hotels on the basis of their maintaining high sanitation standards. The fear was expressed that a high standard of sanitation would be maintained by the hotels only on the day of competition. Moreover, in the prevalent scheme of grading of the hotels the gradation of the hotels was changed from year-to-year depending upon the standard of hygiene maintained by the hotels. The hotels were also inspected regularly by the Health department of the Municipal Corporation. The explanation by the mover-members that the mooted suggestion was supplementary to the prevalent scheme of grading of the hotels and not its substitute was not appreciated by the officials, and so the proposal was negatived in the Committee.

Vegetable Markets

Though an agreement existed between the members and the M.O.H. about the desirability of establishing a vegetable market in a new locality that had come up after the 1961 flood, the exact location had not been fixed up. The statement of the M.O.H. that the place had already been fixed for the construction of the market did not carry conviction with the members who resolved that the market be constructed early and referred the matter to the Municipal Commissioner for his remarks about the location of the market and related matters. In the case of the decision already taken to institute a vegetable market on the Poona-Bombay road, however, members could not settle the exact location, whether behind the P.M.T. bus stand or close to the railway line. The officials pointing to the difficulty of the place belonging to the railways did not satisfy the members who suggested the acquisition of the place. So, a second site inspection visit was fixed, as some members had not attended the first inspection.

Visit to Bombay

Members suggestions for visits to other cities to inspect certain novel civic amenities there for emulation here were ever welcome to the Committee. The suggestion to depute a delegation of members to Bombay to inspect various amenities, like the electric funeral machinery and vegetable markets there, was readily converted into a resolution by the Committee. A damper statement by a member that there was nothing novel about these civic amenities in Bombay city to warrant inspection by the members did not reduce their curiosity to visit Bombay. It was interesting to note that the new vegetable market had already been constructed in Poona and so also the electric funeral machine agreed to be purchased, but even then the visit to Bombay to inspect the variants of amenities there was thought rewarding by the Committee members.

Summing-up

The picture of the decisions on the proposals from the members in regard to the influence carried by the members and the officials is varied. Three items of innovative proposals from members were put aside due to the official opposition, while four proposals of members were pressed by members/Chairman and carried by the Committee. In two items, reference was made to the officials for remarks, or their remarks were accepted by the Committee, though not palatable. On one item co-operation between the officials and the non-officials was evinced. Delay occurred in regard to three items: in two at official level and in one at non-official level. In one item, members relented on their resolution as they wanted to avoid confrontation with the Standing Committee.

D. Decision-making Process in the M.R.P.H. Committee

The matters that came up for consideration at the Medical Relief and Public Health Committee, except a few, like proposals for new hospitals, were of a humdrum nature. If even a few members had acquired factual knowledge of the subjects before the Committee the discussions and dialogues with the officials would have been substantial and the balance in them on the side of the officials would have been titled in favour of the non-officials.

Bureaucracy, by its inherent nature and functional status, is conservative and opposed to innovations. Popular representatives, whether in Parliament, Legislative Assembly or a local body, seek to bring a wind of change in the *status quoist* bureaucratic administration, by reflecting in it popular aspirations and wishes in regard to new policies and their translation into fresh or modified administrative measures. In a Municipal Corporation like Poona, new policies are adopted by the general body, i.e. the Corporation, but they can be initiated by a Committee like the Medical Relief and Public Health. A new policy on being adopted by the Corporation is remitted to the Committee for operationalising it into its administrative and financial details. The Municipal bureaucracy in Poona Corporation blocked the adoption of innovative proposals moved by members of the M.R.P.H. Committee, such as in regard to public baths, mobile dispensaries and award of prizes to hotels maintaining sanitary conditions of high order. Such innovative proposals were backed by a minority of members of the Committee and so fell through for want of majority support. It may be that the members derived satisfaction in putting across their individual constituency-oriented suggestions for sanitary blocks and having these remarked on favourably by the officials. Another reason for their failure to press innovative suggestions into acceptance by the Committee was, as observed above, their weak factual knowledge. The hard wall of resistance on the part of the officials could be pierced, if not broken, by the members only through the marshalling of facts and arguing them skilfully. If the members, collectively or individually, had conceived of a systematic plan of the development of health and medical facilities, projects of mobile dispensaries, cottage hospitals, public restaurants with good dishes at a reasonable tariff, these could have been fitted into this plan, argued with the bureaucracy before being put across in the Committee and got it approved.

The members seemed to be carried away by a notion that all types of medical facilities should be afforded by the Municipal Corporation to the citizens and their dependants at an absolutely nil cost. A graduated scale of fees for medical facilities according to the level of income of the householder/earner should have been evolved and put into execution. The poorest deserved to be served with medical facilities at nil cost, but the higher income groups must be asked to pay their own cost. That was the most effective way of improving the standard of medical services in the hospitals, dispensaries and maternity homes of the Municipal Corporation. The Co-ordination Committee had approved a suggestion that if the cost of a drainage line was agreed to be met by a private person/group of persons, the Municipal Corporation would construct it. This mode of delegation of financial burden and responsibility should have been applied to some other works which the citizens/builders/institutions desired to get executed at earliest.

All members of the Committee were not too keen to preserve the Municipal autonomy amidst the pressures of the incoming government directives and circulars. Members were eager to apply the scheme of incentives for family planning framed by the government to the employees of the Poona Municipal Corporation instead of evolving their own scheme. Similarly, the Committee agreed to the communication from the State Government regarding the conversion of refuse into compost without investigating into its economics. In one matter, however, the Committee maintained its autonomy. For one month of March, at least, the Committee was prepared to foot the bill for the family planning centres conducted with the government grant for most part of the financial year.

In terms of the influentials in the decision-making process in the Medical Relief and Public Health Committee, the Health bureaucracy led by the Medical Officer of Health was most effective. This was in spite of the fact that the relations of the M.O.H. with a few of the members of the Committee were not smooth. This was evident from the unhappy episode on the issue of the approval of the non-practising allowance to the M.O.H. sanctioned by the State Government. In the section on the Standing Committee a few incidents of discord between the M.O.H. and certain members of that Committee have been noted. But the M.R.P.H. Committee also witnessed the discussion on a subject which evoked co-operation between the M.O.H. and the Committee. The Municipal Commissioner would be present at the meetings of the M.R.P.H. Committee occasionally. It was implicit that the remarks of the Municipal Commissioner on various items to be considered by the Committee were in fact those formulated by the Medical Officer of Health. Rarely, on an occasion, like, that of the discussion of the subject of award of prizes to hotels maintaining high standards of sanitation, did the Municipal Commissioner intervene, that too on the side of the health bureaucracy.

Among the members of the M.R.P.H. Committee a medico and the Chairman could be mentioned as having influenced the making of final decisions on a handful of subjects. An S.S.P. member had moved two innovative suggestions regarding public baths and award of prizes to hotels showing high performance in sanitation. Cleavages on the basis of affiliations of political parties were not apparent in this Committee as on some subjects discussed by the Transport Committee. A reason might be that the powers of the M.R.P.H. Committee were not as important in financial and personnel matters as those of the Standing Committee or the Transport Committee. On subjects of setting up sanitary units, an implicit understanding prevailed among the members to second and support one another's proposals. Health and medical facilities were in general not a portfolio of subjects that should have incited differences among the members on the basis of their belonging to different political parties.

THE CITY IMPROVEMENT COMMITTEE

Among the four special Committees, the City Improvement (C.I.) Committee was the weakest in two senses. In one sense, the C.I. Committee did not have independent functional jurisdiction in regard to actual works, not overlapping that of the other three Special Committees, viz., the Public Works, the Medical Aid and Relief and the Law, Revenue and General Purposes. In financial and personnel matters, relevant matters from the C.I. Committee had to go to the Standing Committee for sanction or processing before transmission to the General Body for final approval. In the second sense, in regard to the sphere of consultative competence of the C.I. Committee, viz., the Development Plan, the town-planning schemes, reservation of lands, construction of new works like roads, schools, gardens, etc., its members did not possess the requisite knowledge. Members of the C.I. Committee lacked the knowledge of city or urban planning, so they tended to look at the different works and the land reservations from the short-term point of view of advantage to their own constituencies or to the vested interests whose cause they would espouse.

Twenty meetings of the C.I. Committee were observed by us, almost 12 of these could not be held due to lack of quorum. The discussions observed by us were insubstantial due to the members' lack of competence in urban planning.

A. Development Plan

The members of the C.I. Committee were in general critical of the effects of the Development Plan in the encroachment of the land reservations stipulated in the Development Plan on the lands belonging to private individuals, co-operative housing societies, institutions conducting schools, etc. Another consequence of the Development Plan would have been a huge capital expenditure on the part of the Municipal Corporation in acquiring about 1,375 acres of land reserved in the Development Plan for various public purposes. A major flaw in the process of the framing of the Development Plan for Poona City, according to the members of the C.I. Committee, was the absence of participation of the Poona Municipal Corporation in it. This criticism on the part of the Corporators was not justified because the Draft Development Plan for the City had been referred to the Poona Municipal Corporation for its opinion on it and its alternative suggestions on the various aspects of the Development Plan, such as land reservations, major roads, amenities, etc. Adequate time had also been given for the consideration of the Development Plan by the Municipal Corporation. It was the liberal norms for land reservations for public purposes, such as schools, gardens, roads, etc., which had not found favour with the Corporators.

Lands of Co-operative Housing Societies Affected by Development Plan

The lands of several co-operative housing societies were reserved for various public purposes in the Development Plan of the city prepared by the State Government's Town Planning Department and approved by the State Government. All the members of the C.I. Committee felt unanimously that these lands belonging to the co-operative housing societies tied up in reservations in the City Development Plan should be deleted form it altogether. The Municipal Secretary who attended the meeting of the Committee which discussed this suggestion also stressed that justice ought to be done to the co-operative housing societies in this respect. The Chairman of the Committee was not in favour of the total deletion of the reservations of the lands belonging to the co-operative housing societies from the Development Plan. Instead, he suggested the reference of the members' suggestion to the Municipal Commissioner for his remark. The Committee, therefore, postponed the matter till the M.C.'s remark was received. The matter was also to come up at a meeting of the General Body where Corporators would be free to air their views on the matter.

It was surprising how, during the consultation on the Draft Development Plan with the Municipal Corporation, the Corporators did not raise the matter of the harm that would be done to the co-operative housing societies whose lands were to be reserved for public purposes in the Draft Development Plan.

When at another meeting of the C.I. Committee, two female members mooted a similar suggestion, information was asked to be collected by the Corporation Office. On the information being placed before the Committee, the Committee approved of a hint by the Municipal Secretary to postpone the decision on the subject until the Co-ordination Committee discussed and decided on the matter.

Reservation of a Land of an Educational Institution for Primary School

The construction of buildings for primary and secondary schools on a land belonging to an educational institution had been sanctioned by the Municipal Corporation. This land was reserved for a primary school in the Development Plan of the city. The educational society had addressed a communication to the Chairman of the Standing Committee to look into the matter. He pointed out in the meeting of the C.I. Committee that a primary school already existed in the locality even before the current Development Plan was framed. Hence, the educational society pointed out, no need existed to reserve the land for primary school purposes. The society, therefore, pleaded for the cancellation of the reservation of the land belonging to it. An office-bearer of the society had approached the State Minister for Local Self-Government in this behalf. The item was referred to the Municipal Commissioner for his remark. He agreed with the suggestion of the members of the C.I. Committee and promised to get the reservation of the plot for a primary school lifted by the State Government whom he would approach in the case. A mistake in the Development Plan was thus rectified through the C.I. Committee.

Accommodation of Shops of all Intending Timber Merchants in a Timber Market

The shops of 700 timber merchants were to be located in the timber market reserved area away from the place in the thick of the city which had been affected by the fire earlier. A suggestion was mooted by a member of the C.I. Committee to allow 300 out of 700 timber merchants to locate their shops outside the reserved timber market area. Significantly, another member of the Committee belonging to the same political party to which the mover-member was affiliated was opposed to the mooted suggestion on the ground that the original policy of locating the shops of all timber merchants in the reserved timber market area would be deviated from and eventually nullified if an exception was made of 300 timber merchants. A few members asked for the elucidation about the quantity of timber required, the number of traders (and not of licences issued), etc. A member revealed that when new places were allotted to some timber merchants they sold them at higher prices. The Municipal Commissioner wanted the members of the Committee to adhere to the policy already adopted. Curiously, some members asked the Chairman of the Committee to send the subject again for the opinion of the Municipal Commissioner who had already expressed it in favour of the adopted policy and against the mooted suggestion. These members were not willing to displease the Municipal authorities as well as the vested interests. The main ground of the M.C. in sticking to the adopted policy was that fire had broken out earlier in the old timber market area and so the timber market had to be shifted away from the hubbub of the city to save the timber property from devastation. The Chairman of the C.I. Committee exerted the influence of his position against the mooted suggestion; he argued that if a change in the adopted policy was made at that juncture the timber merchants who had shifted their shopping establishments in the new reserved area would object to it. The C.I. Committee, in the end, rejected the mooted suggestion. The discussion on the subject brought out the importance the members of the C.I. Committee attached to the opinion on it of the Municipal Commissioner and the Committee's Chairman.

Cancellation of a resolution of the C.I. Committee to delete reservation of two survey numbers for timber market development in Development Plan

Two survey numbers had been reserved for timber market development in the Development Plan. To suit the convenience of some private individuals, the C.I. Committee had deleted the reservation of these two survey numbers. The Municipal Commissioner found this resolution of the C.I. Committee inconsistent with an earlier resolution of the Standing Committee approving of the land acquisition proceedings for the purpose as well as the limited jurisdiction of the Municipal Corporation in respect of the Development Plan once it had been finalised. Further, the Government had already commenced the land acquisition process and the measurement of the land was then being done. A member proposed a joint meeting of the C.I. Committee and the Standing Committee, but the members did not heed it. Finally, its own earlier resolution deleting the reservation of the two survey members was cancelled by the C.I. Committee.

B. Town Planning Schemes

The members of the C.I. Committee evinced keen interest in advocating the interests of the persons or institutions affected by the town-planning schemes.

Conversion of an Industrial Plot into Agricultural One

A plot of land earlier reserved for industrial user in a town planning scheme was later converted into the one for agricultural user. This would have caused a heavy loss to the individual plot holder. The Chairman of the C.I. Committee pointed out that as the level of the plot was higher than the level of the water to irrigate the land the conversion of the plot for agricultural user would not help the plot owner. The member who moved the suggestion to revert the plot to its original industrial user argued that as the plot was surrounded by roads and the railway track, nuisance would not be caused to other lands in the proximate area by the industrial user of the plot. An inspection of site was suggested by a few members, while reference to the Municipal Commissioner was mooted by another. Earlier, the Chairman shared the latter course of action. But, later, he wanted the proposer-member to see the Municipal Commissioner in his office and convince him about the propriety of his proposal. At long last, the members of the Committee were persuaded to agree to the mover's suggestion. A reasonable plea of a member, though favouring an individual person, set right the wrong done to him.

Plea for Removal of Reservation of a Private Plot for Market

A plea was moved by a member to remove the reservation of a plot of land belonging to a Corporator earlier for a market. The locality in which the plot was located had recently developed and it needed a market. The ground of the plea that the locality did not need a market was countered by another Corporator living in the same area who knew its essential requirements. The Municipal Commissioner opined against the removal of the reservation. The suggested site inspection was carried out after the meeting of the C.I. Committee at which the above discussion was held. At the next meeting of the Committee the advice of the Municipal Commissioner was upheld by the Committee and the reservation of the privately owned plot of land was retained. The Commissioner thus saw through the play of the vested interest in the discussion and gave the correct guidance to the Committee.

Suggestion to Completely give up the Town Planning (T.P.) Scheme

A suggestion by two members of the C.I. Committee that the whole Town Planning Scheme in operation should be cancelled or modified *in toto* betrayed their ignorance about its legal status and the powers of the Municipal Corporation *vis-a-vis* the T.P. Scheme. The Municipal Commissioner ruled the suggestion out of court; he explained that the existing T.P. Scheme had come into operation only a year before and its effects were yet to be seen. He expressed the fear that complications would arise if the suggestion was accepted. Some members of the Committee and the officials present at the meeting of the Committee were aware that the local body could broach constructive suggestions to modify the T.P. Scheme but could not change it completely or reject it outright; the final decision on these suggestions lay with the State Government. A member queried the Chairman of the Committee whether he had received any suggestions for the consideration of the Committee to which he replied in the negative. Almost all the members of the Committee agreed that there was no need for the entire revision of the T.P. Scheme. So there should not have been postponement of the decision on the subject. But the Chairman desired that as the proposers of the suggestion were absent at the meeting, the Committee did not have the opportunity to hear their point of view. Hence he proposed the postponement of the decision on the subject. This pointed to the decisive role of the Chairman of the Committee.

Reversion of Agricultural User of a Plot to the Original Industrial user

An injustice was done to an individual person in the execution of the

Town Planning Scheme in operation. An individual owning a small-scale industry in the city had purchased a land in an area declared as industrial area by the Municipal Corporation under the T.P. Scheme. He had invested about Rs. 40,000 in the purchase of the land. This land was included in the block of lands omitted from the industrial zone as a result of a recommendation of a government-appointed committee. The inclusion of the plot of land of the individual on the agricultural zone would have entailed a loss to him. A member of the C.I. Committee moved a suggestion in the Committee that the land be reverted as an industrial land. The Municipal Commissioner advised against the member's suggestion on the ground that its implementation would place a lone industrial plot between two agricultural zones. But many members of the Committee were not in agreement with the observation of the Municipal Commissioner and decided to inspect the site of the plot. The inspection convinced them of the injustice done to the plot-holder by the conversion of the industrial plot as an agricultural one. The C.I. Committee, therefore, passed a resolution requesting the Government to declare the area at issue as an industrial area. Here the C.I. Committee, being moved by the injustice done to the individual plot-holder, did not go by the observation of the Municipal Commissioner.

In the matters pertaining to the Town Planning Scheme, the interests of the acquaintances were espoused in the C.I. Committee out of the motive of correcting the wrong done or advancing the private gain at the cost of the public good.

C. New Improvement Proposals

Chawls Construction at a Place to be Acquired

A particular place was suggested by a member of the C.I. Committee to be acquired for constructing *chawls* for residential purposes. Another member who was not pulling on well with the mover-member put across an alternative user, viz., a public garden, of the place to be acquired. But, on being pointed out by some of the other members and the officials that nearby there was already a public garden, the alternative suggestion for the use of the place to be acquired could not find support in the Committee. The Municipal Commissioner's support to the mover's suggestion also added its own weight on the side of the mover-member's suggestion.

Plea for Donation of a Land Acquired for Chawls Construction to an Unknown Association

A land had been acquired by the Municipal Corporation at market cost. A member mooted a suggestion that the land be donated to a social service association, *Harijan Seva Mandal*. Members expressed ignorance about the association and its activities. The Municipal Commissioner, on the other hand, gave the opinion that the land should be utilised for constructing accommodation for the Municipal employees as well as those affected by the recent flood in Poona city. The Committee agreed with the Municipal Commissioner's suggestion rejecting the member's for donating it to a social service association whose credentials had not been established.

A Redundant Road to be Deleted

In a locality a new road was to be laid. But there already was a road close-by to the proposed road, which was going to be widened soon. A member moved a plea to drop the laying of the new road. The member asked his colleagues in the Committee to call upon the officials from the Engineering Department to explain the actual position. But the Chairman of the Committee preferred an observation in writing from the Municipal Commissioner. Accordingly, the Committee sent in the matter for the Municipal Commissioner's remark. The M.C. in his remark was inclined to agree with the viewpoint of the members and withdrew the proposal to construct the new road.

In all the above three matters the good sense of the members of the C.I. Committee prevailed over the unreasonable positions of the minority among them or the officials.

D. Factors in Decision-making in the C.I. Committee

The main handicap of the members of the City Improvement Committee in the meaningful and insightful discussion of the Development Plan and the Town Planning Scheme was their lack of knowledge of urban or city planning. By and large, they did not exercise their right to discuss and get modified the Development Plan and the Town Planning Scheme during the stage of the consideration of their drafts. After these were finalised by the State Government and sent over to the Municipal Corporation for execution, did the General Body and the City Improvement Committee awaken to the inconvenience to the institutions and private individuals that would result from the execution of certain of their parts. Then, it was, therefore, possible to secure amendments to them only in cases of gross injustice to institutions or individuals.

Out of 11 items considered by the C.I. Committee, one item concerned a general matter of the deletion of the Town Planning Scheme; and in three items pertaining co-operative housing societies, an educational institution and the deletion of a new road, respectively, harm would have been done to public institutions or private plots in case of retention of the Development Plan in its form finalised by the State Government. Out of the remaining seven items, only in two items the C.I. Committee resolved in favour of private individuals whose interests (in retaining the industrial use of the lands) would have been affected in case the Town Planning Scheme was executed in its finalised structure in favour of agricultural user. In the rest five items, suggestions benefiting private individuals (two items concerning timber merchants unwilling to locate shops in the new timber market and another regarding a plot reserved for a market) or advancing prejudiced positions taken by some members (opposing use of acquired plots for construction of houses) were not accepted by the Committee or decisions were taken subserving the public good. This is a creditable record on the background that the members lacked specialised knowledge of urban planning and some sought to espouse and promote the interests of their acquaintances.

In two instances where wrong was done in the Town Planning Scheme to private individuals, the Municipal Commissioner's opinion (based on the views of the Engineering Department on conversion of industrial user into agriculture) was not followed, which spoke for the independence the members exercised away from the bureaucratic stand. But, in a large number of cases in which the awareness of the public good *vis-a-vis* private interest prevailed, the Municipal Commissioner[4] (mostly guided by the view of the Engineer officials), guided or supported the stand taken by a majority of the members of the C.I. Committee. The Chairman and a few of the members of the Committee had also advocated the cause of the public good in a number of such items. The Municipal Secretary supported the side of public good in few items.

THE LAW, REVENUE AND GENERAL PURPOSES COMMITTEE

The Law, Revenue and General Purposes Committee of the Poona Municipal Corporation was one of its four Special Committees. Its main function was to frame rules and bye-laws and to consider proposals regarding the rates of taxation. During March-October, 1967, 10 Committee meetings were observed by us. The subjects considered by the Committee included new bye-laws, amendments to the existing bye-laws, donations to applicant public institutions in cash or kind, proposals regarding taxation and procedures for taxes collection, and personnel matters relating to tax assessment and collection not falling within the jurisdiction of any other Special Committee. General matters, like election, hawkers' nuisance, etc., also occupied the attention of the Law, Revenue and General Purposes (L.R. & G.P.) Committee.

A. Taxation

Concession in Property Tax to the Flood-affected

An official proposal moved by the Municipal Commissioner concerned the grant of concession in the property tax to the house-owners affected by the Panshet flood during 1961. Members of the Committee were generally in agreement with the Municipal Commissioner's proposal. But some of them raised queries. Information was elicited about the authorisation by the State Government and the rates of concession and the ensuing loss to the Municipal Corporation. A query also pertained to the types of construction that would be covered in the concession. Some members suggested that the concession be extended to the housing co-operatives and the societies which constructed houses on loan. The Municipal Commissioner then expressed the fear that the loss in tax collection might be heavy. Another suggestion came from some members to postpone the consideration of the matter and to transmit it to the Co-ordination Committee in the meanwhile. At that juncture the issue was postponed to the next meeting. At the postponed meeting a discussion was held over the details of the concession. An amendment to the official proposal to grant the same concession to the tenants, in case they paid the tax, was mooted. Another suggestion was aired to grant the concession to the taxpayers in the slum clearance scheme. The Assistant Municipal Commissioner (A.M.C.) who was present at the meeting at that juncture pointed out that the new Municipal Corporations Act was to come into force soon. Actually this difficulty pointed out by the A.M.C. had nothing to do with the official proposal being discussed in the Committee, but no member seemed to be aware of this. The A.M.C. pointed to another difficulty of properly enforcing the concession. This difficulty mentioned by the A.M.C. spurred the members of the Committee to postpone the item indefinitely. It was gathered that the official proposal was carried later in the Committee.

Exemption to Harijan Housing Co-operatives

An official item brought in later by the Municipal Commissioner at a meeting of the L.R. & G.P. Committee proposed the exemption of the Harijan housing co-operatives from the payment of the property tax, by amending Section 129 of the Municipal Corporations Act. A concession in the payment of the property tax had already been given to the flood-affected house-owners and the industrialists on the *chawls* constructed for the industrial workers. The Assistant Municipal Commissioner raised the point he had broached on the item of property tax concession to the flood-affected house-owners analysed above. The point was that soon the amended Municipal Corporations Act was coming into operation. A valid issue was raised by a member. He advised that this exemption should not be granted to the Harijan housing co-operatives irrespective of merit. Some Harijan house-owners in such co-operatives might derive a high income by renting out the houses. He also suggested that if the house-owners in Harijan housing co-operatives would be given complete exemption from the property tax payment, then the flood-affected be also extended the same exemption. Another member cited the difficulty in verifying details, like, whether the house had been rented; if so, the exact rent, etc. The A.M.C. moved a suggestion to refer the Municipal Commissioner's proposal to the State Government. The suggestion was accepted by the Committee.

In both these items, the official proposals, for a generous treatment in regard to the property tax levy in favour of the flood-affected and the Harijan housing co-operative member house-owners, were supported by the members of the Law, Revenue and General Purposes Committee. The members also pleaded for some more concessions in favour of the tenants of the houses in housing co-operatives, the slum-dwellers, etc. A few members, however, were discrete to indicate that the house-owners who really did not afford to pay the house-tax levied by the Municipal Corporation should be granted exemption or concession and that those who earned a sizeable income from the house-rent did not deserve this exemption or concession.

New Procedure in Collection of Tax on Hand-driven Carts

Still another official proposal was related to a new procedure to be adopted in the collection of tax on hand-driven carts. The Municipal administration found it difficult to collect the tax due to the mobility of the hand-driven carts, a very small amount of tax (Rs. two) levied and the poverty of the owners. The Municipal Commissioner had, therefore, suggested that the tax on hand-driven carts would be collected on the road in the manner the cycle tax was collected by impounding hand-driven cart on the road until the tax was paid. The Assistant Municipal Commissioner present at the meeting doubted the legality of the new procedure proposed as it was not mentioned in the Act and/or the Rules under the Act. A member did well to point out that it was uneconomical for the Municipal Corporation to send the notice to the defaulter to collect the tax of two rupees. No member thought of referring the matter for the opinion of the legal adviser of the Municipal Corporation. Despite the airing of the objection about the legality of the proposed procedure for the tax collection the official proposal got through. This showed the weight the official proposal carried with the Committee.

New Rates for Poultry-keeping

Yet another official item concerned new rates for poultry-keeping. The proposal was moved in response to a communication received from the Director of Animal Husbandry of the State Government. A citizen had represented to the President of India regarding the high rates on hen-keeping levied by the Municipal Corporation, which militated against the policy of the government to encourage poultry-keeping. Accordingly, in the new scheme of rates, persons who kept 10 hens were exempted completely and those who kept them solely for household purposes were also exempted. A few members felt that excluding the exempted categories the proposed rates were higher than the existing ones and so against the policy of the government. But some others replied to the objection by asserting that the government rates were not binding on the Municipal Corporation. The rates proposed were mainly to keep hygienic control over poultry-keeping. The proposed rates would not raise the price of eggs, explained an official. Queries were asked on the administrative difficulties involved in the enforcement of the rules for poultry-keeping. For example:

(i) how control was exercised over the hens kept on open space on upper floors;
(ii) whether any rules existed in regard to the selection of sites; and
(iii) how it was ensured that hens belonging to different persons in the same or different households were not put together in the name of single tax-payer.

Replies were provided to the queries by the officials. In regard to (i) above, rules for house construction had made sure that the open space of upper floors was not misused. In regard to (ii), the rule stipulated that the poultry should be kept away from the house at the minimum distance of 10 feet, and (iii) did not occur generally.

Non-official Suggestion to Fix a Higher Rate of Property Tax for Cinema Theatres

Members also moved their own proposals in the Law, Revenue and General Purposes Committee. A member's proposal suggested the fixation of a higher rate of property tax on the cinema theatres on the ground that they earned a high income from popular films and by renting the theatres during spare hours for the dramas. Another member averred that this would require an amendment to the M.C. Act. As the income of the Cinema theatres fluctuated with each picture and for the same picture at different times, no fixed criteria could be applied for the determination of the rateable value of the property, the same member stated. Though the member did not favour the suggestion, the Committee sent it to the Municipal Commissioner for opinion. At the next meeting, however, the proposal was negatived as per the opinion of the Municipal Commissioner. Here the M.C.'s opinion concurred with the opinion of the Committee except the mover. The proposal seemed to be impracticable, hence the agreement between the majority of the members and the Municipal

Commissioner.

All the four official items got through in the L.R. & G.P. Committee. Two of these secured the whole-hearted support of the members of the Committee since they sought to liberalise the incidence of the property tax for the housing co-operatives of the flood-affected and the Harijans. The other two official proposals sought to partially raise the rates of the tax on poultry-keeping and make the procedure for the collection of the tax on hand-driven carts more stringent. The support the members gave to those two official items indicated that they did lend their hand to the official attempts to increase the Municipal income through higher income from Municipal taxes. On the other hand, a non-official item regarding the fixation of a higher rateable value for the cinema theatres did not find support from the majority of the members of the Committee as well as the Municipal Commissioner due to its unfeasibility.

B. Building Bye-laws

Amendments to the existing building by-laws were suggested by members of the Law, Revenue and General Purposes Committee to meet the demands/difficulties of their constituents in their electoral constituencies or in the city as a whole. The bye-laws were adopted by the Municipal Corporation, but they required the approval of the State Government before they were executed. Three categories of modifications to the bye-laws were suggested by members. In one item before the Committee, a suggestion was aired to exclude the area required for building the stair-case from the built-up area. In another item, permission to construct the second floor in a certain locality where it was prohibited was sought to bring about uniformity between different localities. In the third item before the Committee change in the existing regulations for constructions was sought to allow for a larger floor area. The object underlying all the three items was to enable the house-owners to have a larger space as built-up area.

Exclusion of Stair-case from the Built-up Area

The first item did not evoke any discussion except the intervention of the Assistant Municipal Commissioner that the amendment in the bye-law would entail an amendment to the Municipal Corporations Act itself. The proposal was dropped thereafter.

Permission to Construct Second Floor in a Locality

In the discussion on the second item it was pointed out that in the same locality some buildings had two to three floors. The engineering official informed the Committee that in the locality the space built for motor car parking was not included in the floor area prescribed by the Municipal Corporation. A site inspection was held after this discussion. The facts observed in it were, however, not cited in the next meeting. The Municipal Commissioner had given an unfavourable opinion on the suggestion in the item, while the A.M.C. present at the meeting aired a favourable opinion. He mentioned in support of the suggestion that in Bombay city the construction of as many as 30 floors was allowed. He, therefore, pleaded for the adoption of a more liberal policy in this behalf. Members stressed the need for uniformity in the rules of construction. The suggestion was carried in the Committee by a majority. It was noted that the support to the suggestions came forth from the members irrespective of their party affiliations.

Pleading for a Larger Floor Area

A lively discussion evoking participation by all the members of the Committee took place on the third item. The Municipal Commissioner was opposed to the suggestion of allowing a larger floor area for construction than laid down by the Corporation rules as the amendment involved would be against the policy of the government. The Town Planning Act also stipulated that the final decision in the matter rested with the government. The information regarding the rules on the density of population and their correlation with the building rules called in by the mover-member was placed before the next meeting of the Committee. Some members averred that the government's policy concerning density of population was wrong and that it should depend on the area available for construction. A member suggested that information about the rules of construction in different cities should be collected. The absence of consultation with the Municipal body in policy-making in the matter was regretted by the members. The study of the existing population density in the city was to the members also essential before the rules were framed in the matter. Only heavily populated parts of the city were heeded while framing the rules, was another shortcoming in the process of rules-making. Several members thought they should resort to agitation to get the rules amended. A member went to the extent of asserting that many a time imaginary rules were cited during discussions in the meetings of the Committees. A plea by the Assistant Municipal Commissioner to set up a Sub-Committee to study all the directives, the Town Planning Act, the bye-laws and their inter-relationships, was not heeded by the members. A member intervened to say that the Committee had already corrected all the rules. The same member informed the Committee that an extension by 10 feet to the maximum height allowed under the rules was contained in the amended rules, which practically met the contention of the mover's suggestion. This timely information by the member persuaded the Committee to file the proposal.

In another item regarding the amended rules to regulate the private burials of corpses within the Poona Municipal area, as no objections or suggestions were received from the citizens on their publication, they were placed before the Committee for approval. Members asked for factual information on the number of such burials, etc. The item was postponed by the Committee until the information was furnished.

The officials except the Assistant Municipal Commissioner were not in favour of the non-official suggestions to relax the building rules and bye-laws. Among the officials, the A.M.C. had spent the longest career in the Poona Municipality. He had been Municipal Secretary for several years which might explain his favourable orientation to the Corporators. In the one item out of three disposed by the majority vote in favour of the mover-member by the L.R. & G.P. Committee, obvious discrimination against the locality at issue in respect of the construction of the second floor had been committed. In another item another member argued that the mover's point in favour of a larger built-up area had already been met by the allowed extension in the height of a building. In the remaining item, the concession sought by the mover was thought by the Committee to be less preferable than the trouble of approaching the government for the approval of the modified bye-law.

C. Donations to Public Institutions

Only in one out of four items relating to donations to public institutions was the opinion of the Municipal Commissioner turned down because the application of the institution was received later than the last date prescribed for the receipt of applications.

Grant for an Approach Road to a College

A local collage in the city had requested the Municipal Corporation that an approach road to the college should be laid out by the Corporation at the latter's cost at 100 per cent. The Municipal Commissioner had pleaded for a sympathetic attitude to the educational institution. A member, however, pointed out that the road would be useful to the students of the collage only and not to the public at large and that a precedent once laid might be generalised. After the sight inspection the resolution in favour of the grant to the collage at 50 per cent of the cost of the road was carried unanimously by the Committee.

Donations to Two Colleges

Resolutions of grants to two colleges in the city had already been accepted by the Co-ordination Committee, which was generally consulted in the matter of grants (donations) to public institutions. Some members doubted the representative character of the Co-ordination Committee as the Independent members were not represented in the Co-ordination Committee. A member put across an alternative suggestion that the amount of donation be deposited in government securities, the interest from which should be utilised for the education of the needy and deserving students. But he did not press it. So both the resolutions were adopted unanimously by the Committee.

Donation to a Welfare Institution

The Municipal Commissioner had proposed a grant of Rs. 5,000 from the residuary fund by the end of the financial year to a juvenile delinquent welfare institution as its application for donation had been received later than the last date prescribed. The Municipal Commissioner had opined that, besides this grant, a permanent grant be also donated to the institution in view of its standing as a welfare institution. But the members in general did not entertain a favourable opinion about the institution. So they turned down both the suggestions of the Municipal Commissioner to donate a varying amount and a fixed amount by way of a permanent grant.

Donation to an International Friendship Association

The Co-ordination Committee had agreed to a donation to an international friendship society. The proposal was not sympathised with by the Committee members. They thought that if the donation was granted to this association a mushroom number of small associations might ask for the donations from the Municipal Corporation. The resolution of the Co-ordination Committee was also considered to be not binding on the L.R. & G.P. Committee. The matter was referred to the Municipal Commissioner who gave a favourable opinion. The members felt that the M.C. would always keep a favourable wave-length with the Co-ordination Committee. The proposal was, therefore, carried in the L.R. & G.P. Committee.

Excepting in one item, in other items in regard to the donations to public institutions, the opinions of the Municipal Commissioner and the Co-ordination Committee which were identical in these matters were accepted by the Law, Revenue and General Purposes Committee. In the remaining third item the non-observance of a rule prevented the adoption of the resolution for a grant.

D. Personnel

Selection for the Post of Octroi Superintendent

Taxation was within the jurisdiction of the Law, Revenue and General Purposes Committee. So it was up to the Committee to propose a person for the post of Octroi Superintendent who was the Head of the Octroi Branch of the Tax Department. The post was crucial as the octroi provided the highest amount of income among all the taxes levied by the Poona Municipal Corporation. Besides, there was much scope for augmenting the income from the octroi by plugging the loopholes by prevention of corruption and slack administration and adoption of follow-up measures, etc. The person required for the post had to be honest, hard-working and experienced. The post was vacant for a few months. The Municipal Commissioner had proposed the name of the Assistant Assessor and Collector of Taxes. The name was opposed by the members of the Committee. Members cited various reasons: The official proposed by the M.C. had declined the post of the Assistant Octroi Superintendent earlier on health grounds. His conduct towards the staff in the department was not cordial. He had earned an unfavourable remark from the Chief Auditor. He had less than a year of experience as Assistant Tax Assessor and Collector. In his place members unanimously suggested the name of the Assessor and Collector of Taxes who was present at the meeting. Members thought that he would not only manage the Octroi branch well, but that he would augment the income from the octroi. The members were about to pass the resolution of his selection as Octroi Superintendent. But the official declined the offer due to advanced age. The name of the Municipal Secretary was also suggested by some members but he also declined the offer as the post offered was lower than his own post. The members desired to have detailed information regarding the career record of the Assistant Tax Assessor and Collector whose name had been proposed by the Municipal Commissioner. At the next meeting the A.M.C. could not furnish much information on the service record of the official proposed by the M.C. A member wanted an experienced official for the post. But members were reluctant to wait for an outside person being suggested. Then the name of the Assistant Octroi Superintendent was suggested by some members, which was approved unanimously by the Committee.

The discussions on the item brought out that the members of the Law, Revenue and General Purposes Committee would not falter to reject the choice by the Municipal Commissioner for a key-post like the Octroi Superintendent. They had their own impressions of the Municipal Officers in the course of their own contacts with the Municipal administration and particular departments and branches. They could size up the capacities and the demeanour of different officials. They would make up their own mind at crucial junctures and suggest the name of own nominee for the crucial post of Octroi Superintendent.

E. Miscellaneous

Regulation of Mangal Karyalayas

A lady member had proposed the regulation of *Mangal Karyalayas* (Community Halls for holding auspicious functions like marriages). The practice of converting old large houses or plots into *Mangal Karyalayas* was spreading due to the lucrative income yielded by these. But the tenants in the buildings and the residents in the neighbourhood had to suffer considerable disturbance due to the proximity of the *Mangal Karyalayas* which indulged in immense noise pollution. The non-official resolution sought to completely ban the business in the thick of the city. A member, however, reminded the Committee that granting of the licence of *Mangal Karyalayas* had been accepted earlier by the Committee, so he suggested that detailed regulations for checking the nuisance could be considered later by the Committee. The member's suggestion was approved by the Committee.

Extension of the Prevention of Beggars Act for a Year

At the instance of the government, the Municipal Commissioner had moved a proposal to extend the execution of the State Act for the Prevention of Beggars in the Municipal Corporation area by another year. The Municipal Corporation had to bear an expenditure of a lakh of rupees for the purpose. Many a member pointed out that despite the Act the number of beggars on the streets in the city was considerable. It was explained by the Assistant Municipal Commissioner that the police caught the beggars only when they found them begging and then kept them in beggars homes. The Committee adopted the proposal adding that a more rigorous enforcement of the Act was desirable.

Two other resolutions, one regarding the hawkers and the other to grant concessions to candidates at the Municipal elections in respect of deposit and fee for sky signs, were also adopted by the Committee. The M.C. was requested in the first resolution to stay the actions taken by the Municipal enforcement officials against the hawkers whose carriages were found encroaching on public roads. Both the resolutions were joint exercises by members belonging to different political parties to put across demands of the constituents from among petty hawkers and their own political profession.

Among the miscellaneous items, two were constituency-favouring, one official emanating from a government communication and one regulatory coming from a member.

F. Factors in Decision-making in the L.R. & G.P. Committee

Out of 18 items discussed, 11 were official, including one that came in from the State Government, and seven non-official proposed by the members of the Law, Revenue and General Purposes Committee. Out of the seven non-official items, three pertained to bye-laws, one to taxation and three to miscellaneous matters. The non-official proposals were thus not inconsiderable. The participation of the members in the discussions was substantial. In one item, the members turned down the proposal of the Municipal Commissioner concerning the appointment of the head of the most important tax branch.

The analysis of the items on the basis of their nature would bring out that the constituency-oriented items were seven, regulatory three, welfare seven, income-raising three and administrative related to establishment one. Three items were overlapping, two sharing the nature of constituency-orientation and welfare-orientation and one regulatory and income-raising. The preponderance of constituency-oriented and welfare-oriented items was understandable in view of the elective composition of the Committee and the Municipal Corporation and the tendency of the elected Corporators to seek the relaxation of building restrictions to cater to the demands of the constituents and the inclination of the officials to liberalise taxation to help the calamity-affected and the weaker sections.

In nine items, the officials initiated and carried the decisions, or had the last word where the members had proposed suggestions. In six items the non-officials, i.e. members, dominated. In two items in regard to the relaxation of the property tax both the officials and the non-officials concurred. One item had been sponsored by the government.

The matters that came up for consideration in the meetings of the L.R. & G.P. Committee observed by us were those in which the members were interested and so evoked discussion and their participation.

SUB-COMMITTEES

Statutory Provision

The Municipal Corporations Act, 1949 has provided for the constitution of Sub-Committees by the Standing Committee (Section 24) and the Transport Committee (Section 29), but in the case of the Special and Ad-hoc Committees no such explicit provision exists. Such Sub-Committees for inquiry and report to the parent Committee were appointed by the Standing and the Transport Committees from time to time; however, no delegation of own functions to any of these Sub-Committees or any other Sub-Committee had been done. Some of the Special sub-Committees had also constituted few Sub-Committees, but these were not as effective as some of those appointed by the Standing and the Transport Committees. Ad-hoc Committees had not resorted to this device during the period of our study.

References to a few of the Sub-Committees appointed during the period of our study have been made above in this chapter; here, the Sub-Committees appointed in the years 1962-63, 1963-64 and 1964-65 have been reviewed so that definitive conclusions about their working could be drawn.

I. Standing Committee

Three Annual Sub-Committees

It was the practice of the Standing Committee to appoint three Sub-Committees every year. One Sub-Committee dealt with the suggestions to be remitted to the Municipal Commissioner in regard to the annual report of the working of the Municipal Corporation. The second Sub-Committee concerned the audited accounts of the various departments of the Corporation. The third Sub-Committee went into the disciplinary actions on employees taken by the Corporation.

Eleven Other Sub-Committees Appointed

The Standing Committee appointed eleven other Sub-Committees on various matters during the three years, i.e. 1962-63, 1963-64 and 1964-65. Except in the case of two Sub-Committees, the suggestions of the other Sub-Committees were agreed to by the Standing Committee in entirety. In the case of the Sub-Committee on water rates, a part of its suggestions was accepted by the the Standing Committee. In case of another Sub-Committee on the Municipal Commissioner's recommendation to construct a shade and to accept a tender for the work, the original recommendation of the Sub-Committee suggesting various alternatives for the work was agreed to by the Standing Committee and one of these was accepted by the Public Works Committee.

Varied Subjects

The subjects referred to the Sub-Committees by the Standing

Committee were various: legal in the case of three Sub-Committees, personnel matters in respect of three; financial of two; tenders in respect of two; and one on a miscellaneous subject.

(a) *Legal*: The legal subjects examined by the three sub-Committees were:

(i) a draft of the Standing Orders in respect of the Octroi Department of the Corporation;
(ii) the terms of contract between the Municipal Corporation and the Poona Electric Supply Company for the supply of electricity to the Hadapsar industrial area; and
(iii) the terms of agreement in regard to the Employees State Insurance Scheme and suggestion as to the municipal dispensary for locating the scheme.

In regard to (i) the draft proposed by the Municipal Commissioner was approved by the Sub-Committee and its approval was agreed to by the Standing Committee. In regard to (ii), some clauses of the contract conflicted with the Municipal Corporations Act, hence the Sub-Committee had suggested the revision of the contract. The Standing Committee accepted the suggestion of the Sub-Committee and decided that instead of entering into the proposed contract the format of the earlier contract concluded with the Company would be adhered to. In (iii), the Sub-Committee approved of the conditions of contract for the ESI Scheme and suggested a Municipal dispensary for its location. The proposals of the Sub-Committee were agreed to by the Standing Committee.

(b) *Personnel*: The personnel matters referred to by the Standing Committee to the Sub-Committees were:

(i) To report on the salary-scales and allowances of the Municipal employees embodied in the agreement concluded between the employees and the arbitration panel;
(ii) Advancing the date of the application of the pension-*cum*-gratuity scheme for the Municipal employees from January 1960 (by two years) to January, 1958; and
(iii) To advice regarding the amount of the non-practising allowance to be paid to the allopathic and ayurvedic medical graduate

employees.

In regard to (i), certain changes in the provisions of the agreement were proposed by the Sub-Committee which were agreed to by the Standing Committee. The date of the application of the pension-*cum*-gratuity scheme in (ii) was proposed to be advanced by two years by the Sub-Committee; the proposal was accepted by the Standing Committee. The Sub-Committee for (iii) suggested dual amounts of non-practising allowance for the allopathic and ayurvedic medical graduate employees; the suggestion was cleared by the Standing Committee.

(c) *Financial:* The two Sub-Committees appointed by the Standing Committee to consider and report on financial matters went into (i) the fixation of the water rate as per the size of the water pipeline and also for a temporary pipeline; and (ii) the price of the two road-rollers to be purchased by the Municipal Corporation.

In (i), the suggestion to fix a water rate as per the size of the pipeline was agreed to by the Standing Committee but the exact rate was not; so also its suggestion regarding a temporary pipeline. In regard to (ii), instead of the scrutiny of the price of the two road-rollers, the Sub-Committee inquired about the working condition of the same type of road-rollers purchased by some other clients. The Sub-Committee proposed changes in some conditions of the contract, which were accepted by the Standing Committee.

(d) *Tenders:* Two other Sub-Committees were set up by the Standing Committee to scrutinise tenders for a construction work and for purchase of medical appliances for the Municipal dispensaries and hospitals, respectively. The Municipal Commissioner's recommendation for the construction of a shade was not accepted by the first Sub-Committee, instead it proposed movable iron girders. This suggestion of the Sub-Committee was accepted by the Standing Committee. The Standing Committee had also accepted the different alternatives for the work, which were transmitted to the Public Works Committee. The P.W.C. worked out these. The Second Sub-Committee recommended the Municipal Commissioner's proposal for acceptance of a tender for the purchase of medical appliances to equip the Municipal dispensaries and hospitals and the grant of exemption from the payment of Octroi for these. The Standing Committee cleared the suggestions of the two Sub-Committees.

(e) *Miscellaneous:* A book on Municipal accounts and audit written by a retired Chief Auditor of the Municipal Corporation was recommended for use by the Municipal officials by another Sub-Committee. The recommendation was approved by the Standing Committee.

The Sub-Committees constituted by the Standing Committee were thus helpful in the process of the decision-making in the Standing Committee and the Corporation.

II. Transport Committee

It was the practice of the Transport Committee, as with the Standing Committee, to set up annually three sub-Committees. These were:

(i) To air suggestions on the Draft Annual Report on the Working of the P.M.T. prepared by the Transport Manager;
(ii) to scrutinise the disciplinary actions taken on the P.M.T. employees and their appeals thereon; and
(iii) to examine the bi-monthly reports on the servicing conditions including the break-downs of the transport vehicles. The third annual Sub-Committee was a substitute for the Sub-Committee on Audited Accounts appointed annually by the Standing Committee. As these were the usual Sub-Committees their review has not been taken here. In this chapter, references have already been made to these annual Sub-Committees of both the Standing and the Transport Committees.

One Ad-hoc Sub-Committee was appointed in 1962 by the Transport Committee to advise regarding the ways to appreciate and encourage the good performance of the P.M.T. employees through gifts, prizes, etc. The Transport Manager was opposed to the constitution of the Sub-Committee, but it was set up. However, the Sub-Committee did not submit the report. The Transport Committee, therefore, agreed to the proposal of the Transport Manager to examine which the Sub-Committee had been appointed.

III. Special Committees

The device of Sub-Committees was used sparingly by the Special Committees. Some of the few Sub-Committees constituted by them also did not care to prepare and furnish the reports.

Public Works Committee

One Sub-Committee appointed by the Public Works Committee was on an important subject of delays in the issue of building permissions by the concerned section and the consequent corruption, nepotism and other evils in the administration. On knowing that an Ad-hoc Committee on the same subject had already been set up by the General Body of the Corporation, the Sub-Committee was dissolved by the P.W.C.

Medical Committee

The Medical Relief and Public Health Committee constituted a Sub-Committee to advise on the proposal of the Municipal Commissioner to appoint a trained maternity nurse in the rural area recently incorporated in the Municipal Corporation. The Sub-Committee opined that the appointment should be made on experimental basis and confined to a locality. Among other things, the Sub-Committee gave suggestions on the salary and other payments for the post, the basic medical equipment to be supplied to her and her duties, including furnishing of up-to-date vital statistics. The suggestions of the Sub-Committee were accepted by the M.R. & P.H.

Another Sub-Committee set up since 1965 to check the classification of hotels into grades allotted by the inspectors of the Health Department, however, failed to submit its reports successively for three years.

No Sub-Committee set up by the City Improvement Committee

The City Improvement Committee did not set up any Sub-Committee during the selected period of our study.

Law Committee

Three Sub-Committees were constituted by the Law, Revenue and General Purposes Committee during the three years of our study for this purpose. Out of these, only one Sub-Committee submitted the report, while two failed to do so. The Sub-Committees which did not deliver the goods had been asked to report on the feasibility of the recommendations of the All-India Mayors' Council and to advise on the ways and means to increase the income from the proceeds of the Octroi, an elusive tax in the hands of the tax-collecting officials. The only Sub-Committee which complied was appointed to report on the draft regulations for the post of Transport Manager. The Sub-Committee gave its report within the stipulated fortnight's time limit, which was approved by the Law Committee.

Summing-up

Of all the Committees, the Standing Committee alone utilised the device of Sub-Committees to facilitate the process of decision-making, to some effect. The device was used sparingly by the Transport Committee and the Special Committees. The domination of the Transport Manager *vis-a-vis* the Transport Committee did not generate a proper atmosphere in the Committee for the deliberation in its Sub-Committees, which delayed the approval of the proposals or suggestions of the Transport Manager. The Special Committees themselves were meant to render advice to the Corporation and the Standing and the Transport Committees. On complex subjects, the Special Committees were, in their own right, entitled to constitute Sub-Committees to render advice. But most of the Sub-Committees appointed by them did not discharge their work.

CONCLUSION

In the decision-making process in the different Committees in the Poona Municipal Corporation, the Standing and the Transport Committees engaged the prime attention of the Corporators. The Corporators affiliated to the political parties and the Independent members of the Municipal Corporation in the Poona Municipal Corporation attached greater importance in terms of their status and prestige to their membership of the Standing Committee and Transport Committee than that of the Special Committees. The leaders of the political parties represented in the Municipal Corporation were *ex-officio* members of the Co-ordination Committee. The representation in the Ad-hoc Committees was ad-hoc depending upon the Corporators' interest in the themes of the Ad-hoc Committees and other factors such as the importance attached to these themes by the political parties and the Independent Corporators.

It was not that the best experts or experienced Corporators

belonging to the political parties and the Independents were assigned to the Standing Committee or the Transport Committee. The rule of rotation for the representation in the various Committees was applied by the different political parties and the Independents represented in the Municipal Corporation. So the most proficient Corporators were not concentrated in these two executive Committees with the result that these two powerful Committees had their share of the most competent and non-proficient Corporators. The Special Committees stood to gain in their composition on account of the operation of this rule of rotation among the members of the different political parties and the Independents.

Among the different categories of matters that came up before the Committees for consideration those concerning personnel and those which had constituency orientation and welfare content were discussed most by the members of the Committees. In financial (including budgetary), urban planning, engineering and medical and public health matters, in general, the members, barring a few exceptions, lacked proficiency. This resulted in the members accepting the opinions expressed in the official dockets. In some items, it was found that members had not equipped themselves with the knowledge of the factual data put out in the officials dockets. The appointment, suspension, disciplinary actions and conditions of service relating to the Municipal personnel attracted the attention and forensic skill of the members of the Committees. Contracts and tenders for the purchase and sale of goods and equipments with large amounts of outlay were also occasionally discussed by the members. Proposals for sanitary units, water taps and new outlets to existing water taps in public places, laying of new roads and repairs to existing ones, changes in the Development Plan and the Town-Planning Schemes to undo the harm to the private or institutional plots, changes in the users, were favourite themes broached by the members in the concerned Committees. But, by and large, as the members did not possess expert knowledge of financial, engineering, medical and public health and urban planning, the discussions lacked substantive depth or comprehensiveness. On matters affecting popular or individual interests members came out enthusiastically during the course of the proceedings of the different Committees.

In regard to the official items, the Municipal officials had an upper hand during discussions and in decisions. In the Standing Committee the Municipal Commissioner's opinions on the various official matters were agreed to, in some members put in queries and sometimes own doubts and standpoints. In a few matters, decisions were postponed or members prevailed in the end in taking decisions not in line with the views expressed by the Municipal Commissioner. In few matters, the Municipal Commissioner gave out his dissent from the views of the heads of the departments. He also brought into the focus of discussions of the Standing and other Committees the decisions of the Co-ordination Committee and persuaded these Committees to fall in line. In the Transport Committee, on the other hand, the Transport Manager desired to appear dominant, and he was so. Despite members' views to the contrary, he sought to foist his own views on the Committee, in which except in a handful of matters he was successful. In two matters, suspension of the Works Manager and suggestion of a plaint on the Transport Manager by the State Government, the Transport Manager came to loggerheads with the Committee members, in the latter matter he prevailed while in the former he had to submit to the Committee's decision.

The proposals moved by the members were defended and argued out by them in the meetings of the Committees. But, by and large, in regard to new water taps, sanitary units, etc., unless the proposer members marshalled facts and canvassed support, the officials' remarks were accepted by the Committees. Members took keen interested in pleading for the constituency-oriented and welfare proposals. Matters favouring private individuals, such as withdrawing reservations in the Development Plan and the Town-Planning Schemes or changing the user, were argued by members enthusiastically; in some, they could prevail; in others, they could not.

In subjects that emanated from the State Government, members of the Committees followed the official line except in one matter (provision of Municipal funds for family planning centres for one month) where they acted on their own. Such subjects were, however, very infrequent.

The Chairmen of the two Committees, the Standing and the Transport, which were armed with executive powers to an extent, were vested with a responsible role to play. While the Chairman of the Standing Committee filled the bill to an extent, the Chairman of the Transport Committee could not rise upto it. The Chairman of the Standing Committee stalled the influence of the extraneous vested interests on its decisions in land acquisition and purchase matters. But his insistence on the operation of the rule of consensus in the adoption of resolutions on issues on which opinions of the members were sharply divided thwarted free expression of their views and conclusion of decisions, if needed by voting. The Chairman of the Transport Committee supported the side of aggrieved employees meted out disciplinary actions like suspension, dismissal, etc., but he received scant backing. He did not possess proficiency in transport in general and engineering and financial matters in particular, with the result that he could not provide leadership in the course of the deliberations of the Committee. In each of the six Committees, observed by us, two to three members did participate effectively in their proceedings.

The overall impression was of the leverage exercised by the officials in the decision-making process in the Committees. The position of the Municipal Commissioner was unique in that he did not appear to be dominating over the deliberations of the Standing Committee, though he exercised a balancing role in case of divided voices. In the Special Committees he presented himself on few occasions, leaving the heads of the departments to take the lead in advising and intervening in the deliberations of the Committees. The Transport Manager asserted in the proceedings of the Transport Committee every now and then, both because he had no official of comparable status and capacity below him and because of his disposition.

By and large, the Municipal bureaucracy (except the Municipal Commissioner in one matter of the development of infrastructure in new areas) did not initiate innovative proposals or support innovative policies or measures mooted by the members of the Committees — whether the issue was of public baths, mobile dispensaries or awarding prizes to restaurants for maintaining high standards of cleanliness or setting a binocular at the Parvati hill or laying water tanks in different localities to put out fires quickly. The Municipal Commissioner did take a lead in constructing new facilities, like a sports stadium, a theatre for plays, as per plans blue-printed by the first Municipal Commissioner of the city. But he did not countenance lending support to innovative measures suggested by select members of the Committees. Nor did the majority of the Committees' members extend support to these innovative suggestions mooted by their colleagues.

The Committees of the Poona Municipal Corporation helped raise a popular sanction to the administrative policies, decisions and actions mostly initiated by the officials and in minority of matters by the non-officials. A few among the lawyer, engineer, medico, trader and businessman and political worker members in the Committees did display participative skills during the proceedings of the Committees. Some among them rose to the elective positions of Deputy Mayor and Mayor of the Municipal Corporation and still later to play the elective role of legislators and/or ministers at the State and Central levels.

The Committees of the Poona Municipal Corporation were democratic without being populist, performing their role as delegates-*cum*-representatives with caution and circumspection, at the same not being able to rise to the peak of excellence or even heights of very meritorious performance.

Considerable scope existed for the improvement of the performance of the Committees. By co-opting experts in their composition, the quality of discussions of subjects in engineering, medicine and public health, urban planning, finance, etc., could be improved. Inspections of sites could be made more effective by looking more attentively into the formulation of their reports and soliciting the responses of each one of the participant members. An allowance may be paid to the members for attending the meetings of the Committees separately to enthuse them to be regular and to evoke greater participation on their part. Days and timings of the Committees' meetings may also be fixed to facilitate the members' attendance.

A better term for the Corporators-in-Committees-and-Corporation would be 'Repre-legate' combining the roles of the 'Representative' and the 'Delegate', representing in one's own vision his functions on behalf of the constituents and acting as if constituents themselves are acting. The above improvements would strengthen their capacities as 'Repre-legates'.

NOTES

1. The particulars of the meetings of the Committees such as frequency, membership, attendance, etc., are cited in Appendix II (Part A) and those pertaining to the topics of the items before the meetings in Part B.
2. Two resolutions passed by the Standing Committee, one during 1964-65 and another during 1966-67, also indicated the influence of the Municipal Commissioner on the thinking of a majority among its members. In an item (1964-65) a resolution of the Municipal Commissioner for a compulsory departmental examination before confirmation of a Municipal employee was adopted by the Standing Committee by a majority of 6-2. In another item (1966-67), the purchase of a new car for the Mayor was not approved by majority (3-2) as a sequel to the official noting, despite insistence in favour by the

Chairman. In a third item during 1965-66 also, the Municipal Commissioner's influence was seen. A member had moved a resolution to transfer a land given to the Corporation by the State Government to a charitable institution for a medical dispensary. The Commissioner pointed out that it would be improper to approach the Government in the matter, the matter was therefore filed.

3. During 1962-63 despite official opposition, a resolution was carried by majority (6-2) to increase the budget estimate by Rs. 46,000 for additional works in a vegetable market.
4. During 1963-64, the Municipal Commissioner supported the majority in the Committee (6-2), who expressed themselves against the resolution of a member for the reservation of a land for children's park and playground as it was not necessary. In another item, during the same year the Commissioner had cited a legal point on the side of a member's resolution for the lifting of the reservation of a land earmarked for housing. A person had owned the land earlier and obtained the sanction of its layout also from the Corporation. The resolution was carried by a majority of 7-1 due to the Commissioner's legal plea.

7

COMMITTEES *VIS-A-VIS* THE CORPORATION

THE COMMITTEES, the Municipal Administration and the Corporation (the General Body) formed a triangle of the decision-making mechanism in the Poona Municipal Corporation. The Committees — the Standing, the Transport and the functional (special) — were the primary consultative side of this triangle. The Standing and the Transport Committees, — and to a little extent the functional Committees — within specific limits, decided matters without the need to refer to the General Body for final decision-making. However, beyond these specific limits, the General Body was the decision-making authority. The Municipal Administration headed by the Municipal Commissioner in Municipal matters and the Transport Manager in respect of the Municipal bus transport, formed another side of the triangle, possessing authority to initiate items for decision and, more importantly, to express views on various items proposed by the Corporators in the Committees or the Corporation.

While dealing with the decision-making process in the Committees, we have reviewed the role of the Municipal Administration in it. During the discussions on the recommendations emanating from the Committees, the Commissioner was consulted, but because he had already committed his views in writing while opining on the items in the Committees his interventions were rare except on financial matters, including the budget. On the resolutions initiated by members in the General Body, the Commissioner expressed his views before or after the respective Committees proceeded with them.

During 1966-67, for instance, out of 127 Corporation meetings called, as many as 107 were adjourned. The total number of resolutions passed by it were 566.

In this chapter, unless mentioned specifically or otherwise, it should be taken that the resolutions/recommendations/proposals had emanated from the respective Committee dealt with in the section concerned.

For purposes of the study of the relationship between the decision-making in the Committees and that in the Corporation, select items from the Corporation proceedings during 1961-67 were followed.

STANDING COMMITTEE[1]

A. Financial Matters

In the decision-making in the Committees the financial matters figured prominently. But the matters within the stipulated financial limits were decided by the Standing Committee within its own jurisdiction, these were not required to be placed before the Corporation, that is the General Body. Among these decisions of the Standing Committee which, under the Act and the Rules, were required to be placed before the Corporation, next to the matters related to the personnel, the financial matters figured prominently.

In general, it could be stated that even in those decisions on financial matters of the Standing Committee referred to the Corporation, the Corporation resolved in conformity with the Standing Committee's decisions. If the decisions of the Standing Committee were amended by the Corporation, they had to be referred back to it for its consideration and fresh resolution, which in turn was again placed before the Corporation for its own decision. Then the General Body adopted the Standing Committee's fresh decision, whether it followed the amendments earlier proposed by the Corporation or not. Similarly, in the case of the resolutions proposed by a member or members of the Corporation *suo motu*, the Standing Committee gave due consideration to them; but if the Committee diferred from the Corporation's resolution the Committee's decision was generally kept up by the Corporation.

Most of the financial matters placed before the Corporation after having been resolved upon by the Standing Committee were passed by the Corporation without debate. The resolution of the Standing Committee to fix the water rates for the supply of water to the premises, on the basis of the size of the water tap, was passed by the Corporation without debate. Similarly, the Committee's resolution to increase the period of the contract of tenancy of the residential blocks in a building owned by the Corporation by about 10 years was adopted by the Corporation without debate. The following were the other resolutions of the Standing Committee passed by the General Body without discussions:

(a) The sale by auction of 2,500 empty drums to a person for Rs. 12,000.

(b) To meet a certain percentage of expenditure for the construction of 1,300 rooms under the slum improvement scheme. (The construction work was to be executed by the Maharashtra State Housing Board.)

(c) To rent out a small place in the main Municipal vegetable market to a dealers' association for a nominal amount for conducting a small dispensary for the benefit of the occupants of the market.

(d) To approve of the expenditure incurred on the felicitation of the Mayors of Bombay and Nagpur, and the Chief Minister and the Home Minister of Maharashtra.

(e) To start an Urdu-medium school in a locality inhabited by the Urdu-speaking minority.

(f) To transfer the amount in the budget reserved for the construction of a hospital for building a school considered to be urgent.
(A member sought an assurance to execute the plan of hospital construction in future, which was given by the Mayor.)

(g) To depute a delegation to the State Government to urge upon it not to recover from the Corporation the entire expenditure incurred on repairing the Sambhaji Bridge dilapidated due to the recent flood.
(A few members desired the inclusion of more members in the deputation, to which the Corporation agreed.)

A resolution of the Standing Committee to reduce the fees charged for the buffaloes impounded in the Municipal cattle camp, however, evoked criticism of the cattle camp in which the cattle had to suffer the heat of the sun in the roofless compound, before the resolution was adopted by the General Body.

The estimated expenditure (earlier passed) for the construction of a school, which was found to be superfluous, was resolved to be deleted by the General Body. On being referred back, the Standing Committee followed the General Body's resolution. The resolution of the Standing

Committee recommending the sale of a Municipal plot in public auction, however, gave rise to varied criticisms in the Corporation including the one that the price agreed to in the auction was lower than the market rate. In reply, the Municipal Commissioner pointed out that the plot was not required by the Corporation and was also inconvenient for construction of a building which could be let out.

The Corporation, *suo motu*, provided, by a resolution, an amount of Rs. 1,50,000 from the reserve fund for the construction of a school building on a government plot of land. The school building was an urgent need of a suburban locality whose school-going population was large and, therefore, required a new school building. On reference to the Standing Committee the resolution of the Corporation was approved by it. The Corporation then adopted the Committee's resolution.

Corporators were keen to know when the Mayor's car in disorder would be replaced by a new one. The Commissioner told the Standing Committee about the direction to purchase it through the State Trading Corporation, hence it had to be awaited.

B. Personnel Matters

In personnel matters, in contrast with the financial matters, placed before the Standing Committee for consideration, in the cases of some Municipal officials a bias appeared apparent in its decisions. The General Body tended to follow the decisions of the Standing Committee in such cases, but in some of these the G.B. tried to correct the bias. On the ground of economy, facilities resolved upon by the Standing Committee to be provided to the officials, the General Body intended to reduce them. Rules and norms of propriety were also sought to be adhered to.

The following were the types of items relating to the Personnel, which were placed before the Corporation after having been considered and resolved upon by the Standing Committee:

(a) Conditions of service;
(b) Higher Scale;
(c) Honorarium;
(d) Agreements with Unions;
(e) Changes in Service Regulations;
(f) Re-employment/Extension after Retirement;

(g) Leave;
(h) Incentives;
(i) Transfer;
(j) Deputation;
(k) Appeal by Municipal Employees.

(a) Conditions of Service

The resolution of the Standing Committee to include the employees in the Municipal Secretary's office within the ambit of a contract concluded with the other Municipal employees regarding pay and other conditions of service was adopted by the Corporation without debate. Another item, pertaining to the payment of dearness allowance and the 'B' area allowance to the Municipal employees, however, evoked a sharp reaction from the members of the General Body which adopted an adjournment motion in protest of the delay in the payment of these allowances on the part of the office. It was explained by a member on the floor of the General Body that the Chairman of the Standing Committee, who belonged to the Congress party, was in favour of the payment of these allowances to the employees of the Municipal Corporation but the other members belonging to the Congress party deferred the decision of the issue in their own party. The Chairman of the Standing Committee desired a unanimous decision in the Standing Committee which did not come off due to the above stand of the Congress party members in the Committee. A provision for the payment of these allowances was, however, made in the budget estimates for the next year. Despite the budget provision, the adjournment motion was adopted by the General Body. This indicated the Corporators' sympathy for the cause of the Corporation employees, so also the resentment of the majority among them against the anti-employees stand of the Congress party members of the Standing Committee who formed a majority in it.

(b) Higher Scale/Increment

Injustice was sought to be removed in the case of a sub-engineer by the Standing Committee at the instance of the Municipal Commissioner. The sub-engineer was granted a higher scale, though he lacked the educational qualification considered essential in a State Government department. A Corporator, a member of the Standing Committee, who had concurred with its resolution, raised objection in the General Body regarding the officer's deficiency in respect of educational qualification. On the floor of the General Body the Municipal Commissioner justified the higher scale on the ground of the officer's longer experience. Another Corporator, who was a member of the Standing Comittee seconded it on the floor of the General Body. An attempt to refer back the resolution of the Standing Committee was frustrated due to the pleadings on behalf of it by this member and the Municipal Commissioner.

In two matters concerning grant of additional increments, the General Body held opposite views. The Standing Committee had resolved to grant six additional increments to a lady Medical Superintendent of a hospital, taken over recently by the Corporation from private management. Some members opined in the General Body that six increments granted to the new medical officer were excessive in view of her qualifications and experience. So the Standing Committee's resolution was referred back to the Standing Committee via the Medical Committee. The recommendation of the Standing Committee reduced the increments from six to four; this resolution of the Committee was ratified by the Corporation. On the other hand, the Corporation sought to amend the resolution of the Standing Committee to grant one increment to the medical officers in the employ of the Corporation holding an additional diploma, besides the basic graduation or the post-graduate degree. The Corporation desired that the post-graduates be eligible for two increments being given an edge over the holders of an additional diploma who would be granted one increment as stipulated in the Standing Committee's resolution. On reference back to the Medical and the Standing Committees, both adopted a fresh resolution as desired by the Corporation; the Corporation adopted it later.

(c) Honorarium

A matter that should have in fact been decided by the Municipal Commissioner, or, at the most, at the Standing Committee level, was under the law placed in the jurisdiction of the Corporation. It related to the honorarium to the head of the medical and public health department from the All-India Radio for a talk. The permission to the officer was accorded by the Commissioner on the presumption that both the Standing Committee and the Corporation would agree to it. A

Corporator queried as to why the matter was not placed before the Corporation before the talk was delivered. Another Corporator answered by pointing out the paucity of time between the consent by the Standing Committee and the date of the talk.

(d) Agreements with Unions

Two items related to the agreements entered into with the employees' unions were before the Corporation. One of these was a Standing Committee's resolution in respect of employees in higher category, concerning their pay and service conditions. It was accepted by the Corporation without debate. The other item was the Standing Committee's resolution ratifying an agreement with senior grade employees regarding pay, allowances and leave rules. A Sub-Committee of the Standing Committee had examined the details of the agreement. The main proposals were that:.

(i) the minimum basic grade would be Rs. 100;
(ii) the employees with the basic pay of Rs. 100 and above would be granted one increment; and
(iii) the date of the operation of the agreement was fixed.

An objection was raised by a Corporator as to why the basic pay of Rs. 100 was fixed at a point higher than that agreed to by the joint conciliation board. The reply given was that no increase in the scale proposed earlier was effected by the Sub-Committee and that the Sub-Committee had scrutinised this and other conditions of service thoroughly.

(e) Changes in Service Regulations

For the sake of the convenience of the employees the Corporation did not have any hesitation in adopting necessary resolutions of the Standing Committee in two cases. A number of employees could not pass the higher examination in Hindi, which was obligatory, as they found it rather tough. The Standing Committee, therefore, replaced the higher grade examination in Hindi by the lower grade examination. This necessitated a change in the service regulations. In the other item, to enable the Municipal employees to join the defence forces for a temporary period during the national emergency, the Standing

Committee had resolved to recommend to the Corporation the necessary amendment in the service regulations. The Corporation cleared the amendment. Both the resolutions of the Standing Committee were adopted by the Corporation without debate.

(f) Re-employment/Extension

The Standing Committee had resolved to recommend the appointment of an ex-consulting Surveyor to the State Government as Arbitrator (in town-planning schemes). A Corporator raised an objection to the appointment on the ground that such a senior official with a very high pay and status was not needed for the Municipal post of Arbitrator. But the General Body evinced confidence in the wisdom of the decision of the Standing Committee arrived at after a thorough discussion.

In another case, the Standing Committee had resolved to commend to the Corporation the appointment of a retired Assistant Municipal Commissioner of the Corporation who had already been granted one year's extension on a special duty after retirement. An objection as voiced on the floor of the General Body that the re-employed official's main work was to deal with disciplinary cases, which was a principal function of the Municipal Commissioner that could not be delegated to a subordinate official. It was also alleged that the retired Assistant Municipal Commissioner who was the acting Municipal Commissioner for some time had revised the note in the docket to suit his re-appointment. But these arguments against the re-appointment of the officer for another year did not weigh with the Standing Committee to which the matter was referred back by the Corporation. On reiteration of the resolution by the Standing Committee the Corporation passed it.

(g) Leave

A resolution of the Standing Committee permitted some Municipal employees, who could not enjoy Municipal holidays, privilege leave of additional 10 days. The resolution went through the Corporation without debate.

(h) Incentives

A Corporator had moved a proposal in the Corporation to award prizes to the merited employees. Neither the proposal nor the move to refer it to the Standing Committee was approved of by the Corporation. Opportunities for higher scales in assigned posts and promotions to higher posts were considered by the Corporators adequate incentives for the merited employees.

(i) Transfer

A resolution of the Standing Committee occasioned debate in the Corporation, most of which contained .aspersions on the unbusiness-like proceedings of the Corporation, like the criticism of the resolution on the Krishna-Godavari Water Dispute. The Standing Committee had authorised the transfer of the Provident Fund of an employee from the Municipal (Bus) Transport Department to the Sanitary Department due to his transfer. As the office did not furnish the information in time the matter was delayed. The concerned employee had entered the (Bus) Transport Department in 1956; but, until the Auditor's adverse remark, his service in the department was not regularised. The Standing Committee's resolution was, after the discussion, adopted by the Corporation.

(j) Deputation

Four resolutions of the Standing Committee placed before the Corporation for decision concerned deputation from or to the Corporation service.

The Standing Committee's resolution favouring the extension of the officials from the Land Acquisition Department of the State Government on deputation to the Corporation was adopted by the Corporation without debate. So also the resolution accepting the recommendation of the Law and Judicial Department of the State Government to appoint its experienced and trained staff in the special Municipal court.

Another resolution of the Standing Committee related to deputation was adopted by the Corporation by majority, while still another after reiteration by the Standing Committee on reference back to it.

Four names of the Municipal engineering staff were proposed in a Standing Committee resolution to an institution from the city for study abroad at its instance. Two objections were raised in the discussion on the resolution in the Corporation. One related to the absence of reference to the Public Works Committee by the Standing Committee before its own resolution. The Municipal Secretary replied that during his leave period the matter was placed on the agenda of the Standing Committee without its consideration by the Public Works Committee. Once the item was inserted on the agenda of the Standing Committee, the Municipal Secretary averred, it could not be rescinded. The other objection pertained to the non-inclusion of the City Engineer's name in the list recommended by the Standing Committee even though the Commissioner had recommended it. The Standing Committee's resolution was adopted by the Corporation. The debate revealed the internal 'administrative' politics in the Corporation.

The other Standing Committee resolution that was debated on the floor of the Corporation pertained to the re-extension of the deputation of a Municipal tax officer to the Delhi Municipal Corporation for a period of three years. A few Corporators objected to the delay in placing the matter beyond the end of the earlier period of deputation to the same Delhi Municipal Corporation. The Commissioner expressed helplessness regarding the delay on the part of an external institution. He also pointed to the legal point that the officer could not re-join the parent employer-institution unless released by the external institution.

(k) Appeal by Employees

To decide the case of appeal regarding their employment and service matters, the Standing Committee took its own time. This resulted in the anguish among the employees. A few Corporators, therefore, took up the cause of the employees and urged the General Body to limit this time-limit to three months. The Municipal Commissioner deftly sidelined the confrontation and left the matter of fixing time-limit for deciding the appeal cases to the Standing Committee itself.

A question by a Corporator elicited the answer that the Standing Committee resolution regarding framing of employees service conditions was being attended to and within a month these would be framed.

C. Miscellaneous Matters

The item pertaining to two public gardens in the city from the State Government came up before the General Body, one of which was outside the Municipal limits. Both the public gardens were in a neglected conditions some Corporators, therefore, urged the

Corporation to take them over for a proper upkeep. The General Body referred the item to the Standing Committee. The City Engineer expressed against the taking over of the public gardens, while the Municipal Commissioner favoured it. The negotiations with the State Government were started. At the time of the investigation by us one public garden was taken over by the Corporation.

Another miscellaneous item was concerning a piece of land acquired by the Corporation for the construction of a medical dispensary and a medical department's office. A part of the land had been utilised by the Corporation. Some Corporators pleaded on the floor of the General Body that the remaining (unused) portion of the land should be returned to the landowner. The Municipal Commissioner countered the plea by promising to undertake the work on providing for it in the next year's budget. On reference to the Standing Committee the Commissioner's promise was not heeded and the way was cleared for return of the unused portion of the land to the owner.

In a related matter, resentment was voiced in the General Body by several Corporators, regarding the policy of large-scale land acquisition by the Municipal Corporation, by tabling an adjournment motion. A good number of the land acquisitions were for the purposes of road-widening. Despite the official answer the adjournment motion was adopted by the General Body.

Summing-up

In the bulk of the items before the Corporation, which came from the Standing Committee, the Corporation acquiesced with the decisions of the Standing Committee. In a few items regarding administrative personnel the General Body corrected the bias against the targeted officials. One resolution to return a piece of the acquired land to the owner confirmed the Corporators' interest in protecting the interests of the constituents. An adjournment motion adopted in favour of the grant of Dearness and the 'B' area allowances to the employees showed up the Corporators' sympathy for its employees despite the major party's adverse stand.

TRANSPORT COMMITTEE

A. Structural

(i) Membership of the Transport Committee

In the General Body some Corporators articulated the view that the structure of the Transport Committee should be changed to facilitate a more thorough discussion of the budget of the Poona Municipal Transport in the Corporation. The budget of the P.M.T., on approval by the Transport Committee, would be remitted to the Standing Committee. After the approval of the Standing Committee, the P.M.T. budget would be placed before the Corporation for adoption like the budget of the Municipal Corporation (excluding the P.M.T.). As seen in the chapter on the Structure of the Committees, eight members of the Transport Committee elected by the Corporation (General Body) might be anybody having related "experience" or "capacity", they might be Corporators or from outside the Corporation, only the Chairman of the Standing Committee being necessarily a Corporator. This might create a situation when not a single member of the Transport Committee would be a Corporator, except the Chairman of the Standing Committee who was *ex-officio* member of the Transport Committee. But, as the Chairman of the Standing Committee would participate in the discussion on the budget in the Standing Committee, he did not feel free or necessary to air his views on the P.M.T. budget on the floor of the General Body. At a juncture during 1962 no Corporator except the Chairman of the Standing Committee was a member of the Transport Committee. A Corporator tabled a resolution for re-structuring the Transport Committee, which was seconded by another Corporator. This was a genuine drawback in the statutory provisions regarding the structure of the Transport Committee.

The Corporators availed of this opportunity to ventilate their grievances regarding the working of the P.M.T. in general and the Transport Committee in particular. The persons elected to the Transport Committee, despite the statutory provision that they should possess related "experience" or "capacity", would not include experts in transport, automobile, engineering, transport administration or management, or related fields. This impelled some Corporators to suggest that the Transport Committee ought to include at least one expert in a related field. However, some other Corporators countered this suggestion by pointing out that the then Transport Manager himself was not an expert in transport or engineering, nor did either the Public Works Committee nor the Medical Relief and Public Health Committee necessarily contained any experts in the relevant fields. Resort to the fact of the P.M.T. being a public service instead of a commercial one was also taken by some members for arguing against inclusion of experts in the Committee. Corporators dissatisfied with the

P.M.T. administration of the Transport Manager aired an opinion that the P.M.T. be placed under the supervision and control of the Municipal Commissioner.

Finally, the General Body referred the resolution for re-structuring of the Transport Committee to the Law, Revenue and General Purposes Committee.

The resolution indicated the general discontent in the minds of the Corporators about the working of the Poona Municipal Undertaking, its management by the Transport Manager and the functioning of the Transport Committee.

(ii) Co-option of a Labour Representative

The existing statutory provision was for the co-option of persons having "experience" or "capacity" in an area related to transport. A resolution before the General Body, therefore, urged the co-option of a labour representative to the Transport Committee. The resolution pleaded an appropriate cause of involving a representative of the labour in the P.M.T. in the process of decision-making in the Transport Committee. The stronger of the two unions in the P.M.T. belonged to the INTUC, a trade union affiliate of the Congress party. A Corporator owing allegiance to an Opposition party criticised the resolution as a ploy to afford the representation on the Transport Committee to the puppet union, indirectly controlled by the Transport Manager. But another Corporator of the same Opposition party favoured in principle the representation of the labour in the P.M.T. on the Transport Committee. The resolution was canvassed by the Corporation to the State Government for incorporating an amendment to the (Poona) Municipal Corporation Act.

B. Financial

(i) Income

A resolution of the Transport Committee was tabled before the General Body to bring down the rates of skyline advertisements on the P.M.T. buses, as they adversely affected the P.M.T. revenue from such advertisements. The General Body unanimously referred the resolution to the Municipal Commissioner for his remarks. The M.C. opined that the resolution was discriminatory in favour of the advertisers leaving aside other categories of taxpayers. He had also opined that the new rates of advertisement were quite reasonable and hence needed no change. The opinion of the Commissioner was accepted by the General Body. In the case of difference of opinion between the Transport Committee and the Corporation on this item, the Corporation prevailed.

(ii) Expenditure

(a) *Expenditure on Unforeseen Items*: The P.M.T. was required to expend on two unforeseen items, namely, the payment to the employees on account of a new agreement entered into with them and payment of the increased motor vehicle tax. The P.M.T. had proposed to expend on these two unforeseen items from the annual balance of Rs. 1 lakh with it. There was some misunderstanding among some Corporators whether expenditure could be incurred from the annual balance. On a positive explanation by the Transport Manager the resolution was adopted by the General Body.

(b) *Re-allocation from the Municipal Fund to the Transport Fund*: The P.M.T. requested the General Body to re-allocate a sum of Rs. 5 lakhs from the loan of Rs. 60 lakhs credited in the Municipal Fund to the Transport Fund to meet certain expenses. The re-allocation from the loan amount had to be approved by the Standing Committee. Hence the resolution was referred to the Standing Committee for its recommendation. The Standing Committee declined the re-allocation as the position of the Municipal budget was itself tight. In the meanwhile, the P.M.T. was permitted by the State Government to raise a loan in the market. Hence, the resolution was deleted from the agenda of the Corporation.

Thus, while in one item of unforeseen expenditure the resolution of the Transport Committee was agreed to by the General Body, in the other the Corporation supported by the Committee did not accept the proposal of the Transport Manager.

(iii) Purchases

A question was asked in the General Body whether the Transport Manager had purchased certain parts of the Tata-Mercedez buses, priced at above Rs. 5 lakhs, without the approval of the Transport Committee. The Transport Manager replied that when the order for the parts was placed the price of the parts was below Rs. 5 lakhs but later it went up, and that the matter was then brought to the notice of the Transport Committee.

(iv) Bus Fares

(a) *Questions*: Three questions were asked on the floor of the General Body on the bus fares; two on the possibility of concessions in bus fares for the distant new localities of the flood affected and the Municipal primary teachers serving in suburban areas, and the third on the increased fares for certain long distanced localities. The questions on the concessions in bus fares were answered in the negative on the ground that once concessions were granted to a particular category of passengers they would have to be extended to other similar categories of passengers, which would result in loss of revenue to the P.M.T. The bus fares had been increased recently for certain long-distanced areas because, though the fares for these were lower than those allowed by the Regional Transport Authority, these had been left out from the list of routes on which increased fares had been charged. The Transport Manager added in his answer that on obtaining the sanction of the R.T.O., the matter would be placed before the General Body for approval. The T.M. answers to these questions seemed to have satisfied the General Body.

(b) *Resolution*: A resolution of the Transport Committee urging the General Body to approve increase in bus fares evoked considerable discussion. The main components of the resolution were as follows:

(i) To retain the minimum fare of five paise for the children of the age group of 3-12 years;
(ii) to classify the bus stops into two categories: the request stop and the stage stop — for the sake of fixing the rates the stage stop would be relevant;
(iii) between the age group of 3-12 years the charge would be half of an adult as per the Motor Vehicles Act;
(iv) to raise the fare of the luxury buses for sight-seeing by 50 per cent.

The new fare structure, on sanction by the State Government, would come into effect after a month during which it would be publicised to invite public comments. An amendment suggested to the resolution by a Corporator was to appoint an Ad-hoc Committee of the General Body to examine the bus fares proposed by the Transport Committee/Transport Manager thoroughly, which allegedly was not done by the Transport Committee. On the side opposing the rise in bus fares, it was argued that the rise was excessive leading to a surplus of Rs. 20 lakhs for the P.M.T. The P.M.T's assets were large and it suffered from no deficit, the opponents added. The proponents pointed the instance of Bombay city bus fares which were higher than those in Poona city (which statement was not correct). They also averred that the expansion of the city entailed the expansion of the P.M.T. fleet which required larger funds for which increase in bus fares was necessitated. A surplus of Rs. 4 lakhs and not of Rs. 20 lakhs would ensue, they added. In the end of the discussion, the amendment was defeated and the original resolution was adopted by the General Body. Increase in the bus fares was inevitable due to the rising spiral of prices all round and the needs of expansion of the P.M.T. bus fleet. But the suggestion of an Ad-hoc Committee to scrutinise the periodic increases in bus fares also denoted lack of confidence in the competence of the Transport Committee to engage in a thorough examination of the bus fares.

(c) *An Adjournment Motion*: Another occasion of increase in bus fares evoked an Adjournment Motion in the Corporation. The General Body itself had approved of the resolution of the Transport Committee on the matter. It was, therefore, pointed out during the discussion that the Transport Committee alone could not be held responsible for the increase in the bus fares, the onus also lay on the General Body. Despite the assurance to the General Body by the Transport Manager to inform the Transport Committee on the incidence of the rise in the bus fares on the different routes and its effect on the income of the P.M.T. on these respective routes and the possibility of reduction in the bus fares on these routes, the General Body was in no mood to relent from adopting the Adjournment Motion. It was notable that the leader of the major party in the Corporation, the Congress, himself supported the Motion which was adopted unanimously. This indicated the casual manner with which the General Body sometimes treated important matters like the increase in the P.M.T. bus fares.

C. Personnel

(i) C.I.D. Report about Meeting of Employees Sympathetic to the Transport Manager

A question by a Corporator sought to elicit information regarding a meeting held in a nearby village by some P.M.T. employees who were sympathetic to the suspended Transport Manager. The interrogating Corporator reported that these employees decided at the meeting to harass the Acting Transport Manager by resorting to break-downs of vehicles, slow driving and so on. Even the names of some employees who held the meeting were divulged by another Corporator. The same member asked whether the report from C.I.D. about the meeting was received by the Acting Transport Manager. The T.M. replied that the C.I.D. report was precautionary and that nothing more could then be done on it. The suspended Transport Manager's strong personality but dubious administrative ways were evident from this question.

(ii) Motor Car Allowance of the T.M.

The Transport Committee had resolved to recommend the increase in the motor car allowance of the Transport Manager from Rs. 100 to Rs. 200 in view of the rise in the cost of petrol, etc. The General Body accepted the T.C.'s resolution with a cut of Rs. 20 in the increase proposed by the T.C. The General Body thereby asserted its supremacy over the Transport Committee.

(iii) Questions about Employees' Training

Two questions were asked in the General Body about the availability of training in bus driving to the P.M.T. employees. Such facility was available in the nationalised motor transport undertakings. Chances of promotion would be available to the training employees. After six months of the experiment a report on the scheme would be given to the Transport Committee, the Transport Manager promised the General Body. The Transport Committee would then be in a position to decide about the continuation of the scheme. Another question asked whether partiality prevailed in the selection of trainees for bus duties. The Transport Manager replied that the Transport Committee had framed the rules about the selection of trainees and that the selection of all employees was done accordingly.

D. Operational

Three questions were asked in the General Body, respectively, on the public announcement about some discontinued request stops, the correctness of the information regarding the breakdown of buses during the period from 1961-62 to 1963-64 and the number of buses required to provide adequate space to the pass-holders and the school-going children. On the request stops discontinued recently neither the Transport Committee nor the public was informed. The Transport Manager promised that in future he would keep the Transport Committee posted in the matter. The statistics on the bus breakdowns during 1961-62 to 1963-64 furnished to the Transport Committee were incorrect although a breakdown register was maintained in the T.M. office. The Transport Manager admitted that the existing fleet of P.M.T. buses was inadequate to cope with the then number of pass-holders and the school-going children. He promised the General Body that information would be collected on the number of these categories of passengers and the number of buses required to meet the requirement.

All the above questions brought out the inadequacies or failings in the administration of the Poona Municipal Transport.

Summing-up

The General Body aired grievances regarding the working of the P.M.T. as well as that of the Transport Committee. Members were particularly not happy over the functioning of the suspended Transport Manager whose style of conduct with the staff as well as the Corporators left much to be improved upon. The structural position of the Transport Committee *vis-a-vis* the Municipal Corporation left much to be desired and the Corporators desired an overhauling of this relationship. Over the rise in P.M.T. bus fares, the Corporators had discontent which they articulated in the meetings of the General Body. It was surprising to find the General Body adopting an adjournment resolution disapproving of the increase in the bus fares which had been cleared by itself a few months ago. This indicated the casual attitude of most of the Corporators to the business relating to the Poona Municipal Transport in the Corporation meetings. The General Body was keen to maintain its supremacy in financial matters particularly when the demands of the Poona Municipal Transport tended to cut into the sanctioned funds and reserves for the requirements of the Corporation excluding those of the Poona Municipal Transport. In rest of the matters the General Body gave due regard to the requirements of the P.M.T.

In the matters within the strict jurisdiction of the Standing Committee to which the General Body referred the concerned P.M.T. matters, it preserved its identity without offending the genuine interests of the P.M.T.

PUBLIC WORKS COMMITTEE

A. Works Proper

(i) Provision of Public Drinking Water Taps

A good number of resolutions, namely nine, from the Public Works Committee, placed before the Corporation, pertained the provision of public drinking water taps in different localities. All the resolutions were unanimously adopted by the Corporation, without any debate. Out of nine, three resolutions were initiated by the Corporators living in the respective localities where public taps were needed. The remaining resolutions were initiated by the Municipal Commissioner on the recommendations of the departmental officials or the Corporators.

A seemingly minor item but important from the point of view of the Corporator from the locality concerned regarding the re-location of a proposed public water tap, near an Octroi post, was referred back to the Public Works Committee for re-consideration. On reference by the Committee, the Municipal Commissioner opined that instead of the location proposed earlier the public water tap should be set up at a convenient place. The recommendation of the Committee based on the remark of the Municipal Commissioner was accepted by the General

Body unanimously.

The important factor in the location of the public water taps by the Municipal Corporation was the need of the locality. A number of resolutions on the matter were initiated by the Corporators through the Public Works Committee, but the Corporation office recommended only deserving cases. Without an on-the-spot inspection no public water tap was approved of. On the department's satisfaction about the need of the locality the docket on the item was kept before the Public Works Committee and then before the General Body. This information was furnished to the Corporation in the course of the answer to a question raised by a Corporator by the Development Engineer.

(ii) Filtered Water Supply Scheme

An important matter that was raised by a Corporator through a resolution concerned the re-consideration and abandonment of the filtered water scheme approved already by the Corporation. The mover adduced various reasons for re-consideration of the scheme. The filtered water scheme was no doubt necessary for the improvement of the health of the people for which filtered water supply was considered desirable. Various grounds were pleaded against the execution of the filtered water scheme in Pune. It was an expensive scheme entailing a burden on the tax-payers. The health of the residents did not improve necessarily as was evident in the adjacent Cantonment. The employment of the additional staff up-scaled the current expenditure on the scheme. The house-owners were expected to fix the meters for the assessment of the charge for filtered water supply, on this matter there were bound to be disputes between the house-owners and their tenants. Filtered water would be wasted on gardens and for other reasons. When other crucial health and development works were stalled for want of funds, expenditure of Rs. 1 crore on the scheme would be an extravagance. The resolution for the re-consideration of the scheme was referred to the Public Works Committee. The Committee recorded that the scheme had already been accepted by the Co-ordination Committee and, further, the Life Insurance Corporation had been approached for an adequate loan. The item was, therefore, filed. It was natural for the Corporators to be concerned about an expensive scheme, like the filtered water supply scheme, but the mover Corporator ought to have inquired in this behalf in the office before he moved the resolution.

(iii) Query regarding two Minor Works

A Corporator put across a query regarding two minor works on the floor of the General Body. One was about the levelling of a road in a Municipal colony and the other was about the setting up of a mercury lamp there. The Municipal Commissioner replied that the process of road levelling had already been completed and that in the other matter the Public Works Committee re-considered its own earlier resolution and decided to set up two ordinary lamps instead of one mercury lamp.

B. Financial Matters

(i) Estimates

Out of 21 estimates for public works which had emanated from the Public Works Committee, 19 were adopted by the Corporation unanimously without debate; only two estimates evoked a little discussion, but these also were accepted. One of these two debated estimates was for Rs. 35,000 for the construction of school rooms near a police headquarters. Two objections were raised in the matter. Why sanitary blocks and watchmen's quarters were not included in the estimate was one objection. The other objection related to the rent that would be charged by the State Government for its land — leased to the Municipal Corporation for the purpose; it was feared that the rent would be too high. To the first objection the Development Engineer replied that the estimates for the sanitary blocks and watchmen's quarters, which were not included in the docket by mistake, would be placed before the Committee and, later, the Corporation in the near future. On the second objection, he told members that the Corporation had requested the State Government to charge a token rent on the land and that he was confident about the granting of the request. The Corporation adopted the estimate after this explanation. The other discussed estimate of Rs. 81,000 was for the construction of an additional floor on a Corporation's high school building. The high school catered in the main for the pupils of backward castes living in the locality. A point raised against the resolution was that the high school building did not figure in the package of school buildings approved earlier by the Corporation. The resolution was, on the other hand, defended on these grounds. The item was for the extension of a high school building and not for a new construction referred to in the objection. The objection raised was political and did not touch the substantial issue that the high school catered to the needs of the pupils of backward people in the locality. The House adopted the resolution on elucidation. The Corporators seemed to be inquisitive on minor matters, but they glossed over matters involving large amounts.

Three resolutions on Works estimates from the P.W.C. and the Standing Committee, which were debated in the General Body, were adopted eventually, one unanimously and the other two with majority. The resolution adopted unanimously was regarding the estimate of expenditure of Rs. 3,000 for constructing a fence to Corporation primary school building. The need for the fence was questioned during the debate, but even then the resolution was adopted. The resolution for an estimate of expenditure of Rs. 17,000 for constructing a protective wall around a school of the Corporation was passed with majority vote which was merely one-fifth of the cost of the school building. In the other resolution adopted by the Corporation with a majority, it sought to withdraw an earlier resolution in favour of the expenditure of Rs. 30,000 on construction of three class-rooms in a Corporation school. It was argued against the cancellation of the earlier resolution for the expenditure that the school catered for the pupils of backward classes. Despite the argument, the resolution for deletion of expenditure was passed by a majority vote.

These three instances showed that the General Body on occasions awakened to its responsibility of keeping vigilance on unnecessary expenditure.

(ii) Financial Provision for Works from Residue of Current Budget

Eleven items to make financial provision for certain works from the residue of the current budget were passed by the Corporation unanimously without discussion. Two items invoked some debate before being adopted by the General Body. In one item, the Municipal Commissioner had proposed (in June, 1963) Rs. 55,000 for certain road-widening works which had not been provided for in the current year's budget. The item had been recommended by the Public Works Committee and the Standing Committee. It was pointed out by a member in Opposition to the resolution on the matter that the provision in the current budget on the head had not been exhausted so far. The member also opined that within the remaining three months in the current financial year the proposed amount would not be exhausted. The Standing Committee had also cut down the proposed amount. But the leader of the major Congress party explained that many houses had been demolished for road widening and further road repairing work necessitated by the demolition would require the proposed amount. On this intervention, the resolution was adopted by the General Body.

The other item asked for a total sum of Rs. 3 lakhs for fixing diesel engines as an alternative source of power supply in cases of frequent power breakdowns, setting up a pumping house at a high place to facilitate the supply of water to high population density localities, installation of pipes for water storage on a high plane and to lay a concrete bed on one of the water tanks. A query was put in by a member as to how many years would be taken for the completion of these works. It was replied by the leader of the Congress party, who was a member of the Standing Committee, that the officials had assured the Standing Committee of early completion of the works if cement was made available expeditiously by the authorities. Thereafter the resolution was adopted unanimously.

The observation noted earlier, that the Corporators expressed concern on small matters but ignored items requiring big outlays, would apply in regard to the financial provisions from the residue of the current budget.

(iii) Tender for Construction of a School Building

A tender for Rs. 75,000 for the construction of a school building attracted considerable discussion in a Corporation meeting. Both the Public Works Committee and the Standing Committee had recommended the tender. Criticism voiced in the meeting was that the construction rate approved was Rs. 30 per sq ft which was above the market rate of Rs. 25 per sq ft. The building was ordinary, not having any special features. In reply the Mayor pointed out that the walls of the school building would be high (the Engineer had earlier opined that the foundation of the building had to be deep to be strong). It was also said that the Municipal Commissioner was discriminatory in favour of the particular contractor whose tender had been recommended by the Subject and the Standing Committees. Another point of criticism cast aspersions on the composition of the Public Works Committee. A member opined frankly that the Committee lacked experts, engineers in the case, among its members and so they could not judge the cost of the work and the rate of tender called for. The members of the Committee who were present at the Corporation meeting, however, rebutted this criticism, pointing out that the Committee had examined the cost and the rate of the tender carefully. The Corporation, however, heeding the criticism, referred back the matter to the Public Works and the Standing Committees. The P.W.C. decided to invite new tenders and advised the tenderers to reduce their rates in view of the criticism voiced in the Corporation. The same tenderer whose tender had been recommended earlier reduced the rate of his tender. The P.W.C. and the Standing Committee recommended the revised tender. The General Body accepted it. This instance brought out the Corporation's vigilance in this particular case, but such cases were few.

(iv) Plot-holders to give Deposits to the Municipal Corporation for Water and Drainage Connections to be adjusted against Municipal Taxes

It was a statutory responsibility of the Municipal Corporation to provide drainage and water lines on the roads belonging to it, but it was unable to do so due to financial difficulties. The above via media was suggested by the Commissioner, which, on being recommended by the Public Works and Standing Committees, was adopted by the General Body. The gravity of the financial situation was realised by the General Body.

(v) A Question on Repair of Old Cars

A question was asked in a meeting of the Corporation: Why some of the old cars in the Vehicle Department were not repaired and used further? The Municipal Commissioner replied that those cars were too old to be brought into use after repairs. The supplementary, whether the matter was placed before the Committee, evoked the reply that the relevant information would be placed before the Committee.

C. Property

(i) Leasing of a Municipal Plot to an Educational Institution

A resolution to lease a plot of land for a hostel of an educational institution catering to the pupils from backward classes was moved by a Corporator directly at the General Body. The conditions laid down by the Corporation were that the hostel had to be constructed within two years and the managing committee of the hostel had to co-opt two representatives of the Corporation. An objection to the resolution raised the issue of the low rent for the lease. Another objection voiced was that as the matter was financial it should be referred to the Standing Committee. But the members seemed to sympathsise with the cause of the backward class students for whom the hostel was to be built, so they rejected both the objections and passed the resolution. This was an instance when the prescribed procedure would be set aside to press forward a cause with which a large number of the Corporators sympathised.

(ii) To Replace a Plot Donated to an Athletic Association for building a Gymnasium by Another Suitable Plot

A resolution in the matter was placed before the General Body directly. A point was raised that the building plan for the Gymnasium at the recommended place had already been approved by the authorities and the Government had also donated an amount to the Association. The item was referred to an Ad-hoc and the Public Works Committees, both of which recommended another suitable place for the purpose. Thereafter, the General Body agreed to it.

(iii) To sell a Municipal Plot of Land of Two Acres to the Central Government

The Central Government approached the Municipal Corporation for the sale of a Municipal plot of land of two acres for constructing residential quarters for the staff of the Food Ministry. The Corporators asked the office to insert an additional condition in the sale agreement that the Central Government should pay the Municipal property tax. This was an eyewash in view of a Constitutional provision exempting the Central Government properties from the payment of the Municipal property tax. A plea in favour of the resolution was that the area in which the plot was located would develop due to the location of an administrative building there.

(iv) A Query regarding Possibility of Acquisition of Excess Land for Road Widening

A Corporator pointed out that in some cases for road-widening land acquired was in excess, beyond the limits of road-widening. The member wanted to know whether the Public Works Committee had been consulted in the matters concerned; he was under the impression that only the Standing Committee had been consulted. Neither the Municipal Commissioner nor the Municipal Secretary gave a satisfactory answer to the query of the member.

D. Personnel

The personnel matters also figured in the resolutions before the General Body which came from the Public Works Committee and the Standing Committee. These were about:

(i) appointments in a substantive vacancy,
(ii) appointments in leave vacancies,
(iii) increment for a new incumbent in a post, and
(iv) deputation of the officials to training or conferences.

(i) Appointment in a Substantive Vacancy

The General Body had confirmed the appointment of the Development Engineer to the post of City Engineer. The vacancy of Development Engineer had, therefore, to be filled. The Municipal Commissioner had recommended a particular person to the post on permanent basis. The P.W.C. had approved the Commissioner's recommendation which was placed before the General Body for approval. An amendment to the resolution sought to appoint the recommended person on a temporary basis on the ground that the post was a responsible one and so the new incumbent should be put on test for some time before he was made permanent. The amendment was passed with majority.

(ii) Appointments during Leave Vacancies

The resolution regarding appointments to the temporary vacancies of City Engineer and Development Engineer, respectively, on the deputation of the City Engineer for training abroad in town-planning and the promotion of the Development Engineer to the post of City Engineer during leave vacancy, was approved by the General Body unanimously.

(iii) Increment for a New Incumbent in a Post

The Development Engineer was promoted to the post of City Engineer.

He drew the salary of Rs. 610 and as City Engineer his starting salary would have been Rs. 620. The Municipal Commissioner opined that the post of City Engineer being that of the head of the engineering department, the new incumbent should be granted one increment in the starting salary as an indicator of his promotion. The M.C.'s recommendation was accepted unanimously by the General Body.

(iv) Deputation of the Officials to Training or Conferences

A resolution to depute the Depot Superintendent in the Vehicle Department to attend a diesel engine course held by a private company at Madras was adopted unanimously. The deputationist was to draw a daily allowance of Rs. 10 in addition to a paltry allowance of Rs. 3.87 given by the company to make up for the higher cost of living at Madras. A member had queried on this, but on the M.C.'s reply the General Body adopted the resolution unanimously.

Two resolutions, authorising the participation of the City Engineer in a conference convened by the Public Health Engineering Institute at Nagpur and of the Development Engineer in another conference, were adopted unanimously by the General Body. A member questioned about the delay in placing the docket on the item after the participation of the City Engineer in the conference. The P.W.C. had approved the necessary expenses in time before the participation, but there was a delay in the placing of the docket before the General Body.

Thus, in personnel matters at times the General Body showed up bias against certain officials whose promotion or deputation to conference was there for a decision.

E. Miscellaneous

Two resolutions seeking to renew the contract with the Poona Suburban Electrical Company for the power supply (failing an alternative source) for a further period of three years and recommending to have another road scheme suggested by the Town-Planning Arbitrator, instead of the one already approved leading to a public garden, were adopted unanimously.

Summing-up

The bulk of the resolutions which emanated from the Public Works

Committee alone or from the P.W.C. through the Standing Committee were adopted by the General Body without discussion and those among a few that evoked discussion were also adopted by it. Only a handful of the resolutions were referred back to the P.W.C. or the P.W.C. and the Standing Committee. In revised form assumed through these Committees the General Body passed these. Most of the estimates of expenditure for proposed works were cleared by the General Body. The proposals for public water taps were also okayed without hesitation. Only a few of the Works expenditure estimates evoked debate just to indicate the awareness of the Corporators of their responsibility, one of which even attracted criticism regarding the absence of experts in the P.W.C. Proposals of appointment, promotion, advanced increment, deputation to conference/training of targeted officials invoked adverse opinions of some Corporators. Major proposals, like the renewal of the agreement with the Poona Suburban Electric Company, escaped uncriticised while a desirable proposal like the filtered water supply scheme, unnecessarily evoked an adverse resolution.

MEDICAL RELIEF AND PUBLIC HEALTH COMMITTEE

The financial matters regarding an additional grant of Rs. 6,000 to a charitable hospital, which had been declined earlier, and the sanction of expenditure on certain works, from the residue of the current budget, were cleared by the Corporation without hesitation.

The General Body had referred back a resolution passed by the M.R.P.H. directing that the collected refuse be burnt instead of turning it into fertiliser, which was expensive in comparison with the cost involved. Few Corporators had pointed to a communication from the State Government suggesting the conversion of refuse into fertiliser. But the financial aspect weighed more certainly on the General Body than the communication from the State Government. The Committee reiterated its earlier resolution on back reference. The General Body did not demur in adopting the confirmed resolution of the Committee.

A Corporator had placed a proposal before the General Body to take action for the control of rabid dogs. The proposal was referred to the M.R.P.H.C. The Committee recommended that the Corporation should start issuing licences to the dogs which had undergone anti-rabies treatment. The General Body adopted the Committee's recommendation.

The members felt concerned about the unhygienic conditions in the eastern part of the city. On receiving an assurance in the matter from the Commissioner that the Administration would take action, the adjournment motion was withdrawn.

A plot of land was offered to the Corporation by a person for the construction of a Municipal dispensary. The M.R.P.H.C. had recommended the acceptance of the offer. But the General Body felt that the cost of the construction of the dispensary would be much more than that of the plot of land. On reference back, the Committee negotiated with the person who offered in addition the donation of an amount of Rs. 10,000 towards the dispensary construction. The Committee recommended the supplementary donation. The General Body accepted the new resolutions of the Committee.

Members were keen to know more about the Employees' State Insurance Scheme of the State Government in which the Corporation desired to participate through its hospitals. On the provision of necessary information by the Commissioner, the General Body agreed to the proposal.

On two resolutions from the Committee, concerning, in one instance, the payment of an honorarium of Rs. 100 to the Medical Officer of Health for conducting a course for Sanitary Inspectors of the All-India Institute of Local Self-Government and, in the other, regarding a statement made by the same officer in the M.R.P.H.C. some members had compunctions. In the second instance they moved an adjournment motion. Both these items showed up the grudge against the officer in the minds of some Corporators. On explanation by the Municipal Commissioner, the frayed tempers of the Corporators were assuaged and the actions urged by the Administration were agreed to.

The status of the resolutions before the General Body which came from the Medical Relief and Public Health Committee was in general uneventful, barring a few ones. The reasons were: First, there was near unanimity on the urgency of conceding the demands from the Administration or proposals from the Corporators; and, secondly, the nature of the subject was too technical for the following and pursuing of details and subtleties of the matters in the resolutions on the part of the members. In the resolutions from this Committee also, Corporators seemed to harbour a grudge against the Medical Officer of Health, who was head of the department of medicine and health.

LAW, REVENUE AND GENERAL PURPOSES COMMITTEE

I. Constitutional

Three constitutional matters were placed before the Corporation for consideration and decision:

(i) The application of Municipal building bye-laws to plots adjacent to the national highways and district roads;
(ii) inclusion of certain bordering areas in Municipal limits; and
(iii) the position of the Transport Committee *vis-a-vis* the Corporation.

(i) It was pleaded on behalf of the resolution recommended by the Law Committee that the rules of ribbon development were applicable to the plots adjacent to the national highways and district roads, which put stringent conditions on construction, for example on the frontage space. These rules had an adverse effect on the building activity in the city. After inspection of these areas only, the resolution was recommended. But the Mayor was in favour of the postponement of the item. The members on the side of the resolution, however, desired the decision at the meeting itself. Voting was equal, the Mayor gave his casting vote against the resolution, so it was negatived.

(ii) The Law Committee had resolved to include certain areas in the Corporation limits and exclude others. Areas presently included in the *Zilla Parishad* were fit to be detached from it and joined to the Corporation as they were close to it. On the other hand certain areas within the Corporation limits were not manageable by it, these should have been merged in the *Zilla Parishad*. Several new suggestions were mooted in the General Body meeting. So the resolution was referred back to the Law Committee for a fresh look. The Committee consulted the Municipal Commissioner in the matter. The Committee in its revised resolution suggested two principles. The first principle was that areas with a maximum of 75 villages in the Corporation should be included within the Corporation. The second principle emphasised the factors of nearness, easy access and financial advantages likely to accrue to the Corporation. These principles were readily accepted by the General Body at its next meeting.

(iii) An Independent Corporator had forwarded a resolution to the General Body in which he desired the Law Committee to introduce an amendment whereby after every Municipal election the whole of the Transport Committee should consist of newly elected Corporators. The various viewpoints reviewed earlier in the section on the Transport Committee cropped up in the context of discussion of this resolution also. None of the Corporators was present in the Transport Committee to report truthfully the transactions in the Committee, was the main difficulty deliberated upon. That one-half of the Transport Committee should comprise the present Corporators was one suggestion aired at the meeting. Another suggestion mooted was that the members of the earlier Committee should continue until new members were elected. The issue of the essential inclusion of experts was also discussed attracting both favourable and unfavourable responses from the members. The meeting was adjourned after the debate; the resolution fell through.

II. Financial

The following were the categories of financial items discussed by the Corporation:

(i) Octroi (seven);
(ii) Other taxes (two);
(iii) Estimates/Proposals of Expenditure (three);
(iv) Grants of Institutions (four) and
(v) Donation to the Corporation (one).

(i) Octroi

Two items were concerning concession or exemption in Octroi incidence to certain categories of taxpayers. Two others (one each) proposed reduction or increase in the Octroi rates. One item pertained the cancellation of the existing Octroi rules for industry and trade. Two items were queries about certain legal cases in Octroi payment.

The Law Committee had recommended concessions to an industrial area in Octroi incidence on Poona-Ahmednagar road so that more employment opportunities were available. An objection was raised in the meeting of the General Body, which considered the resolution, that the names of the industrial concerns located in the area be deleted to skirt the charge of partiality. The suggestion was agreed to; the resolution with the suggestion was passed. In another item, a communication was forwarded from the State Government suggesting exemption to certain industries located in a particular survey number, with recommendation. The main ground for a favourable observation by the Municipal Commissioner was the same as in the previous resolution. After some discussion the resolution was adopted by the General Body.

While one item proposed to increase the Octroi rates on consumables like tea and coffee, and to include new items, another sought to reduce it on silver. The General Body felt compunctions in adopting the first item, so it referred it back to the Law Committee which reiterated the earlier resolution. The reiterated resolution was later cleared by the General Body. The other resolution had come from the Law Committee, it had recommended the reduction in the Octroi duty on silver. The goldsmiths (in this case silversmiths, to be exact) were affected by the Gold Control Order of the Government of India, the workers in their shops were deprived of jobs. It was pleaded on behalf of the resolution that the reduction in the Octroi duty on silver would increase its sale for ornaments, which would not only lead to the rise in the income of the Corporation from the Octroi duty on silver, but also to the re-employment of the jobless workers in goldsmiths' shops. A few other members, however, differed from this plea. According to them, whether the Corporation's income was due to the reduction of the Octroi duty on silver was uncertain, so also whether workers would benefit, besides the wholesale traders in silver. The resolution was, therefore, referred back to the Law Committee which confirmed it. The General Body had, therefore, no hesitation in adopting it later.

Certain Octroi rules regarding industry and trade framed a few months earlier were ought to be cancelled by a resolution. The views of the representatives of industry and trade expressed in the Mayor's office had not been taken into consideration by the General Body before it passed the resolution now sought to be cancelled. A point was raised whether the resolution could be discussed by the General Body before the Law Committee's opinion on it was obtained. But as the General Body had adopted the earlier resolution it was competent to reconsider it. But the General Body negatived it by 24 voting against and 19 for.

A question was asked in the General Body whether the Corporation had lost in an Octroi case in which it was required as the result of the Court judgment to pay an amount of Rs. 8 lakhs and whether the

Commissioner would consult the General Body and/or the Law Committee. The Commissioner cited both precedents of the Commissioner having and not having consulted the Law Committee before filing appeal, but he averred that he had no objection to consultation with the representatives of the people in the nature of give and take. In another question on another legal case, regarding the refund of octroi, the reply given was that an appeal was filed in the Supreme Court on a resolution to that effect by the Law Committee though the Corporation's Senior Legal Adviser had advised against it, the legal expenses involved being Rs. 7,000.

(ii) Other Taxes

The Law Committee had passed a resolution recommending the abolition of the Hotel Tax for the consideration of the General Body which adopted it without any discussion. The Corporation had not levied such tax on any other profession. In another item, a proposition moved by a member wanted tax concessions to newly merged rural areas of the Corporation. This was also the policy endorsed by the State Government. On reference to the Law Committee, it prepared a schedule of tax rates to be levied on these recently merged rural areas. The General Body adopted the schedule and forwarded the resolution for the approval of the State Government, which was essential in the law.

(iii) Estimates Proposals of Expenditure

While one estimate of expenditure of Rs. 7 lakhs for stores was passed by the General Body without any queries or questioning though the amount involved was large, the two other estimates evoked some discussion before adoption. One of the latter two estimates was concerning an amount of Rs. 50,000 proposed to be expended on repairs of schools damaged by the recent Panshet floods. The State Government would assist to the extent of Rs. 16,000. A member who had been Deputy Mayor thought the estimate to be excessive, his guess was about Rs. 10,000 to Rs. 15,000. But the house was in a mood to approve of the estimate, the voting was 44-1 (of the dissenting member). The other item had asked an amount of Rs. 65,500 for setting up an Octroi *naka* (checkpost) and providing for the increase in the salaries of the employees in the department. It was alleged in the course of the discussion that the provision for the increase in the employees' salaries was proposed to accommodate an official who had resigned earlier to contest an election, but later resumed the service. The reply was that all the parties in the Corporation had agreed to the official's rejoining the service. The reply satisfied the General Body which accepted the Law Committee's resolution regarding the estimate for the Octroi department.

(iv) Grants

Varying approaches were exhibited on the issue of grants to different institutions by the General Body during the consideration of the resolutions on the matter of the LRGP Committee. While some members were reluctant to raise the amount of grant to the All-India Libraries Conference, to be held in the city, from Rs. 250 approved by the Standing Committee to Rs. 1,000 originally recommended by the LRGPC, in the case of the Deccan Agricultural Association the amount of Rs. 1,000 was adhered to. The grounds on which some members would reduce the grant to the libraries conference were, first, that the Poona University had given the needed grant of Rs. 2,500 and, secondly, the State Government had set an example of the grant of Rs. 250 before the Corporation. At long last, the pleading by some other members to stick to the amount of Rs. 1,000 because the Municipal Corporation ought to give the grant of Rs. 1,000 to an All-India Conference of a learned association, being hosted in the city, was heeded. Similarly, while the proposal of the Law Committee to pay a grant of Rs. 5,000 to an institution in the city engaged in social work was reduced by the General Body to Rs. 1,750 as the grant had to be not more than one-third of its annual income, the proposal of grant of Rs. 5,000 to the Municipal Sports Club engaged in the activity of sports of its own (Municipal) employees was sustained by the General Body.

(v) Donation

Reluctance was seen in the attitude of the G.B. to a resolution of the Law Committee accepting a donation of Rs. 300 by a person for educational purposes on the ground that the expenses on administering the donation would exceed the interest on the amount. Twice the G.B. referred the item to the Law Committee which re-affirmed the resolution on both the occasions. Finally, the G.B. deleted the item indicating its disapproval to accept the small donation.

III. Relationship with the State Government

Two pleas of the State Government to the Corporation, one to share the expenditure on beggars' homes conducted by the State Government and the other to share the expenditure on the construction of houses for the families affected by the recent Panshet floods, were accepted by the Corporation, the latter declined initially but agreed to it a little later. The expenditure on the beggars' homes of the State Government in the city was going up as the city attracted them from outside in growing numbers. To take care of the housing of the flood-affected, though morally a concern of the Corporation, it was financially not capable to do so. So, reluctantly, finally, the G.B. agreed to share the expenditure, which was as large as Rs. 45.5 lakhs on the construction of the 1,300 rooms for the flood affected families.

IV. Personnel

The stipulated 12 per cent reservation of posts for the scheduled castes had been observed by the Corporation, an answer to a question by an S.C. Corporator revealed.

Summing-up

It should be noted the majority of the items that came from the Law Committee to the General Body were adopted by it without any discussion. The discussions on those which evoked some discussion have been related above. The own jurisdiction of the Law Committee was confined to legal and constitutional matters as well as proposals for taxation, but omnibus matters like education and grants to institutions were referred to it as they did not fall within the area of any other Committee.

The response of the General Body to the Law Committee's resolutions was varying. Sometimes large amounts of expenditure were cleared without discussion while small amounts were discussed. So also was its approach to different proposals of grants. It was gratifying to find legal and constitutional matters debated in the General Body.

CITY IMPROVEMENT COMMITTEE

The draft development plan, reservations of plots and zones, de-reservations, open spaces and the like matters were the preserve of the City Improvement Committee. Certain construction activities like housing which were a part of city development, were also included in the jurisdiction of the City Improvement Committee (C.I.C.), but these could also have been placed in the area of the Public Works Committee.

Except two items, all other (13) were adopted by the General Body unanimously. Out of these 13 items, three were cleared without discussion and 10 after discussion. Only two items out of the total of 15 caused division; one was passed while the other lost. While five items were referred back by the General Body to the Committee, another emanated as a resolution moved by Corporators in the General Body itself and later on referred to the C.I.C.

(i) Draft Development Plan

During our period of study of two years, the General Body adopted resolutions twice for the extension of the time-limit for the submission of the Draft Development Plan to the State Government, first, for one year beyond the two years already granted by the State Government and, secondly, for six months more. The occurrence of the Panshet floods was one important reason adduced by the members and the officials. The close of the term of the C.I.C. and the resultant delay in the acclimatisation of the new members of the Committee to the agenda of its meetings, was another reason cited in the meetings of the G.B. Continual disfiguring of the plan by the resolutions adopted for de-reservations and change of the user was still another reason for the completion of the plan at a stretch. On both the occasions, the General Body resolved to request the State Government for the needed extensions.

(ii) Reservations, De-reservations and Change of User

Out of six items under this heading, three were concerning inclusion of more area in industrial zones in the city, one pertained de-reservation of two plots from a public user, another was about withdrawing a layout of a plot from an industrial zone and the remaining concerned the change of user. The most important plea in favour of the expansion of the industrial zones in the city by including non-industrial plots was the dire need of industrial development which would provide more employment to the jobless. A ground for the postponement of the consideration of the items was the need for considering them together while discussing the draft.

All except one item were agreed to by the General Body. The item was development plan at a later stage, not accepted by the G.B. since the Commissioner had not approved it. Another item concerned the conversion of industrial user to residential; this was brought in at the instance of a housing co-operative, which was granted after some discussion. Another item still asked for de-reservation of two plots in Shivajinagar area, one of which in *Gaothan* (the old village) was cleared by the C.I.C. and the G.B. The item regarding an open space (200′ × 80′) to be reserved for a playground was also voted by the General Body.

(iii) Cancellation of a Road-widening Scheme

The C.I.C.'s resolution to cancel a road-widening scheme was passed by the G.B. unanimously. The reason was that the recent Panshet floods had damaged several roads in the city, so the P.M.C. had to reconsider the whole roads map in the city.

(iv) Purchase of a land owned by the State Government for the Construction of houses for slum-dwellers

A proposal from the C.I.C. was before the Corporation to purchase a land owned by the State Government for the construction of houses for the slum-dwellers. The Corporation expected grants and loans from the State and the Central Governments as assistance in the project. A few Corporators were opposed to the proposal as they found the cost of the land too high, but the reply was that there was no ground for comparison as the land had been acquired by the State Government. The Mayor was among the opponents of the proposal. The resolution was referred back to the Committee which reiterated it after an on-the-spot inspection. But the General Body turned it down on the point of its exorbitant cost.

(v) Improvement of a Bus Stand and Construction of Railway Crossing

C.I.C.'s recommendations in both the matters were accepted by the General Body.

(vi) Appointment of a Junior Assistant in the Town-Planning Arbitrator's Office

An official in the State Government's Town-Planning Department was recommended for appointment to a new post of Junior Assistant by the Town-Planning Arbitrator in the Corporation. The members approved of the resolution of the C.I.C. in the matter, but advised the Commissioner to consider the Corporation's own officials for the posts in the office in future.

(vii) Donation

A donation was sought from the Corporation by a private wrestling club in the city. The C.I.C. had recommended the grant of Rs. 12,000 to the club on two conditions, viz., that the Corporation's three representatives (two Corporators and one official) be co-opted on the managing committee of the club and that prior consent of the National Wrestling Association be obtained by the club for holding the wrestling contests. Some discussion was held on the latter condition as to why such consent was necessary. But, finally the C.I.C.'s recommendation with these two conditions was adopted by the General Body.

As in the case of some other Committees, the City Improvement Committee also was keen about certain small matters, while important issues like, the draft development plan and reservations or de-reservations eluded its firm grasp and immediate attention. The draft development plan was a complex matter, even the experts entertained differing views on its aspects and details. Corporators were likely to be swayed by their own or their constituents' immediate interests neglecting the requirements and desiderata of the long-term development of the city and its environs. In the third place, since the financial resources with the Municipal Corporation were limited in comparison with the dimensions of urban development and the available physical space within the city limits had competing demands, the draft development plan and the related issues of reservation and de-reservation should have claimed keener and sustained studied attention of the Corporators (and the officials also). This necessitated systematic training and frequent orientation of the Corporators as well as the officials in the different departments.

CONCLUSION

A majority of the recommendations of the different Committees were adopted by the General Body, a few ones after discussion. Even those which had been referred back to the Committees were adopted by the General Body on reiteration by the Committees. A handful of matters within the jurisdiction of each Committee occasioned division in the House. Personal biases towards a few officials were evidenced during the discussions and, in few cases, even in the voting in the General Body. Large momentous matters escaped the keen attention of the Corporators, while small ones engaged debates.

Party affiliations did not figure prominently in the discussions or the rare votings in the Corporation. Interests of the individual Corporators varied with their personal likings, affiliations on individual basis with co-members, and/or stakes in the constituents.

In several matters, developmental, health and works, the rank and file of membership of the Corporation needed to be oriented periodically to make their participation in it more meaningful.

NOTES

1. The Standing Committee and the General Body took a progressive view on educational matters. On an item from the School Board during 1962-63 to sanction the opening of an Urdu medium school attached to an existing Marathi medium one, the resolution favouring the opening of the Urdu school was adopted by the Committee by 8-1, despite reasons advanced against it, viz. paucity of space and funds. The General Body later approved the resolution unanimously. On another educational item during the same year, this time regarding the provision of an adult education class for women in a children's school, the Committee gave favourable verdict by 7-1. The grounds pleaded against the resolution were the superfluity of the additional responsibility besides the obligatory one of primary education, shortage of funds and the exclusive coverage of women in the class. As in the item above, the General Body approved the Committee's resolution unanimously..

   The deputation of the Mayor to the World Mayors' Conference was resented by a minority (3-4) in the Committee during 1964-65. In the General Body, the replacement of an official to accompany the Mayor by the Deputy Mayor was turned down by 3-24. In the Committee the Congress party tried to block (4-4) the invitation to the Chief Minister to inaugurate an industrial school building as it was not consulted. The Chairman's casting vote saved the resolution. In the General Body, however, the Congress party was generous in extending its support to the resolution and making its unanimous passage a smooth affair (1965-66). During 1964-65, the General Body reversed a majority resolution (6-3) of the Committee on another matter of the cancellation of an earlier resolution for exchange of a land of the Corporation and that of the Swastik Company. This it did because the Commissioner averred that the legal transaction in the land had already taken place.

8

CONCLUSION

MAIN FINDINGS

Democratic-Bureaucratic Decision-making

ESSENTIALLY THE decision-making mechanism and process in the Poona Municipal Corporation as studied by us was democratic-bureaucratic. It was neither absolutely democratic nor entirely bureaucratic. The Administration, that is bureaucracy, was the custodian of the knowledge of the administrative facts, i.e. data, of the resources available to the Municipal Corporation, including financial and human, particularly by way of expertise, and of the precedents. By virtue of its command of knowledge of data and precedents it could place before the Committees and the Corporation different alternative lines of action, which were limited on account of the financial constraints. The expertise available to the Administration also suffered from limitations both due to the paucity of financial resources and constricted prospects, as, for example, in town-planning or specialised branches of engineering like cement construction. In a large majority of items of decision, the advice or opinions of the Municipal Commissioner or heads of the departments were accepted by the Committees and/or the Corporation. So, partly, the decision-making mechanism and process was bureaucratic.

In matters in respect of which the demands of the people were basic and pressing, and realisation of which required reasonable amount of financial resources, the Corporators were effective in securing approval of the Committees and the Corporation despite in some cases opposition by the officials. Such matters were water tap connections and sanitary facilities in public places. In change of the user of plots of land from industrial to residential or *vice versa*, or de-reservation of plots from user as sports ground or school location or any other public amenity, sections of the Corporators, sometimes, prevailed. In these matters the demands of the clientele were pressing and affected their individual interests and the Corporation did not lose financially, but did so in long-term ecological prospects or healthy development of the city and its surroundings. The democratic nature of the decision-making process was also evident in the reflection of the needs of the long-term development of the city and its constituents in the resolutions of the Committees — particularly the Ad-hoc and Co-ordination Committees — and of the Corporation. These resolutions did not project well-thought out, coherent policies, which was a major shortcoming of both the Corporators and the officials.

Few Corporators were found to be knowledgeable in regard to the items placed for consideration and decision before the Committees and the Corporation. This was another factor making for the inability on the part of most of the Corporators to play a significant role in the decision-making process in the Municipal Corporation. A sufficiently high level of education or a long spell of professional experience or experience as a Corporator would contribute to their knowledgeability *vis-a-vis* the subjects which came up for consideration in the Committees and the Corporation. Members did not seem to be keen to discuss matters which had policy implications or which had a large financial outlay or an administrative or political significance.

The vesting of the functions or subjects with policy significance in the State Government and financial paucity of the Municipal Corporation in relation to the long term tasks involved, in terms of the State or Municipal functions proper, were the two major difficulties in the realisation of the role of the Municipal Corporation in evolving policy goals or policies themselves. The political parties, which were expected to play a significant role in the development and articulation of policies, faulted. In terms of composition they were loosely organised, nor had they developed any infrastructure towards that objective.

Decision-making in Ad-hoc Committees

Among the different Committees of the Municipal Corporation , the Ad-hoc Committees were the best suited to deal with long-term policies. Not all the Ad-hoc Committees constituted by the Municipal Corporation dealt with long-term policies. Five of the Ad-hoc Committees were concerned with long-term changes: two of them dealt with changes in the Municipal Corporations Act and one each with secondary education, housing and miscellaneous subjects like water supply, industry and transport facilities.

Out of the two Ad-hoc Committees which dealt with changes in the provision of the Municipal Corporations Act, one expressed opinion on the recent Zakaria Committee Report of the State Government on the Act. The Committee gave vent to its dissatisfaction with the important recommendations of the Zakaria Committee Report. The Ad-hoc Committee had served its purpose, but it had no impact on the State Government's acceptance of the Zakaria Committee's recommendations and the amendment of the Act. The second Ad-hoc Committee was concerned with the Poona Municipal Transport. The Committee articulated its dismay over the inadequate competence of the Transport Manager and expected that he be from the cadre of the Indian Administrative Service to cope with the onerous responsibilities of the (Bus) Transport Undertaking which had grown significantly over years since its inception. The Committee's report was also infructuous. But, at least, these two Ad-hoc Committees had done their assigned job in relation to the matters having policy implications on some aspects of the constitution of the Municipal Corporation.

The third Ad-hoc Committee sought to tackle problems that arose out of he increase in the number of the secondary schools (including the technical school and technical classes) conducted by the Municipal Corporation and could not be sorted out in the normal course of administration. The recommendation of the Ad-hoc Committee on secondary education in favour of the institution of a fifth Special Committee on the subject in the Corporation was also not acted upon by the State Government immediately; however, it was realised in due course. So also with the proposals of the Ad-hoc Committees on housing and on municipalisation of trades, transfer of vacant government lands to the Municipal Corporation and assistance towards construction of houses by the Corporation.

The other issues that engaged the attention of the remaining Ad-hoc Committees were of short-term significance. The one on riverside residents and constructions had acquiesced in the State Government's action in the cancellation of the flood-line on the banks of the Mutha river to prevent destruction of the riverside houses and residents in the floods in future.

The Municipal Corporation should have associated more knowledgeable Corporators and even outside experts with the Ad-hoc Committees on long-range subjects to ensure weightier reports. More effective follow-up action was also called for to put into immediate action the recommendation of the Ad-hoc Committees on matters with long-range policy implications through the relevant Committees and the General Body.

Co-ordination Committee

The Co-ordination Committee in the Poona Municipal Corporation was another device which could tackle subjects of long-term policy significance. But it failed to deal with policy proposals concerning slum clearance, building regulations, house tax, and so on. These matters were looked upon as of no great consequence and so possible of being processed leisurely through different statutory Committees. The agenda of the meetings of the Co-ordination Committee was studded with items of short-term significance and of subsidiary, temporary nature.

Scarce Policy Outputs

The Standing Committee could have discussed policy matters with long-term significance, particularly in the context of the budget and other financial proposals. But, obviously, because the Standing Committee did not fulfil the expectations in this behalf, the devices of the Ad-hoc Committees and the Co-ordination Committee were employed by the Municipal Corporation.

The offices of the Municipal Commissioner and the finance branch should have policy sections marshalling data and thinking in the different departments in the Municipal Corporation. Obviously the Municipal Commissioner, being the administrative head of the Municipal Corporation, is expected to play a pivotal role in evolving long-term policies regarding Municipal functions in general and city development scenario in particular.

The development plan of the city did not engage adequate attention of the Corporators through the Committees (particularly the City Improvement Committee) and the General Body. A majority of them lacked adequate knowledge of the development plan and its components. The keenest discussions held in the City Improvement Committee and the General Body were regarding changes in the user of plots of land and of the zones and de-reservation of plots reserved for public amenities in the development plan. Proper and adequate orientation with the help of the State Town-Planning Department and experts — both academics and practitioners — outside the Corporation and the State Department should be imparted to the Corporators and the concerned Municipal officials.

The Ad-hoc Committees were particularly useful in suggesting solutions to short-term issues both relating to the formulation and execution of decisions. The Co-ordination Committee facilitated the formal decision-making in the statutory Committees and the General Body. This evoked a criticism that the Co-ordination Committee pre-empted the competence of the statutory Committees in regard to decision-making. This criticism had some substance in it; however, the informal nature of discussions in the Co-ordination Committee particularly helped the speeding up of formal decision-making in regard to the formulation as well as implementation of the decisions on large development projects like a stadium, a drama theatre, etc. All and sundry matters of subsidiary and temporary nature should not have been put in the basket of the Co-ordination Committee, which distracted the attention of the Committee from policy and weighty issues and matters. The Ad-hoc Committees took an inordinately long time in deliberating over and submitting reports on important issues, and the follow-up of their recommendations was also arduous and time-consuming.

The Co-ordination Committee more or less endorsed the stand taken by the Administration on several issues that came up for its consideration. The Ad-hoc Committees, however, though helped in its discussions by the briefing by the Administration, ventilated their own views on the matters before them and could include some of these in their reports.

Standing Committee

The Standing Committee was the most pivotal Committee in the decision-making process in the Poona Municipal Corporation, particularly in financial (including budget making) and personnel matters. Its decisions were guided, except in very few matters, by the notings in the official dockets on these. Here also the decision-making was democratic-bureaucratic in essence; the Municipal Commissioner, the head of the administration of the Municipal Corporation, wielded considerable influence. The paucity of knowledge on the issues placed before the Committee for discussion on the part of a majority of the members of the Standing Committee was the prime obstacle in thorough discussions on these, particularly on their policy implications. The annual budget evoked discussion on items of small expenditure while those with large outlay escaped the attention of the members of the Standing Committee. Apart from the paucity of knowledge on most of the important issues of the majority of the members, the multi-political-party affiliation of the members and the changing personnel of the Committee every year accounted for *ad-hocism* in decisions on policy matters taken by the Standing Committee.

Experts, particularly on the financial and personnel aspects, need to be co-opted in the Standing Committee to make the decision-making in it based on substantial discussion.

Transport Committee

Transport Committee was still more bureaucratic in substance; only in some personnel matters some of its members expressed their opinions different from the views of the Transport Manager, but in a few others pressed them to the point of adoption by the Committee. Paucity of knowledge of the items before the Committee on the part of most of its members, even of the facts mentioned in the official dockets, was the prime reason for the dilution of the democratic element in the decision-making process in the Transport Committee. The aggressive character of the Transport Manager, in contrast with the suave disposition of the Municipal Commissioner *vis-a-vis* the Standing Committee, was also another factor underlying the predominantly bureaucratic nature of the decision-making in the Transport Committee.

This would also bring in the structural aspect of the Transport Committee *vis-a-vis* the Standing Committee and of the status of the Transport Manager in relation to the Municipal Commissioner. Though the Transport Manager should be autonomous in the internal operations of the Transport Undertaking, he should be organisationally accountable to the Municipal Commissioner. The virtual independence of the position of the Transport Manager of a commercial (albeit public) undertaking, coupled with the not so attractive remuneration of the post, has accounted for the suspect nature of his financial dealings in the Undertaking.

Special Committees

In respect of the Special Committees also, our finding regarding the Standing and the Transport Committees, that the nature of the decision-making was democratic-bureaucratic, was confirmed. The principal reason again was the same, viz., a majority of their members lacked adequate knowledge of the subjects that came up for discussion in the Committees. The officials, on the other hand, were the custodians of the factual information as well as of the knowledge of the financial resources available and the alternatives possible in each case. In the case of some members they even did not care to read the official information cited in the dockets of the items, leave apart eliciting more or supplementary information from the office.

Members not getting any extra allowance to attend the meetings of the Special Committees was another disincentive in regard to the attendance at these. The timings of their meetings were, therefore, preceding the General Body meetings, which did not leave an adequate length of duration for substantial discussions in these.

The matters which interested the Committees' members were constituency-oriented and welfare-oriented ones. The items on appointment, promotion, disciplinary proceedings, deputation, etc. of the officials also engaged the attention of the members, sometimes evoking their personal likes or dislikes towards them.

Setting of water taps or additional outlets in public places, new roads or re-alignment of the proposed roads were pet items proposed and discussed in the Public Works Committee. Creation of sanitary facilities, setting up of new dispensaries and lowering the fees charged on the patients in the Municipal dispensaries, hospitals and diagnostic centres were the items which evoked the interest of the members in the Medical Relief and Public Health Committee. In the City Improvement Committee, changes in the user of plots of land and de-reservation of lands reserved for public amenities attracted the attention of its members. In the Law, Revenue and General Purposes Committee, exemptions from the assessment and payment of taxes, particularly Octroi, were argued persuasively by the interested members. The arguments against such constituency-oriented or welfare-oriented proposals were in some cases contested by officials, but the mutual support of the members overcame the official opposition.

Reluctance in general among the majority of the members of the Special Committees to the innovative proposals by a few of their colleagues was observed. They, therefore, willingly sided with the officials who generally opposed such innovative proposals of select members. This again proved the preponderantly bureaucratic nature of the decision-making in the Poona Municipal Corporation.

Prominent Members in Decision-making Process

The Chairmen of the Standing and the Transport Committees, the two Committees armed with executive powers to an extent, had a responsible role to play. The Chairman of the Standing Committee fulfilled this role to an extent, while the Chairman of the Transport Committee could not rise up to it. The chairmen of the Medical Relief and Public Health and the City Improvement Committees met the expectations to a certain extent. In the Transport Committee a rare spectacle was observed of the Chairman being opposed by the members who supported the stand of the Transport Manager against which the Chairman pleaded seeking to press the cause of the employees in the Municipal Bus Undertaking.

In each of the six Committees observed by us, two to three members participated effectively in their proceedings. These were the lawyer, engineer, medico, trader, businessman and political worker members of the Committees. One wished their example was emulated by the other members who were in majority.

'Repre-legates'

In the concluding section in the Chapter on the Decision-Making in the Committees we have used a new term 'Repre-legates' for the Corporators-in-Committees-and-Corporation. The Corporators acted better as the representatives of their constituents than as their delegates, because they were more keen to reflect the short-term interests of their constituents than their long-term interests or the public good of the city. The majority of the Corporators could not fulfil the function as delegates because they were not equipped for it in terms of the factual and conceptual knowledge about the subjects that came up for decision in the Committees and the Corporation.

Overlaps

Function-wise the four Special Committees had overlapping

jurisdictions. Mutual understanding and goodwill helped them to tide over the mistakes of omission and commission arising out of these overlaps. Some items were referred to the Standing Committee without the consultation of the concerned Special Committee. Among the six Committees the Standing and the Transport Committees were looked upon as prize Committees by the Corporators due to their having some executive authority.

The Co-ordination Committee could have played informally an effective mediating role to sort out the question of overlapping areas between the different Special Committees, but it did not.

Predominantly Bureaucratic Nature of Decision-making

The Corporation shared with the Committees the democratic-bureaucratic nature of the decision-making process which was predominantly bureaucratic in substance. In the decision-making process regarding a large majority of the items the Corporation played a role secondary to that of the Committees. Only in respect of a marginal number of items did the Corporation reverse the decisions of the Committees. This was of course the underlying intent of the structural pattern adopted in the Municipal Corporations Act of the State Government. But even in those items in which the decisions of the Committees were biased or improper from the point of view of the long-term public good, the Corporation did not rectify. A genuine desire to adhere to the decisions of the Committees, or reluctance to face a body much larger than the Committee which had taken the earlier decision and which would not heed the dissenting view of a member or a group of members, might be the reason for this reluctance.

The Corporation's Unique Role in Decision-making

In three respects, however, the Corporation performed a unique role, distinguished from the role of the Committees. The Corporation discussed matters where it had flawed, as, for example, in respect of the neglect of the eastern parts of the city or newly incorporated suburbs or the growth of slums. As a result of these discussions Ad-hoc Committees were set up by it to examine these matters and to suggest remedial actions. The reports of the Ad-hoc Committees were again discussed by the Corporation, albeit not as avidly as the original issues that led to the constitution of the Ad-hoc Committees. Secondly, the members asked various questions on facts or on administrative deficiencies or on the happenings or decisions in the Committees. The questions ventilated the grievances or doubts in the minds of the Corporators and so cleared the atmosphere for a better administration. In the third place, the adjournment motions were moved by members. Most of the adjournment motions were, however, on extraneous or frivolous issues and these wasted the precious time spent by the Corporators in attending the infructuous meetings of the Corporation. For example, during the year 1966-67, out of 107 adjourned Corporation meetings (out of the total of 127 meetings called), 64 were adjourned on grounds not connected with the Municipal Corporation or in substantial ones. Only a few of the adjourned meetings were concerned with genuine causes, like, expression of condolences on the death of ex-Corporators or the articulation of sympathy for the employees who did not receive dearness allowance on par with the State Government employees.

SHORTCOMINGS IN THE DECISION-MAKING MECHANISM

The pattern of decision-making mechanism in the Poona Municipal Corporation studied in this project suffered in the main from three shortcomings:

(a) Slow pace of decision-making in the Municipal Corporation taken as a whole mechanism;
(b) low quality of decisions barring a few decisions; and
(c) absence of effective and durable instruments for co-ordination and coherence, both in the short-term and intermediate-term administrative measures and aspects of actions.

(a) **Slow Pace of Decision-making**

The existing structures of decision-making mechanism and process were not conductive to a pace in keeping with the urgency, required to tackle and solve the problems and issues in the city's growing and complex administration and development, like, road-widening, slum improvement, proper zoning of lands, to name a few sectors. The Municipal administration no doubt was a unified structure headed by the Municipal Commissioner leading the heads of departments, like, engineering, medicine and health, tax assessment and collection, accounts and audit. City and urban development planning and its follow-up was a significant lacuna in the present structure of Municipal administration.

Municipal Bus Undertaking administration was an autonomous enterprise, but financially it was dependent on the Municipal Corporation for its initial invested and supplementary recurring capital, borrowing power and appointment of superior personnel. The Municipal Bus Undertaking was a State within a State subject to the overall oversight and sustenance by the Municipal Corporation. This structural feature also contributed to the slow pace of administration, which depended upon the approval of the Standing Committee and the Corporation. The way out is not the complete isolation of the Municipal Bus Transport Undertaking from the body of the Municipal Corporation but the appointment of a high level administrator, say, in the cadre of the Indian Administrative Office or in bus transport management and administration. The present low level of administrative or managerial expertise of the Transport Manager is the principal reason for the absence of efficiency in the administration of the Poona Municipal (Bus) Transport (P.M.T.).

The structure of decision-making in the four Special Committees, the Standing and the Transport Committees, and the Corporation (General Body) also made for delay in the pace of decision-making. In the items in the annual budget, because they were time-bound, expeditious decision-making was observed. But the urgency of expeditiousness in decision-making in budgetary items did affect the quality of decisions except those which had been considered over a long time as parts of projects and proposals undergoing gestation over a long period. The plea here is not for the abolition of the scheme of the Committee system altogether, but for either empowering the Standing Committee with expediting decisions or making the Co-ordination Committee statutory and putting teeth in it so as to turn it into an expediting mechanism.

(b) **Quality of Decision-Making Not Satisfactory**

The absence of knowledgeability among most of the Corporators and the lack of a modicum of expertise among the majority of the administrative officials accounted for the low quality of the decisions on most of the significant matters arrived at by the Committees and the

Corporation. The absence of knowledgeability among most of the Corporators had made for the predominantly bureaucratic complexion of the seemingly democratic-bureaucratic nature of the decision-making in the Poona Municipal Corporation. The lack of expertise among the majority of the administrative officials was responsible for the insubstantial quality of the notings in the dockets accompanying the items prepared for the perusal of the members. The absence of high level experts in the administration by way of education or training in subjects, like, engineering, health and medicine, urban development and planning, including town-planning, etc., was also another reason for the inferior quality of decisions in the democratic structures laid down by the Municipal Corporations Act.

Apart from the induction of expertise at the middle-level and high-level rungs of the administration in the various departments of the Municipal Corporation, continual, periodic training of the officials, through refresher and orientation courses in workshops at the Corporation and courses in specialised institutions outside, is very essential. The inefficiency of the majority of the Municipal employees was due both to the lack of expertise and the absence of congenial attitudes. Periodic training is as much necessary as a measure of discipline as to motivate the officials to tone up the quality of their fibre and work.

(c) Absence of Coherence

The annual or biennial elections of the Mayor, Deputy Mayor, Chairmen of the Committees and their members, among other factors, led to the absence of coherence in the considerable number of decisions taken by these bodies. We have noted in the Introductory Chapter the reasons for the near absence of long-term policies figuring in the thinking of the Municipal Corporation. The Administration headed by the Municipal Commissioner had to shoulder the major responsibility for projecting the short-term and intermediate term policies in the piecemeal items for decision-making placed by it before the different Committees and/or the Corporation. The short-term triennial deputation of an I.A.S. Officer from the State administration as Municipal Commissioner affected this process. A longer term of appointment of the Municipal Commissioner is desirable from this point of view.

A cell should be constituted in the Municipal Commissioner's office for framing of long-term and intermediate-term policies and breaking these up into the short-term policies and the latter into pieces of items of decisions on the part of the Committees and the Corporation. An Assistant Municipal Commissioner should be placed in charge of this Cell so that the process of its work is conducted continuously at a high level of efficiency. The processing and follow-up of the reports of the Ad-hoc Committees would be a function of this Cell.

Political Parties did not Perform Their Role in regard to Coherence

The political parties were expected to bring about coherence and co-ordination among the policies and the decisions, on the one hand, and among the various decisional items, on the other. But our observation has been that even members of a single political party, among the different political parties, did not share the same or common views on various decisional items, leave alone the unanimity among the different political parties. Whatever pronouncements were made by the political parties on the eve of the general elections to the Municipal Corporation did not seem to guide the lines of action, if any, adopted by them or their members in the Corporation and the Committees. The political parties were represented in the Co-ordination Committee by their leaders. But the discussions or informal decisions in the Co-ordination Committee did not lead to coherence in terms of the evolution of concerted long-term or even intermediate-term policies.

From the point of view of all the three aspects discussed above, namely, (a) the slow pace of decision-making, (b) low quality of decisions, and (c) absence of effective and durable instruments for co-ordination and coherence both in the short-term and intermediate-term administrative measures and aspects of actions, the existing decision-making mechanism and process was found wanting.

The Simonian model of Satisficing Decision-Making would be applicable to the decisions studied in this project. The factors in decision-making here were numerous, some of them being external to the Municipal organisation like the State Government's policies *vis-a-vis* the municipal government. Quantitative evaluation of the decisions was possible to an extent; qualitative assessment, howsoever inadequate, had, therefore, to be resorted to in our study.

The separation of the deliberative and executive wings of

Municipal Corporation administration was conceived and actualised by the closing decades of the last century. Today, as brought out in the above analysis, neither the administrative structures nor the elective ones, devised a century ago, can cope up with the challenges of the growing populations and the consequent complexity of the problems of the cities. In the Introductory Chapter, we have briefly delineated the gravity of the urban situation today and could scan it in the specific context of the Poona City and its decision-making mechanism and process.

ALTERNATIVES SUGGESTED

The alternative decision-making structures which could be thought out are:

(i) the present Corporators to elect a Mayor-in-Council with executive authority;
(ii) the Mayor being helped by three or four executive councillors elected by the Municipal Corporation;
(iii) the Mayor being elected directly and vested with executive authority;
(iv) the directly elected Mayor being assisted by a City Manager appointed co-terminous with the elective term of the Mayor.

The Calcutta Municipal Corporation has recently adopted the system of Mayor-Council equipped with the executive authority. It is a break-away from the long-established pattern in which separation of executive wing from deliberative wing was enshrined. It is a long-awaited innovation in the urban government in the country. The main objection to the different variants of the elected executives including the Mayor-Council and the directly elected Mayor is that they would politicise the administration. The objection misses the existing reality of a politicised administration without the dynamic drive of the elected executive. Moreover, the elected executive does not mean administrative personnel being recruited without the merit principle being followed. The usual safeguards for the tenure security and merit would be adhered to in the elected executive system also. In the rural local governments in the country the elected executives are coupled with merited bureaucracy with the usual safeguards for the security of tenure.

In another alternative, the Mayor would be elected directly with the ward-wise election of the Corporators. In Madhya Pradesh the presidents of the municipalities are elected directly; in Maharashtra also for a term of five years direct election of the Municipal presidents was in vogue. The direct election of the Municipal Corporation Mayor would arm the Mayor with a direct popular mandate and also enliven the citizens with consciousness of their needs and of the possibilities of their realisation. This would establish a direct link between the elected executive and the people and introduce an element of dynamism in the elected executive's administration which so far has been static.

The directly elected Mayor could select his executive council from the Corporators. This would facilitate his administration of the Municipal functions. On the other hand, this might create rivalries and possibly chasms in the executive administration.

Regarding the administrative services, the existing headship of an I.A.S. officer from the State administration could continue. Or the directly elected Mayor could be assisted by a City Manager inducted for a term of five years co-extensive with the term of election of the Mayor. The same person could continue as City Manager with the re-election of the same person as Mayor or even with a new person as Mayor. A dynamic expert administrator with proven capacity would translate the proposals and plans of the directly elected Mayor into reality.

These alternatives would remedy the shortcomings of the existing decision mechanism and process analysed above, viz., delay in decision-making, low quality of decisions, and absence of coherence and co-ordination. The existing Committee system may continue, but the directly elected Mayor assisted by an efficient administrator would activise the Committee system and obviate the delays in decision-making. Correspondence between the Mayor's plans and proposals with the Corporation's views is necessary to ensure a large democratic consensus within the Municipal set-up.

To ensure a reasonable quality of decisions in terms of expertise, high level experts in different functions, like engineering, urban planning and development, health and medicine, have to be inducted at lateral levels along with the departmental heads.

The structural innovations have to be accompanied by proper changes in attitudes, motivation and orientation of the elected elements, administrative personnel and the people. Without people's co-operation the best of the plans would be frustrated, hence it is a must in any governmental reform.

EXTRACTS FROM THE BOMBAY PROVINCIAL MUNICIPAL CORPORATIONS ACT, 1949

CHAPTER VI

DUTIES AND POWERS OF THE MUNICIPAL AUTHORITIES AND OFFICERS

Obligatory and Discretionary Duties of the Corporation

63. IT SHALL be incumbent on the Corporation to make reasonable and adequate provision, by any means or measures which it is lawfully competent to it to use or to take, for each of the following matters, namely:

(1) erection of substantial boundary marks of such description and in such positions as shall be approved by the State Government defining the limits or any alteration in the limits of the City;

(2) the watering, scavenging and cleansing of all public streets and places in the City and the removal of all sweepings therefrom;

(3) the collection, removal, treatment and disposal of sewage, offensive matter and rubbish and, if so required by the (State) Government, the preparation of compost manure from such sewage, offensive matter and rubbish;

(4) the construction, maintenance and cleansing of drains and drainage works, and of public latrines, water-closets, urinals and similar conveniences;

(5) the entertainment of a fire-brigade equipped with suitable appliances for the extinction of fires and the protection of life and property against fire;

(6) the construction or acquisition and maintenance of public hospitals and dispensaries including hospitals for the isolation and treatment of persons suffering or suspected to be infected

with a contagious or infectious disease and carrying out other measures necessary for public medical relief;

(7) the lighting of public streets, municipal markets and public buildings vested in the Corporation;

(8) the maintenance of a municipal office and of all public monuments and open spaces and other property vesting in the Corporation;

(9) the naming or numbering of streets and of public places vesting in the Corporation and the numbering of premises;

(10) the regulation and abatement of offensive and dangerous trades or practices;

(11) the maintenance, change and regulation of places for the disposal of the dead and the provision of new places for the said purpose and disposing of unclaimed dead bodies;

(12) the construction or acquisition and maintenance of public markets and slaughter-houses and the regulation of all markets and slaughter-houses;

(13) the construction or acquisition and maintenance of cattle ponds;

(14) public vaccination in accordance with the provisions of the Bombay District Vaccination Act, 1892;

(15) maintaining, aiding and suitably accommodating schools for primary education;

(16) the reclamation of unhealthy localities, the removal of noxious vegetation and generally the abatement of all nuisances;

(17) the registration of births and deaths;

(18) the construction, maintenance, alteration and improvement of public streets, bridges, sub-ways, culverts, cause-ways and the like;

(19) the removal of obstructions and projections in or upon streets, bridges and other public places;

(20) the management and maintenance of all municipal water works and the construction or acquisition of new works necessary for a sufficient supply of water for public and private purposes;

(21) preventing and checking the spread of dangerous diseases;

(22) the securing or removal of dangerous buildings and places;

(23) the construction and maintenance of residential quarters for the municipal conservancy staff;

(24) fulfilment of any obligation imposed by or under this Act or any other law for the time being in force;

(25) subject to adequate provision being made for the matters specified above, the provision of relief to destitute persons in the City in times of famine and scarcity and the establishment and maintenance of relief works in such times.

64. The Corporation shall make payments at such rates and subject to such conditions as the State Government from time to time by general or special order prescribes for the maintenance and treatment in any institution which the State Government declares by notification in the Official Gazette to be suitable for the purpose either within or without the City and for other necessary expenses or persons undergoing anti-rabic treatment as indigent persons according to the rules applicable to such institutions:

Provided that the Corporation shall not be liable under this section for the maintenance, treatment and other expenses of any person undergoing anti-rabic treatment as an indigent person in any such institution as aforesaid, unless such person immediately previous to his admission thereto has been resident in the City for at least one year and has proceeded to such institution from the City.

65. (1) The Corporation shall make payments at such rates for each person as the State Government from time to time by general or special order prescribes for the maintenance and treatment at any asylum, hospital or house, within or without the City, which the State Government declares by notification in the Official Gazette to be suitable for the purpose of pauper lunatics, not being persons for whose confinement an order under Chapter XXXIV of the Code of Criminal Procedure, 1898, is in force and of lepers resident within, or under any enactment for the time-being in force removed from the City:

Provided that the Corporation shall not be liable under this section for the maintenance and treatment of any lunatic or leper in any such asylum, hospital or house as aforesaid, unless such lunatic or leper immediately previous to his admission thereto has been resident in the City for at least one year:

Provided further that the rates prescribed by the State Government under this section shall not exceed half the total cost of maintenance and treatment incurred for each person on account of the lunatics for whose maintenance and treatment the Corporation shall be liable under the section:

Provided also that where an application is made to the Court under section 88 of the Indian Lunacy Act, 1912, no order for the payment of the cost of maintenance of the lunatic by the Corporation shall be made without any opportunity being given to the Corporation to show that the lunatic is not pauper and has an estate applicable to his maintenance or that there is a person legally bound and having the means to maintain him.

(2) The Officer incharge of the asylum, hospital or house to which lunatics or lepers for whose maintenance and treatment the Corporation is liable under this section are admitted shall maintain a clear account of the cost of maintenance and treatment incurred on account of such persons detained in the asylum, hospital or house and shall furnish a copy thereof to the Corporation.

66. The Corporation may, in its discretion, provide from time to time, either wholly or partly, for all or any of the following matters, namely:

(1) The organisation maintenance or management of institutions within or without the City for the care of persons who are infirm, sick or incurable, or for the care and training of blind, deaf, mute or otherwise disabled persons or of handicapped children;

(2) the organisation, maintenance or management of maternity and infant welfare homes or centres;

(3) the provision of milk to expectant or nursing mothers of infants or school children;

(4) the organisation, maintenance or management of chemical or bacteriological laboratories for the examination or analysis of water, food or drugs, for the detection of diseases or for researches connected with public health;

(5) swimming pools, public wash houses, bathing places and other institutions designed for the improvement of public health;

(6) dairies or farms within or without the City for the supply, distribution and processing of milk or milk products for the benefit of the residents of the city;

(7) the construction and maintenance in public streets or places of drinking fountains for human beings and water-troughs for animals;

(8) the planting and maintenance of trees on road sides and elsewhere;

(9) the provision of music for the people;
(10) the provision of public parks, gardens, playgrounds and recreation grounds;
(11) the holding of exhibitions, athletics or games;
(12) the regulation of lodging houses, camping grounds and rest houses in the city;
(13) the maintenance of an ambulance service;
(14) the construction, establishment and maintenance of theatres, rest houses and other public buildings;
(15) the organisation or maintenance, in times of scarcity, of shops or stalls for the sale of necessities of life;
(16) the building or purchase and maintenance of dwellings for municipal officers and servants;
(17) the grant of loans for building purposes to municipal servants drawing a monthly salary of not more than four hundred rupees on such terms and subject to such conditions as may be prescribed by the Corporation;
(18) any other measures for the welfare of municipal servants or any class of them;
(19) the purchase of any undertaking for the supply of electric energy or gas or the starting or subsidising of any such undertaking which may be in the general interests of the public;
(20) the construction purchase, organisation, maintenance or management of light railways, tramways, trackless trams, or motor transport facilities for the conveyance of the public or goods within or without the City;
(21) the furtherance of educational objects other that those mentioned in clause (15) of section 63 and making grants to educational institutions within or without the City;
(22) the establishment and maintenance or the aiding of libraries, museums and art galleries, botanical or zoological collections and the purchase or construction of buildings therefor;
(23) the construction or maintenance of infirmaries or hospitals for animals;
(24) the destruction of birds or animals causing a nuisance, or of vermin, and the confinement or destruction of stray or ownerless dogs;
(25) contributions towards any public fund raised for the relief of human suffering within the City or for the public welfare;
(26) the preparation or presentation of addresses to persons of

distinction;

(27) the registration of marriages;

(28) the granting of rewards for information which may tend to secure the correct registration of vital statistics;

(29) paying the salaries and allowances, rent and other charges incidental to the maintenance of the Court of any stipendiary magistrate or any portion of such charges;

(30) the acquisition and maintenance of grazing grounds and the establishment and maintenance of a breeding stud;

(31) establishing and maintaining a farm or factory for the disposal of sewage;

(32) supplying, constructing and maintaining, in accordance with the general system approved by the Corporation, receptacles, fittings, pipes and other appliances whatsoever on or for the use of premises for receiving and conducting the sewage thereof into drains under the control of the Corporation;

(33) granting rewards for information regarding the infringement of any provisions of this Act, or of the rules, bye-laws, regulations or standing orders;

(34) laying out, whether in areas previously built upon or not, new public streets and acquiring land for that purpose and land required for the construction of buildings or curtilages thereof to abut on such street or streets;

(35) the building or purchase and maintenance of suitable dwellings for the poor and working classes, or the grant of loans or other facilities to any person, society or institution interested in the provision of such dwellings;

(36) the provision of shelter to destitute or homeless persons and any form of poor relief;

(37) the building or purchase and maintenance of sanitary stables or byres for horses, ponies or cattle used in hackney carriages or carts or for milch-kine;

(38) surveys of buildings or lands;

(39) measures to meet any calamity affecting the public in the City;

(40) making contributions to the funds of the Local Self-Government Institute, Bombay;

(41) with the previous sanction of the State Government, the making of a contribution towards any public ceremony or entertainment in the City;

(42) any measure, not hereinbefore specifically named, likely to promote public safely, health, convenience or instruction.

CHAPTER XI

MUNICIPAL TAXATION

127.(1) For the purposes of this Act, the Corporation shall impose the following taxes, namely:-

(a) property taxes;
(b) a tax on vehicles, boats and animals,

(2) In addition to the taxes specified in sub-section (1) the Corporation may for the purposes of this Act and subject to the provisions thereof impose any of the following taxes, namely:

(a) octroi;
(b) a profession tax, subject to the provisions of (article 276) of the (Constitution);
(c) a tax on dogs;
(d) a theatre tax;
(e) a toll on animals and vehicles entering the city;
(f) any other tax which the State Legislature has power under the Constitution to impose in the State.

(2A) Notwithstanding anything contained in sub-section (1) or sub-section (2), no tax or toll shall be levied on motor vehicles save as provided in section 20 of the Bombay Motor Vehicles Tax Act, 1958.

(3) The municipal taxes shall be assessed and levied in accordance with the provisions of this Act and the rules.

(4) Nothing in this section shall authorise the imposition of any tax which the State Legislature has no power to impose in the State under the Constitution.

128. A municipal tax may be recovered by the following processes in the manner prescribed by rules:

(1) by presenting a bill,
(2) by serving a written notice of demand,
(3) by distraint and sale of a defaulter's moveable property,

(4) by the attachment and sale of a defaulter's immoveable property,
(5) in the case of octroi and toll, by the seizure and sale of goods and vehicles,
(6) in the case of property tax, by the attachment of rent due in respect of the property,
(7) by a suit.

Property Taxes

Property-Taxes leviable

129. For the purposes of sub-section (1) of section 127 property taxes shall comprise the following taxes which shall, subject to exceptions, limitations and conditions hereinafter provided, be levied on buildings and lands in the city:

(a) a water tax at such percentage of their rateable value as the Corporation shall deem reasonable, for providing a water supply for the city;
(b) a conservancy tax at such percentage of their rateable value as will in the opinion of the Corporation suffice to provide for the collection, removal and disposal, by municipal agency, of all excrementitious and polluted matter from provies, urinals and cess-pools and for efficiently maintaining and repairing the municipal drains constructed or used for reception or conveyance of such matter, subject however to the proviso that the minimum amount of such tax to be levied in respect of any one separate holding of land or of any one building or of any one portion of a building which is let as a separate holding shall be eight *annas* per mensem and that the amount of such tax to be levied in respect of any hotel, club or other large premises may be specially fixed under section 137;
(c) a general tax of not less than 12 per cent of their rateable value, which may be levied, if the Corporation so determines, on a graduated scale:

Provided that the Corporation may, when fixing under section 99 or section 150 the rate at which general tax shall be levied for any official year or part of an official year, determine that the rate leviable in respect of buildings and lands or portions or buildings and lands in which any particular class of trade or business is carried on shall be higher than the rate fixed in respect of other buildings and lands or portions of buildings and lands by an amount not exceeding one-half of the rate so fixed.

Explanation: Where any portion of a building or land is liable to a higher rate of the general tax such portion shall be deemed to be separate property for the purpose of municipal taxation.

130. (1) Subject to the provisions of section 134, the water tax shall be levied only in respect of premises:

(a) to which private water supply is furnished from, or which are connected by means of communication pipes with, any municipal water works; or
(b) which are situated in a portion of the city in which the Commissioner has given public notice that the Corporation has arranged to supply water from municipal water works by means of private water connections or of public stand-posts, fountains or by any other means.

131. (1) The conservancy tax shall be levied only in respect of premises–

(a) situated in any portion of the City in which public notice has been given by the Commissioner that the collection, removal and disposal of all excrementitious and polluted matter from privies, urinals and cess-pools will be undertaken by municipal agency; or
(b) in which, wherever situated, there is a privy, water-closet, cess-pool, urinal, bathing place or cooking place connected by a drain with a municipal drain:

Provided that the said tax shall not be levied in respect of any premises situated in any portion of the City specified in clause (a), in or upon which, in the opinion of the Commissioner, no such matter as aforesaid accumulates or is deposited.

(2) Premises in respect of which the Commissioner has directed that a separate water-closet, privy or urinal need not be provided shall

be deemed to be liable to the levy of conservancy tax if, but for such direction, the tax would be leviable in respect thereof.

132. (1) The general tax shall be levied in respect of all buildings and lands in the City except–

(a) buildings and lands solely used for purposes connected with the disposal of the dead;
(b) building and lands or portions thereof solely occupied and used for public worship or for a public charitable purpose;
(c) buildings and lands vesting in the Government used solely for public purposes and not used or intended to be used for purposes of trade or profit or vesting in the Corporation, in respect of which the said tax, if levied, would under the provisions hereinafter contained by primarily leviable form the Government or the Corporation, respectively.

(2) The following buildings and lands or portions thereof shall not be deemed to be solely occupied and used for public worship or for a public charitable purpose within the meaning of clause (b) of sub-section (1), namely:

(a) buildings or lands or portions thereof in which any trade or business is carried on; and
(b) buildings or lands or portions thereof in respect of which rent is derived, whether such rent is or is not applied solely to religious or charitable purposes.

(3) Where any portion of any building or land is exempt form the general tax by reason of its being solely occupied and used for public worship or for a public charitable purpose, such portion shall be deemed to be a separate property for the purpose of municipal taxation.

133. (1) The State Government shall pay to the Corporation annually in two half-yearly instalments payable by the 30th day of September and the 31st day of March in every year in lieu of the general tax from which buildings and lands vesting in the State Government are exempted by clause (c) of sub-section (1) of section 132, a sum ascertained in the manner provided in sub-sections (2) and (3).

(2) The rateable values of the buildings and lands in the City

vesting in the (Government) and beneficially occupied, in respect of which, but for the said exemption, general tax would be leviable from the State Government shall be fixed by a person from time to time appointed in this behalf by the State Government with the concurrence of the Corporation. The said value shall be fixed by the said person with a general regard to the provisions contained in this Act and the rules concerning the valuation of property assessable to property taxes, at such amount as he shall deem to be fair and reasonable. The decision of the person so appointed shall hold good for a term of five years, subject only to proportionate variation, if in the meantime the number of extent of the buildings and lands (in the City vesting in the State Government) materially increases or decreases.

(3) The sum to be paid annually to the Corporation by the (State) Government shall be eight-tenths of the amount which would be payable by an ordinary owner of buildings or lands in the City, on account of the general tax, on a rateable value of the same amount as that fixed under sub-section (2).

Special Provisions Relating to Water and Conservancy Taxes

134. (1) The Commissioner may–

(a) in such cases as the Standing Committee shall generally approve, instead of levying the water tax in respect of any premises liable thereto, charge for the water supplied to such premises by measurement at such rate as shall from time to time be prescribed by the said Committee in this behalf or by the size of the water connection with the municipal main and the purpose for which the water is supplied at such rates as shall from time to time be prescribed by the Corporation,

(b) in such cases as the Standing Committee shall generally approve, compound with any person for the supply of water to any premises for a renewable term of one or more years not exceeding five, on payment of a fixed periodical sum in lieu of the water tax or charge by measurement or by the size of the water connection which would otherwise be leviable from such person in respect of the said premises.

(2) The Standing Committee may, for the cases in which the

Commissioner charges for water by measurement or by the size of the water connection under clause (a) of sub-section (1), from time to time prescribe such conditions as it shall think fit as to the use of the water and as to the charge to be paid for water consumed whilst a meter is out of order or under repair; and for the cases in which a composition is made under clause (b) of the said sub-section the said Committee may prescribe such conditions as to the use of the water as it shall think fit:

Provided that no condition prescribed under this sub-section shall be inconsistent with this Act or rules or bye-laws.

(3) A person who is charged for water by measurement or by the size of the water connection or who has compounded for a fixed periodical sum shall not be liable for payment of the water-tax, but any sum payable by him on account of water shall, if not paid when it becomes due, be recoverable by the Commissioner as if it were an arrear of water-tax.

135. If, in respect of premises used solely for public purposes and not used or intended to be used for purposes or profit or for residential, charitable or religious purposes, water tax would be leviable under this Act from the (Government), the Commissioner, in lieu of levying such tax, shall charge for the water supplied to such premises, by measurement, at such rate as shall be prescribed by the Standing Committee in this behalf not exceeding the minimum rate at the time being charged under clause (a) of sub-section (1) of section 134 to any other person; and such charge shall be recoverable as provided in sub-section (3) of the said section.

136. No tax or charge of any kind shall be levied or demanded for the use of water in or from any drinking fountain, tank, reservoir, cistern, pump, well, duct, stand-pipe or other work used for the gratuitous supply of water to the inhabitants of the City and vesting in the Corporation:

Provided that the water in or from any such work shall be used only for personal or domestic purposes and not for the purpose of business or sale.

137.(1) The Commissioner may, whenever he thinks fit, fix the conservancy tax to be paid in respect of any hotel, club, stable or other large premises at such special rate as shall be generally approved by the Standing Committee in this behalf, whether the service in respect of which such tax is leviable be performed by human labour or by substituted means or appliances.

(2) In the case of premises used solely for public purposes and not used or intended to be used for purposes of profit or for residential or charitable or religious purposes in respect of which the conservancy tax is payable by the Government the Commissioner shall fix the said tax at a special rate approved as aforesaid.

(3) In any such case the amount of the conservancy tax shall be fixed with reference to the cost or probable cost of the collection, removal and disposal, by the agency or municipal conservancy staff, of excrementitious and polluted matter from the premises.

138.(1) Any person who has paid to the Commissioner any water tax or conservancy tax in respect of any premises shall, if he was not himself in occupation of the said premises during the period for which he has made such payment and subject to any agreement or contract to the contrary, be entitled to receive the amount of the said payment from the person, if any, in actual occupation of the said premises for the said period.

(2) For the recovery of the said amount from the person aforesaid, the person who has paid the same shall have the same rights and remedies as if such amount were rent payable to him by the person from whom he is entitled to receive the same.

Liability for Property Taxes

139.(1) Subject to the provisions of sub-section (2) property taxes assessed upon any premises shall be primarily leviable as follows, namely:

(a) if the premises are held immediately from the (Government) or from the Corporation, from the actual occupier thereof:
Provided that property taxes due in respect of buildings vesting in the Government and occupied by servants of the Government or other persons on payment of rent shall be leviable primarily from the Government;

(b) if the premises are not so held –

(i) from the lessor if the premises are let;

(ii) from the superior lessor if the premises are sub-let;
(iii) from the person in whom the right to let the premises vests if they are unlet.

(2) If any land has been let for any term exceeding one year to a tenant and such tenant has built upon the land, the property taxes assessed upon the said land and upon the building erected thereon shall be primarily leviable from the said tenant or any person deriving title from the said tenant by the operation of law or by assignment or transfer but not by sub-lease or the legal representative of the said tenant or person whether the premises be in the occupation of the said tenant or person or legal representative or a sub-tenant.

140.(1) If the sum due on account of any property tax remains unpaid after a bill for the same has been duly served under the rules upon the person primarily liable for the payment thereof and the said person be not the occupier for the time being of the premises in respect of which the tax is due, the Commissioner may serve a bill for the amount upon the occupier of the said premises, or, if there are two or more occupiers thereof, may serve a bill upon each of them for such portion of the sum due as bears to the whole amount due the same ratio which the rent paid by such occupier bears to the aggregate amount of rent paid by them both or all in respect of the said premises.

(2) If the occupier or any of the occupiers fails within thirty days from the service of any such bill to pay the amount therein claimed, the said amount may be recovered from him in accordance with the rules.

(3) No arrear of a property-tax shall be recovered from any occupier under this section which has remained due for more than one year, or which is due on account of any period for which the occupier was not in occupation of the premises on which the tax is assessed.

(4) if any sum is paid by, or recovered from, an occupier under this section, he shall be entitled to credit therefor in account with the person primarily liable for the payment of the same.

141. (1) Property-taxes due under this Act in respect of any building or land shall, subject to the prior payment of the land revenue, if any, due to the State Government thereupon, be a first charge, in the case of any building or land held immediately from the Government, upon the interest in such building or land of the person liable for such taxes and upon the moveable property, if any, found within or upon such building or land and belonging to such person; and, in the case of any other building or land, upon the said building or land and upon the movable property, if any, found within or upon such building or land and belonging to the person liable for such taxes.

Explanation: The term "property taxes" in this section shall be deemed to include charges payable under section 134 for water supplied to any premises and the costs of recovery of property taxes as specified in the rules.

(2) In any decree passed in a suit for the enforcement of the charge created by sub-section (1), the Court may order the payment to the Corporation of interest on the sum found to be due at such rate as the Court deems reasonable from the date of the institution of the suit until realisation, and such interest and the cost of enforcing the said charge, including the costs of the suit and the cost of bringing the premises or movable property in question to sale under the decree, shall, subject as aforesaid, be a fresh charge on such premises and moveable property along with the amount found to be due, and the Court may direct payment thereof to be made to the Corporation out of the sale proceeds.

Tax on Vehicles, Boats and Animals

142. (1) Except as hereinafter provided, a tax at rates not exceeding those prescribed by order in writing by the (State) Government in this behalf from time to time shall be levied on vehicles, boats and animals of the descriptions specified in the order, when kept for use in the City for the conveyance of passengers or goods in the case of vehicles and boats and for riding, racing, draught or burden in the case of animals:\

Provided that no tax shall be levied on motor vehicles save as provided in section 20 of the Bombay Motor Vehicles Tax Act, 1958.

Explanation: A vehicle, boat or animal kept outside the limits of the City but regularly used within such limits shall be deemed to be kept for use in the City.

(2) The Corporation shall from year-to-year, in accordance with section 99, determine the rates at which the tax shall be levied.

143. (1) The said tax shall not be leviable in respect of-

(a) vehicles, boats and animals belonging to the Corporation other than vehicles or animals used exclusively for the purposes of the

Transport Undertaking;

(b) vehicles, boats and animals vesting in the Government and used solely for public purposes and not used or intended to be used for purposes of profit, including vehicles, boats and animals belonging to the Defence Forces;

(c) vehicles and boats intended exclusively for the conveyance free of charge of the injured, sick or dead;

(d) children's prambulators and tricycles;

(e) vehicles belonging to Municipal officers or servants who are required by the terms of their appointment to maintain a conveyance for the discharge of their duties:

Provided that the exemption granted by this clause will not be available in respect of more than one vehicle for each officer or in respect of a vehicle which does not belong to the class of conveyance which the officer is required to maintain;

(f) vehicles or boats kept by *bona fide* dealer in vehicles or boats for sale merely, and not used:

Provided that a tax, at such rate as the Corporation shall with the approval of the State Government fix in this behalf, shall be levied half yearly in advance from every dealer in motor vehicles for every seven motor vehicles in respect of which a Trade Certificate is issued to him under rules made under the Motor Vehicles Act, 1939.

(2) if any question arises under clause (b) of sub-section (1) whether any vehicle, boat or animal vesting in the (Government), is or is not used or intended to be used for purposes of profit, such question shall be determined by the State Government whose decision shall be final.

144. The Commissioner may, with the approval of the Standing Committee compound with any livery-stable keeper or other person keeping vehicles or horses or bullocks for hire, or with any dealer having stables in which horses are kept for sale on commission or otherwise, for the payment of a lump sum for any period not exceeding one year at a time, in lieu of the taxes leviable under section 142 which such livery-stable keeper or other person or dealer would otherwise be liable to pay.

145. (1) The Commissioner may make an inspection of any stable, garage or coach-house or any place wherein he may have reason to believe that there is any vehicle, boat or animal liable to a tax under this Act.

(2) The Commissioner may, by written summons, require the attendance before him of any person whom he has reason to believe to be liable to the payment of a tax in respect of a vehicle, boat or animal, or of any servant of any such person, and may examine such person or servant as to the number and description of vehicles, boats and animals owned by or in the possession or under the control of such person; and every person so summoned shall be bound to attend before the Commissioner and to give true information, to the best of his knowledge or belief, as to the said matters.

Exemptions from Octroi

146. (1) No octroi shall be leviable on any article which, at the time of its importation, is certified by an officer empowered by the Government concerned in this behalf to be the property of the (Government), to be used or intended to be used solely for public purposes and not to be used or intended to be used for purposes of profit.

(2) If any article on which octroi is paid is imported under a written declaration signed by the importer that such article is being imported for the purpose of fulfilling a specified contract with the Government or otherwise for the use of the (Government), the full amount of the duty paid thereon shall be refunded on production, at any time within six months after importation, of a certificate signed by an officer empowered by the Government concerned in this behalf certifying that the article so imported has become the property of (Government) is used or intended to be used solely for a public purpose and is not used or intended to be used for purposes of profit.

147. Until the contrary is proved any goods imported into the City shall be presumed to have been imported for the purposes of consumption, use or sale therein unless such goods are conveyed from the place of import to the place of export by such routes, within such time, under such supervision and on payment of such fees therefor as shall be determined by the standing orders.

Exemptions from Theatre Tax

148. The theatre tax shall not be leviable in respect of–

(a) any entertainment or amusement for admission to which no charge is made or only a nominal charge is made;
(b) any entertainment or amusement which is not open to the general public on payment;
(c) any entertainment or amusement the full proceeds of which, without the deduction of expenses, are intended to be utilised for a public charitable purpose.

Explanation: For the purposes of this section a nominal charge shall be such charge as may be fixed by the rules.

Other Taxes

149. (1) In the event of the Corporation deciding to levy any of the taxes specified in sub-section (2) of section 127, it shall make detailed provision, insofar as such provision is not made by this Act, in the form of rules, modifying, amplifying or adding to the rules at the time in force for the following matters, namely:-

(a) the nature of the tax, the rates thereof, the class or classes of persons, articles or properties liable thereto and the exemptions therefrom, if any, to be granted;
(b) the system of assessment and method of recovery and the powers exercisable by the Commissioner or other officers in the collection of the tax;
(c) the information required to be given of liability to the tax;
(d) the penalties to which persons evading liability or furnishing incorrect or misleading information or failing to furnish information may be subjected;
(e) such other matters, not inconsistent with the provisions of this Act, as may be deemed expedient by the Corporation:

Provided that no rules shall be made by the Corporation in respect of any tax coming under clause (f) of sub-section (2) of section 127 unless the State Government shall have first given provisional approval to the selection of the tax by the Corporation.

(2) The rules shall be submitted by the Corporation to the State Government and the State Government may either refuse to sanction them or refer them back to the Corporation for further consideration or sanction them either as they stand or with such modifications as it thinks fit, not, however, involving an increase in the rate or rates of the levy or the extent thereof.

(3) Any sanction given by the State Government under sub-section (2) shall become operative on such date not earlier than one month from the date of the sanction as the State Government shall specify in the order of sanction, and the Corporation shall be competent to levy the tax covered by the sanction as from the date so specified.

(4) The Corporation and the State Government shall take such steps as may be practicable to ensure that the date specified in the order of sanction is the first day of April, unless the sanction is given in pursuance of a proposal for supplementary taxation under section 150:

Provided that nothing in sub-section (4) shall affect the power of the Corporation to levy a tax as from a date later than the first day of April if the sanction of the State Government is not given by the first day of March Immediately preceding and if the State Government in the order of sanction specifies a date later than the first day of April for the commencement of the levy of the tax.

(5) The provisions of this section shall apply, as far as may be, to any alterations which the Corporation may from time to time decide to make in the rates fixed for any tax, or in the class or classes of persons, articles, or properties liable thereto or in the exemptions therefrom, if any, to be granted.

Supplementary Taxation

150. Whenever the Corporation determines under section 104 to have recourse to supplementary taxation in any official year, it shall do so by increasing, for the unexpired portion of the said year, the rates at which any tax impossible under this Act is being levied, subject to the limit and conditions for such tax prescribed in this Act or in the orders or sanction of the (State) Government or by levying, with due sanction, a tax impossible under this Act but not being levied at the time being.

Refunds

151. Refunds of a Municipal tax shall be claimable in the manner and subject to the conditions prescribed by rules.

Writing off of Taxes

152. The Commissioner may, with the approval of the Standing Committee, from time to time write off any sum due on account of any tax or of the costs of recovering any tax, which shall, in his opinion, be irrecoverable.

APPENDIX IIA

PARTICULARS OF THE COMMITTEE MEETINGS OF THE POONA MUNICIPAL CORPORATION DURING 1962-1966

I. Standing Committee

1962-63:(a) Strength of Members: 12
(b) Total number of meetings called from 1 April, 1962 to 31 March, 1963: 71
(c) Meetings held: 65
(d) Meetings adjourned due to lack of quorum: 6
(e) Number of resolutions adopted: 547
(f) Average attendance of members per meeting: 9.6

1963-64:(a) Strength of members: 12
(b) Total number of meetings called from 1 April, 1963 to 31 March, 1964: 87
(c) Meetings held: 83
(d) Number of meetings adjourned: 4
(e) Number of resolutions adopted: 665
(f) Average attendance of members per meeting: 8.70

1964-65:(a) Strength of Members: 12
(b) Total number of meetings called from 1 April, 1964 to 31 March, 1965: 92
(c) Meetings held: 85
(d) Number of meetings adjourned: 7
(e) Number of resolutions adopted: 727
(f) Percentage of members present: 8.50

1965-66:(a) Strength of Members: 12
(b) Total number of meetings called: 79
(c) Number of meetings held: 77
(d) Number of resolutions adopted: 655
(e) Number of meetings adjourned: 2

(f) Percentage of members present: 7.42

II. Transport Committee

1962-63:(a) Strength of Members: 9
(b) Total number of meetings called during the year: 46
(c) Meetings held: 42
(d) Meetings adjourned: 4
(e) Number of resolutions adopted: 92
(f) Average attendance of the members: 6.01
(g) Percentage of the attendance of the members: 68.30

1963-64:(a) Strength of Members: 9
(b) Total number of meetings called: 71
(c) Meetings held: 66
(d) Meetings adjourned: 5
(e) Number of resolutions adopted: 172
(f) Average attendance of the members: 5.8
(g) Percentage of the attendance of the members: 62.5

1964-65:(a) Strength of Members: 9
(b) Total number of meetings called: 57
(c) Meetings held: 57
(d) Meetings adjourned: 0
(e) Number of resolutions decided: 215
(f) Average attendance of the members: 6.74
(g) Percentage of the attendance of the members: 75

1965-66:(a) Strength of Members: 9
(b) Total number of meetings called: 50
(c) Meetings held: 49
(d) Meetings adjourned: 1
(e) Number of resolutions adopted: 81
(f) Percentage of members present: 78

III. Public Works Committee

1962-63:(a) Strength of Members: 9
(b) Total number of meetings called: 38

(c) Meetings held: 29
(d) Meetings adjourned: 9
(e) Total number of resolutions adopted: 171

1963-64:(a) Strength of Members: 9
(b) Total number of meetings called: 46
(c) Meetings held: 43
(d) Meetings adjourned: 3
(e) Total number of resolutions adopted: 403

1964-65:(a) Strength of Members: 9
(b) Total number of meetings called: 38
(c) Meetings held: 30
(d) Meetings adjourned: 8
(e) Total number of resolutions adopted: 288

1965-66:(a) Strength of Members: 9
(b) Total number of meetings called: 37
(c) Number of meetings held: 27
(d) Number of meetings adjourned: 10
(e) Number of resolutions adopted: 53

IV. Medical Relief and Public Health Committee

1962-63:(a) Strength of Members: 9
(b) Total number of meetings called: 36
(c) Meetings held: 29
(d) Number of meetings adjourned: 7
(e) Total number of resolutions adopted: 105

1963-64:(a) Strength of members: 9
(b) Total number of meetings called: 31
(c) Number of meetings held: 24
(d) Number of meetings adjourned: 7
(e) Number of resolutions adopted: 165

1964-65:(a) Strength of Members: 9
(b) Total number of meetings called: 34
(c) Number of meetings held: 21
(d) Number of meetings adjourned: 13

(e) Total number of resolutions adopted: 184

1965-66:(a) Strength of Members: 9
(b) Total number of meetings called: 30
(c) Number of meetings held: 18
(d) Number of meetings adjourned: 18
(e) Number of resolutions adopted in the year: 57

V. Law Committee

1962-63:(a) Strength of Members: 9
(b) Total number of meetings called: 36
(c) Meetings held: 22
(d) Meetings adjourned: 14
(e) Total number of resolutions adopted: 42

1963-64:(a) Strength of Members: 9
(b) Total number of meetings called: 38
(c) Meetings held: 28
(d) Meetings adjourned: 10
(e) Total number of resolutions adopted: 139

1964-65:(a) Strength of Members: 9
(b) Total number of meetings called: 39
(c) Meetings held: 30
(d) Meetings adjourned: 9
(e) Total number of resolutions adopted: 80

1965-66:(a) Strength of Members: 9
(b) Total number of meetings called: 45
(c) Meetings held: 22
(d) Meetings adjourned: 23
(e) Total number of resolutions adopted: 137

VI. City Improvement Committee

1962-63:(a) Strength of Members: 9
(b) Total number of meetings called: 36
(c) Meetings held: 26
(d) Meetings adjourned: 10

(e) Total number of resolutions adopted: 41

1963-64:(a) Strength of Members: 9
(b) Total number of meetings called: 39
(c) Meetings held: 28
(d) Meetings adjourned: 11
(e) Total number of resolutions adopted: 89

1964-65:(a) Strength of Members: 9
(b) Total number of meetings called: 26
(c) Meetings held: 21
(d) Meetings adjourned: 5
(e) Total number of resolutions adopted: 80

1965-66:(a) Strength of Members: 9
(b) Total number of meetings called: 30
(c) Meetings held: 12
(d) Meetings adjourned: 18
(e) Total number of resolutions adopted: 10

APPENDIX IIB

NUMBER OF RESOLUTIONS PASSED BY THE COMMITTEES OF POONA MUNICIPAL CORPORATION DURING 1962-1967

I. Standing Committee

Topic	1962-63	1963-64	1964-65	1965-66	1966-67
1	2	3	4	5	6
1. Consent to execute the tender contracts	83	140	140	238	251
2. Consent to execute the contract with the parties without inviting tenders or advertising	32	36	43	55	46
3. The property of Municipal Corporation: Auction, purchase and sale; rates-consent of Corporation	65	58	65	59	109
4. Employees	84	113	142	82	72
5. Finances	183	190	174	111	81
6. Trade Union agreements, compensation claims, etc.	3	1	Nil	1	3
7. Administrative reports, audit reports, etc.	30	26	51	6	8
8. Land acquisition, road widening, etc.	35	38	44	51	33
9. Corporation dues and filing suits in courts, expenses, etc.	4	7	4	4	5
10. Miscellaneous	28	56	64	48	9
Total	547	665	727	655	617

II. Transport Committee

Topic	1962-63	1963-64	1964-65	1965-66	1966-67
1	2	3	4	5	6
1. Full pay leave to employees met with accidents and injured	5	13	18	Nil	2
2. Postponed Subjects	6	34	6	1	2
3. Consideration of accident report Charts sent to Sub-Committee	Nil	Nil	22	Nil	Nil
4. Audit Reports consent sent to Sub-Committee	Nil	Nil	7	4	Nil
5. Appeals of employees sent to Sub-Committee	Nil	Nil	7	6	1
6. To send delegation to attend conference/course	2	3	Nil	1	1
7. Labour Welfare Scheme	1	7	Nil	5	7
8. Decisions on appeals of employees	1	11	1	Nil	Nil
9. Increase in allowance of various employees	3	1	1	Nil	Nil
10. Increase in the strength of employees	1	1	Nil	Nil	Nil
11. Creation of new posts	1	2	6	4	5
12. Negotiations with P.M.T. Union and labour relations	3	2	5	4	10
13. Finances recommendation to Corporation	1	4	10	4	Nil
14. Finances recommended to Stg. Committee	1	Nil	1	1	1
15. Investment of Funds	1	Nil	1	Nil	Nil
16. Investment in Banks	2	3	6	6	2
17. Subjects at the time of budget consideration	2	Nil	3	Nil	Nil
18. Sanction of expenses without inviting tender/contract	5	18	10	15	16
19. Sanction of reports of expenses incurred within the sum of Rs. 1,000 to Rs. 5,000	13	15	21	Nil	Nil
20. Repayment of the amount to Corporation	1	Nil	1	Nil	Nil
21. Budget accepted with changes	2	Nil	Nil	3	2
22. Sanction to contract	9	9	7	7	10
23. To call tender again	1	Nil	Nil	Nil	Nil
24. Sanction to purchase of material	3	Nil	5	1	6
25. To make payment of the bill in the next financial year	1	1	Nil	Nil	Nil
26. Reports of breakdown of buses and Municipal transport earnings	14	32	38	Nil	Nil
27. Permission to change the routes	3	3	6	Nil	3

1	2	3	4	5	6
28. Request to State Government	1	Nil	Nil	Nil	Nil
29. Filing the letters in the records (letters of members and Transport Manager)	4	1	14	2	4
30. Consent of the schemes of administrative improvement	1	2	11	14	11
31. Appointment of Spl. Sub-Committee	1	Nil	4	Nil	11
32. Sent for publication and information	3	2	Nil	1	Nil
33. Correspondence with other admn. and other insttns.	1	1	Nil	1	Nil
34. Misc. resolutions about the matters not in the jurisdiction of Transport Committee	2	7	4	1	Nil
Total	95	172	215	81	94

III. Public Works Committee

Topic	1962-63	1963-64	1964-65	1965-66	1966-67
1	2	3	4	5	6
1. For the recommendation of Municipal Commissioner	50	145	91	Nil	6
2. Requests from members, accepted	30	Nil	10	23	40
3. Recommendation of M.C. accepted	36	22	42	17	27
4. Matters about employees decided	6	5	4	Nil	1
5. The negative advice tendered by M.C. on members' requests accepted	11	Nil	9	Nil	Nil
6. Implementation of Letters of members	3	1	8	Nil	3
7. Official reports and explanations accepted and filed	6	18	17	7	12
8. Favourable advice of M.C. on members' requests accepted	3	22	24	6	39
9. Consideration of the site inspection postponed	12	148	50	Nil	3
10. Expenditure from the balance recommended to Stg. Committee and Corpn.	4	17	13	Nil	Nil
11. Recommendation of the Estimate to Stg. Committee	3	19	15	Nil	3
12. Remitted for the recommendation of M.C.	1	Nil	2	Nil	Nil
13. Request to Govt. of Maharashtra	2	Nil	2	Nil	1
14. Previous resolution of P.W. Committee cancelled	1	1	1	Nil	Nil
15. Resolution for the consideration of the Standing Committee	3	15	Nil	Nil	2
Total	171	413	288	53	137

IV. Medical Committee

Topic	1962-63	1963-64	1964-65	1965-66	1966-67
1	2	3	4	5	6
1. Remitted for the recommendation of M.C.	55	67	67	2	2
2. Subject postponed	8	33	27	Nil	Nil
3. M.C's affirmative recommendation on member's request accepted	9	11	25	4	8
4. M.C's negative recommendation on member's request accepted	22	22	30	13	6
5. Request to M.C.	1	10	20	14	12
6. Request to Standing Committee and Corpn. for provision of additional amount	4	10	6	Nil	Nil
7. Recommendation to make provision in next year's budget	2	1	2	3	Nil
8. To recommend to Corpn. about employees	3	10	7	1	Nil
9. Resolution on other Committee's resolution	1	1	Nil	1	Nil
Total	105	165	184	38	28

V. City Improvement Committee

Topic	1962-63	1963-64	1964-65	1965-66	1966-67
1	2	3	4	5	6
1. Recommendation of M.C. sent	12	27	28	Nil	Nil
2. Recommendation of M.C. accepted	4	9	16	3	6
3. Sent with request to M.C.	1	7	6	5	2
4. Recommendation to Corpn.	6	11	10	2	Nil
5. Request to State Govt.	1	Nil	Nil	Nil	Nil
6. Letter of member filed	3	Nil	7	Nil	Nil
7. Subject-matter postponed	13	34	13	Nil	1
8. Resolution of Corpn. confirmed	1	1	Nil	Nil	Nil
Total	41	89	80	10	9

VI. Law Committee

Topic	1962-63	1963-64	1964-65	1965-66	1966-67
1	2	3	4	5	6
1. Sent for recommendation of M.C.	10	22	29	Nil	2
2. Recommendation of M.C. accepted	1	3	2	7	6
3. Request of members not accepted due to recommendation of M.C.	3	2	5	4	5
4. Suggestion of M.C. not accepted	2	2	4	1	Nil
5. Consideration of subject-matter postponed	11	62	42	Nil	Nil
6. Recommendation to Stg. Committee and Corporation (financial matters)	7	35	37	5	5
7. Recommendation to Stg. Committee and Corporation (non-financial matters)	4	11	16	2	2
8. Resolution to call Spl. meeting of G.B. (M.C.)	1	1	Nil	1	Nil
9. Request to State Govt.	1	Nil	2	Nil	Nil
10. Petition to M.C.	1	Nil	Nil	2	1
11. Request to other Committees	1	1	Nil	Nil	Nil
Total	42	139	137	22	21

BIBLIOGRAPHY

Ashraf, Ali (1966). *City Government in Calcutta : A Study of Inertia* Asia, Bombay.

—— (1977). *Government and Politics of Big Cities – An Indian Case Study*, Concept, Delhi.

Avasthi, A. (1972). *Municipal Administration in India*, Lakshmi Narain Agarwal, Agra.

Bhatt, Anil (1978), "Municipal Commissioner in Gujarat : Structure, Process and Style", *Nagarlok*, 10-2 April-June.

Bhattacharya, Mohit (1970). *Essays in Urban Government*, The World Press, Calcutta.

—— (1976). *Management of Urban Government in India*, Uppal, New Delhi.

—— (1973), "Municipal Decision-Making", *Nagarlok*, 4, Oct-Dec.

—— (1986). "Growth of Towns and Administration of Urban Areas", *A Survey of Research in Public Administration, 1970-1979* (ed.) Kuldeep Mathur, (ICSSR-sponsored Project). Concept, New Delhi.

Church, Rodevich (1973). "Authority and Influence in Indian Municipal Politics : Administrators and Councillors in Lucknow" *Asian Survey*, XIII-4, April.

Clark, T.N. (1968). *Community Structure and Decision-Making: Comparative Analysis*, Chandler, San Francisco.

Cross, Martin and David Mallen (1978). *Political Realities: Local Government and Realities*, Longman, London.

Dahl, Robert (1961). *Who Governs? Democracy and Power in an American City*, Yale University Press, New Haven, Conn.

Dutta, Abhijit (ed.) (1985). *Municipal Executives in India*, CUS, Ind. Inst. of Pub. Admn., New Delhi.

Dutta, V.R. (1984). "Social Background and Decision-making role of Municipal Councillors – Study of Varanasi Municipal Corporation", *Quarterly Journal of Local Self-Government Institute*, LV-2, April-June, pp. 86-96.

Elcock, Howard (1982), *Local Government Politicians, Professionals and the Public in local authorities*, Methuen, London.

Government of India, Central Council of Local Self-Government (1963). *Augmentation of Financial Resources of Urban Local Bodies*, New Delhi.

Ministry of Health and Family Planning (1966). *Report of the Rural-Urban Relationship Committee*, I, New Delhi.

Government of Maharashtra (1964). *Report of the Committee for Unification of the Acts relating to Municipalities in Maharashtra State*, Bombay.

— (1967). Government of Maharashtra (1967). *Maharashtra Municipalities Act*. 1965, Bombay.

Haywood, Stuart (1976). "Decision-Making in Local Government : The Case of an Independent Council", *Local Government Studies*, 3-4 March.

Hill, D.M. (1974). *Democratic Theory and Local Government*, G. Allen & Unwin, London.

Hutchinson, P. (1959). "Committee System in East Suffolk", *Public Administration*, Winter.

Inamdar, N.R. (1968). "Metropolitan Planning in Maharashtra", *Indian Journal of Public Administration*, XIV-3, July-Sept., pp. 670-81.

— (1971). "Draft Metropolitan Regional Plans for Bombay and Poona", *Nagarlok*, III-2, April-June, pp. 25-34.

— (1972). "Municipal Administration in Maharashtra", in Avasthi A., *Municipal Administration in India*, L.N. Agarwal, Agra.

James, P.A. and M. Murlidhar Rao (1972). "The Councillors and the Commissioners in Hyderabad: Their Roles & Relations", *Nagarlok*, 4:1, Jan-Mar.

Jones, R.W. (1975). *Urban Politics in India*, Vikas, Delhi.

Kaushik, S.L. (1986). *Leadership in Urban Government in India*, Kitab Mahal, Allahabad.

Mangudkar, M.P. (1960). *Centenary Volume of Poona Municipality* (in Marathi), Poona Municipal Corporation.

Martin, R. (n.d.). *Decisions in Syracuse*, Syracuse University Press, N.Y., U.S.A.

Mishra, S.N. and Haridwar Singh (1982). "Political Process and Decision-Making in Municipal Government", *Q.J.L.S.G.I.*, LII-4. June.

Masson, J.K. (1975). "Decision-making Patterns of floating coalitions in Urban City Council", *Canadian Journal of Political Science*, 8-1, March.

Mukherjee, Bharati (1984). "Cabinet Government in Municipal Administration : An Indian Experiment", *Q.J.L.S.G.I.*, Bombay, LV-4, Oct.-Dec., pp. 223-33.

Muttalib, M.A. (1967). "City Government by Committees", *Nagarlok*, I, 1969, "The Municipal Commissioner, *Public Administration*, 45, August.

Newton, K. (1976). *Second City Politics : Democratic Processes and Decision-making in Birmingham*, O.U.P., London.

Ripley, B.J. (1973). *Administration in Local Authorities*, Butterworths, London.

Rosenthal, D.B. (1970). *The Limited Elite : Politics and Government in Two Indian Cities*, University of Chicago Press.

Srinivasan, R. and B.A.V. Sharma (1965), "Politics in Urban India : A Study of Four Corporations", in S.P. Aiyar and R. Srinivasan (eds.), *Studies in Indian Democracy*, Allied, Bombay.

Staffing of Local Government (1967). Committee Report, HMSO, London.

Stewart, John (1986). *The New Management of Local Government*, Allen & Unwin, London.

Tinker, H. (1967). *The Foundations of Local Self-Government in India, Pakistan and Burma*, 2nd edn., Lalwani Publishing House, Bombay.

U.K. Government (1976). (Min. of Housing & Local Govt.), *Management of Local Government* (Committee Report, 1, HMSO, London.

Villalan R. Thillai (1975). "Powers of the Commissioner of the Corporation of Madras", *Madras Law Journal*, 148 : 2, January 16.

Wiseman, H.V. (1963). "The Working of Local Government in Leeds : Part I Party Control of Council and Committees", *Public Administration*, Spring.

INDEX